POLITICAL SCIENCE AND HISTORY

THE HISTORY OF THE THIRTEEN COLONIES OF NORTH AMERICA 1497-1763

POLITICAL SCIENCE AND HISTORY

Additional books in this series can be found on Nova's website
under the Series tab.

Additional e-books in this series can be found on Nova's website
under the eBooks tab.

POLITICAL SCIENCE AND HISTORY

THE HISTORY OF THE THIRTEEN COLONIES OF NORTH AMERICA 1497-1763

REGINALD W. JEFFERY

Copyright © 2018 by Nova Science Publishers, Inc.

All rights reserved. No part of this book may be reproduced, stored in a retrieval system or transmitted in any form or by any means: electronic, electrostatic, magnetic, tape, mechanical photocopying, recording or otherwise without the written permission of the Publisher.

We have partnered with Copyright Clearance Center to make it easy for you to obtain permissions to reuse content from this publication. Simply navigate to this publication's page on Nova's website and locate the "Get Permission" button below the title description. This button is linked directly to the title's permission page on copyright.com. Alternatively, you can visit copyright.com and search by title, ISBN, or ISSN.

For further questions about using the service on copyright.com, please contact:
Copyright Clearance Center
Phone: +1-(978) 750-8400   Fax: +1-(978) 750-4470   E-mail: info@copyright.com.

NOTICE TO THE READER

The Publisher has taken reasonable care in the preparation of this book, but makes no expressed or implied warranty of any kind and assumes no responsibility for any errors or omissions. No liability is assumed for incidental or consequential damages in connection with or arising out of information contained in this book. The Publisher shall not be liable for any special, consequential, or exemplary damages resulting, in whole or in part, from the readers' use of, or reliance upon, this material. Any parts of this book based on government reports are so indicated and copyright is claimed for those parts to the extent applicable to compilations of such works.

Independent verification should be sought for any data, advice or recommendations contained in this book. In addition, no responsibility is assumed by the publisher for any injury and/or damage to persons or property arising from any methods, products, instructions, ideas or otherwise contained in this publication.

This publication is designed to provide accurate and authoritative information with regard to the subject matter covered herein. It is sold with the clear understanding that the Publisher is not engaged in rendering legal or any other professional services. If legal or any other expert assistance is required, the services of a competent person should be sought. FROM A DECLARATION OF PARTICIPANTS JOINTLY ADOPTED BY A COMMITTEE OF THE AMERICAN BAR ASSOCIATION AND A COMMITTEE OF PUBLISHERS.

Additional color graphics may be available in the e-book version of this book.

Library of Congress Cataloging-in-Publication Data

ISBN: 978-1-53613-640-1

Published by Nova Science Publishers, Inc. † New York

Contents

Preface		**vii**
Chapter 1	Introduction: Early English Voyages to North America	1
Chapter 2	Virginia: The First Great Colony of the British	15
Chapter 3	The Colonisation of Maryland and the Carolinas	41
Chapter 4	The Puritans in Plymouth and Massachusetts	57
Chapter 5	Connecticut; Rhode Island and Providence Plantation; New Haven; Maine; New Hampshire	79
Chapter 6	The Fight with the Dutch for Their Settlement of New Netherland	95
Chapter 7	The Quaker Settlements and Georgia	109
Chapter 8	The Social and Economic History of New England	125
Chapter 9	The Social and Economic History of the Southern and Middle Colonies	139
Chapter 10	The French Colonies in North America	149
Chapter 11	French Aggression	167
Chapter 12	The Climax: The Struggle Between English and French Colonists	189

Chapter 13	Chronology of Colonial History	**211**
Chapter 14	Bibliography	**231**
References		**235**
Index		**247**

PREFACE*

This book, originally published in 1908, is a short narrative of the History of the Thirteen Colonies. The author endeavoured to give as often as possible the actual words of contemporaries, hoping that readers may thereby be tempted to search further among the mass of documentary evidence which still needs so much careful study.

---

* This is an edited, reformatted and augmented version of the book written by Reginald W. Jeffery, published by Methuen & Company, London in 1908.

George Washington from the painting attributed to Gilbert Stuart in the National Portrait Gallery.

Chapter 1

INTRODUCTION: EARLY ENGLISH VOYAGES TO NORTH AMERICA

It would be out of place in this small book to give in detail a history of all the discoveries which were made along the shores of North and South America at the end of the fifteenth and beginning of the sixteenth centuries. As the main object is to depict briefly the political history of the Thirteen English Colonies on the North American seaboard, it will be unnecessary to say more than a few words about the discoverers whose enterprise and bravery made colonisation possible. With the Spanish, French, and Dutch voyagers it is not proposed to deal; their stories are well known, and affected but little the establishment of our early settlements in the West. Like the British nation, these three peoples also strove to create lasting empires in America; but unlike their rival, they failed. The Spaniards made the fatal error of attempting to settle during the period of exploration. They based their colonies upon slavery, and a mistaken commercial policy; and the sparseness of their colonists made them incapable of contending against the pressure of surrounding savagery. The result was that they, who were without the traditions of public morality and who were to a certain extent lacking in administrative powers, became intermixed with the inferior races with whom they came in contact. The French were no more successful in their endeavours to establish a New

France beyond the sea; they failed, partly because of the French temperament, and partly through obvious errors. The French character was buoyant and cheerful—both excellent natural gifts for colonists—but they were unable to combine the spirit of adventure with that patient commercial industry which so wonderfully distinguished the Puritan emigrants. The Dutch might have proved serious rivals to the British in the West had they been able to rise from the position of mere traders, and had they had a sufficiently large population on which to draw. Their commercial system deteriorated, becoming uneconomic and non-progressive; while their arduous and gallant struggle against Philip II. and Alva had necessarily handicapped them in the race for colonial aggrandisement.

The English, in strong contrast to these competitors, never drew a distinct or sharp line between the soldier and the trader. The story of Great Britain's expansion contains the names of hundreds of gallant heroes, but they were at the same time sober and industrious men. The plodding and commercial characteristics possessed by the British colonial saved him from perpetrating those foolish errors of the Spaniard which arose from a desire to gain rapid wealth and a tawdry glory. One fact stands out pre-eminent amongst the reasons of British success—the English kept their period of exploration almost entirely separate from their epoch of settlement. The glorious dreams of Eldorado, the visions of the golden city of Manoa had been dispersed like a morning mist when the period of colonisation dawned bright and clear at the beginning of the seventeenth century.

The period which coincides with the reign of Henry VII. forms one of the greatest epochs of history; it was indeed the veritable Renaissance, the birth of the New World. It was at this moment that the history of America, the modern history of England, and the present history of Europe practically began. These startling facts were due to the simultaneous discoveries in the East and the West. The voyages of Bartholomew Diaz, of Christopher Columbus, and of Vasco de Gama might well have astonished the world, but seem to have had very little effect upon the English as a nation. England was not yet ready to take up the position of

Mistress of the Seas; the time was not yet ripe for colonial advancement. The country, from both political and social points of view, was still suffering from the confusion and anarchy which had resulted from the rule of the Lancastrians, and from the chaos left by the Wars of the Roses. Two men, however, seem to have understood something of the possibilities that lay open to them in the West. John and his son Sebastian Cabot, of Genoese stock, but sometime resident in Venice, sailed, under the patronage of Henry VII., from Bristol, in 1497, to discover the island of Cathay. John Cabot is described as one who had "made himself very expert and cunning in knowledge of the circuit of the world and Ilands of the same, as by a Sea card and other demonstrations" [1]. The royal charter, granted to these men in March 1496, contained a most important clause, "to saile to all parts, countreys, and seas of the East, of the West, and of the North, under our banners and ensignes, ... to set up our banners and ensignes in every village, towne, castle, isle, or maine land of them newly found ... as our vassals, and lieutenants, getting unto us the rule, title, and jurisdiction of the same" [2]. Bacon, in his History of Henry VII. , refers to Cabot's now celebrated voyage. "There was one Sebastian Gabato, a Venetian living in Bristow, a man seen and expert in cosmography and navigation. This man seeing the success and emulating perhaps the enterprise of Christopherus Columbus in that fortunate discovery towards the south-west, which had been by him made some six years before, conceited with himself that lands might likewise be discovered towards the north-west. And surely it may be that he had more firm and pregnant conjectures of it than Columbus had of his at the first. For the two great islands of the Old and New World, being in the shape and making of them broad towards the north and pointed towards the south, it is likely that the discovery just began where the lands did meet. And there had been before that time a discovery of some lands which they took to be islands, and were indeed of America towards the north-west" [3]. Bacon is here calling attention to what has since become the great controversial question of whether or not the Norsemen discovered the American continent in the eleventh century. It is very improbable that the Cabots knew anything of this tradition; and this voyage was solely the outcome of the discoveries of

Columbus. Their object is definitely stated to have been a "great desire to traffique for the spices as the Portingals did" [4]. It is a remarkable fact that very little is known of this voyage, and there are practically no English records available in which to find the history of so great an event. A Bristol book contains this terse mention of the exploring expedition: "In the year 1497, the 24th of June, on St John's day, was Newfoundland found by Bristol men in a ship called the Mathew" [5]. Carrying out the commands of the charter, John Cabot and his son planted the English standard upon American soil, but they did little besides: no explorations were made into the interior; they were completely satisfied with the all-important fact of discovery. As a proof of their success, Sebastian Cabot brought back three Indians "in their demeanour like to bruite beastes," but who seem to have settled down and taken up English customs, for Robert Fabian says, "of the which upon two yeeres after, I saw two apparelled after the maner of Englishmen in Westminster pallace, which that time I could not discerne from Englishmen" [6].

The restless ambition of the Cabots incited them to a further voyage in February 1498, the charter on this occasion being granted only to the father. They again started from Bristol, and sailed along the North American coasts from the ice-bound shores of Newfoundland [7] to the sunny Carolinas or Florida. The younger Cabot afterwards wrote that he sailed "unto the Latitude of 67 degrees and a halfe under the North Pole ... finding still the open Sea without any maner of impediment, he thought verily by that way to have passed on still the way to Cathaia which is in the East." [8] This voyage is recorded by Sir Humphrey Gilbert, and was frequently quoted as a reason for England's claim to North America. "The countreys lying north of Florida, God hath reserved the same to be reduced unto Christian civility by the English nation. For not long after that Christopher Columbus had discovered the Islands and continent of the West Indies for Spaine, John and Sebastian Cabot made discovery also of the rest from Florida northwards to the behoofe of England" [9]. The Cabots disappear from English history for a time and there are no records of the reception of this voyage. It was undoubtedly of twofold importance; it started that "will o' the wisp" of the North-West Passage, that led so many men to risk and lose their lives; and it may also be regarded as the foundation-stone of the English power in the West.

The next few years of the history of the exploration of America is filled with the records of Spaniards, Italians, and Frenchmen. The voyage of the Bristol merchants by which North America had just been discovered had no effect, and awakened no enthusiasm in the hearts of the English during the early portion of the sixteenth century. Henry VII. and his more adventurous son were both such severe and orthodox Catholics that they hesitated to trespass upon the limitations laid down by the bull of Alexander VI., by which everything on the western side of an imaginary line between the forty-first and forty-fourth meridians west of Greenwich belonged to Spain; while the Brazil coast, the East Indies, and Africa south of the Canary Islands fell to Portugal. Between 1500 and 1550 only two true voyages of discovery have been chronicled. The first was in 1527, when a canon of St Paul's, erroneously named Albert de Prado, sailed with two ships in search of the Indies. It is probable that this was the voyage of John Rut of the Royal Navy, with whom, there is reason to suppose, a Spaniard, called Albert de Prado, sailed. They failed to make any real discoveries, but brought back a cargo of fish from the inhospitable shores of Newfoundland and Labrador. The second voyage was that of Master Hore, in 1536, who, it is supposed, set out in the spirit of a Crusader, but who was more probably a briefless barrister accompanied by "many gentlemen of the Innes of Court and of the Chancery" [10]. They were shipwrecked on the Newfoundland coast, where, as none of them knew how to fish, and although Hore told them they would go to unquenchable fire, they began to eat one another. "On the fieldes and deserts here and there, the fellowe killed his mate, while he stooped to take up a roote for his reliefe, and cutting out pieces of his bodie whom he had murthered, broyled the same on the coles and greedily devoured them" [11]. Luckily for the remainder, a French ship was blown into the harbour, and they seized her with all the food she had on board, sailing home in safety, leaving the French sailors to a horrible fate, which they seemed to have escaped; for "certaine moneths after, those Frenchmen came into England and made complaint to King Henry the 8: the king ... was so mooved with pitie, that he punished not his subjects, but of his owne purse made full and royale recompense unto the French" [12].

The two voyages here set forth are the only ones that are actually recorded, but there is reason for supposing that English ships were quite familiar with the coast of what was afterwards called Maine. Between 1501 and 1510 there are many scattered intimations of English voyages; and one patent in particular, in the first year of the sixteenth century, shows that men of some importance were granted leave to sail and discover in the West. In 1503 a man brought hawks from Newfoundland to Henry VII.; and in the next year a priest is paid £2 to go to the same island. In or about the eighth year of Henry VIII., Sebastian Cabot was again in the employ of the English and in command of an expedition to Brazil, which only failed owing to "the cowardise and want of stomack" of his partner, Sir Thomas Pert [13]. It is evident from the first Act of Parliament relating to America, passed in 1541 that the Newfoundland fishery was carried on by Devonshire fishermen almost continuously from the discovery of the island; and the Act of 1548, prohibiting the exaction of dues, shows "that the trade out of England to Newfoundland was common" [14]. Anthony Parkhurst corroborates this fact in a letter to Richard Hakluyt in 1578, in which he says, "The Englishmen, who commonly are lords of the harbors where they fish, and do use all strangers helpe in fishing if need require, according to an old custome of the countrey" [15]. It may, therefore, be inferred that the growth of the Newfoundland fisheries, together with the increasing knowledge of the country and its products, helped to suggest to the Englishmen of the period the possibilities of future colonisation.

The great voyager Sebastian Cabot returned to England in 1548 from his sojourn in Spain. Under the patronage of Charles V. he had made several voyages, including one of particular importance to the Rio de la Plata. On his arrival in England he was rewarded by Edward VI. with a pension of £166, 13s. 4d., as a slight evidence of that king's appreciation of his manifold services. Old man though he was, his mind still ran on the discovery of a North-West, or North-East Passage to the Indies, and he became the governor of a company of merchant adventurers for the discovery of regions beyond the sea. He did not participate in any of these discoveries, "because there are nowe many yong and lustie Pilots and Mariners of good experience, by whose forwardnesse I doe rejoyce in the fruit of my labours and rest with the charge of this office" [16]. Amongst the young and lusty pilots were Sir Hugh Willoughby and Richard Chancellor, who turned their attentions to a North-East passage. The former died on his vessel in the midst of the ice floes in 1553, while the latter succeeded in reaching Archangel, and so brought about, through a successor, Anthony Jenkinson, the foundation of the Muscovy Company.

It was, however, the discovery of America, and in particular of the North-West Passage, that offered great inducements to Englishmen. The American continent had an ever fascinating attraction, for the reports of its vast wealth drew adventurous spirits as with a magnet. The gold of Mexico and Peru dazzled their eyes and made them hope to find some similar hoard on every barren strip of shore from Patagonia to Newfoundland. "It was thought that in those unknown lands, peopled by 'anthropophagi and men whose heads did grow beneath their shoulders,' lay all the treasures of the earth. That was an irresistible temptation to the great merchants of England, citizens of no mean city, pursuing no ignoble nor sordid trade" [17]. Thus early in the reign of Elizabeth there was an attempt at American plantation; it certainly was only an attempt, for it in no way furthered the schemes of colonisation. Thomas Stukeley, a member of a good Devonshire family, planned, with the sanction of the queen, in 1563, to colonise Florida. He made the fatal mistake of so many others, of converting a colonising expedition into one of mere buccaneering. Spanish and French vessels were his real objects, not the foundation of an English settlement in the New World. The scheme naturally failed; and Stukeley removed his activities to Barbary, where he met a glorious death amongst the chivalry of Portugal upon the classic field of Alcazar. The search for the North-West Passage was even more tempting than the projection of imaginary colonies in the South; it opened before the eyes of speculative voyagers a promise of all the wealth of the East. A large proportion of Hakluyt's great prose epic—that marvellous work of adventure—is filled with the search for Cathay. That mystic land became the purpose and the goal of hundreds of seamen who, during the centuries, struggled and toiled through overwhelming perils, ever to be baffled by the solid and impenetrable ice. Those wild north seas seem to have caused little terror to the Tudor sea-dogs; Master Thorne, for example, deserves to live in the memory of Englishmen for all time simply for one remark with which he is credited. When the objection of the ice was proposed to him, he waived it on one side with words which might well be taken as the motto of the British Empire: "There is no land unhabitable and no sea innavigable" [18]. Sir Humphrey Gilbert, in particular, tried to encourage men to push forward in their adventurous discoveries, and there is no doubt that his famous work, A Discourse to prove a passage by the North West to Cathaya and the East Indies , did a great deal to stimulate men in their hopeless task.

It was largely due to this Discourse that Martin Frobisher sailed to find the tantalising passage, in June 1576, under the patronage of the all-powerful Earl of Warwick. He sighted Greenland, and then reached that inlet on the American coast which he called Frobisher Bay. He brought back with him samples of a black stone which were supposed to contain gold, and thus added the temptation of easily acquired wealth to the sufficiently delusive and dangerous task of discovering the passage. The possibility of mineral wealth in the Arctic Regions brought about the formation of the Company of Cathay, under the government of Michael Lok; and as its Captain-General, Frobisher undertook a second voyage in May 1577. His object was "the further discovering of the passage to Cathay, and other Countreys, thereunto adjacent, by West North-West navigations: which passage or way is supposed to be on the North and North-West part of America ... where through our Merchants may have course and recourse with their merchandise" [19]. Frobisher took possession of the barren territory, and on his return Queen Elizabeth "named it very properly Meta Incognita, as a marke and bound utterly hitherto unknown" [20]. The gold-refiners of London were still deceived by the black stones; and again Frobisher sailed, in May 1578, to work this imaginary mine. He took with him on this occasion "a strong fort or house of timber" for the shelter of "one hundreth persons, whereof 40 should be mariners for the use of ships, 30 Miners for gathering the gold Ore together for the next yere, and 30 souldiers for the better guard of the rest, within which last number are included the Gentlemen, Gold finers, Bakers, Carpenters & all necessary persons" [21]. This might be regarded as an early attempt to found a colony, for Frobisher seems to have hoped to establish a thriving industry in this desolate and ice-bound land; but as a matter of fact these "necessary persons" did nothing at all except to discover an island which existed only in their imaginations, and they returned to England in the autumn. Frobisher's efforts as a discoverer now ceased; for his seamanship and courage were required in home waters for the protection of his native land.

Sir Humphrey Gilbert, half-brother of Raleigh, was the "first of our nation that carried people to erect a habitation and government in those northerly countreys of America" [22]. He was a man bold in action and chivalrous in character; he was one of those giants of the Elizabethan period, and if he had any faults they were only those of his age, while his virtues were all his own. As early as 1563 he was connected with schemes for colonisation in the formation of a company for the discovery of new trades. He it is who has the proud position of being the founder of our premier colony, Newfoundland. In 1578, letters patent were granted to him by Queen Elizabeth for establishing a colony in North America. He made his first voyage in that year, sailing from Dartmouth in September. The expedition was a complete failure, and fearing lest his patent should expire, he undertook that voyage which has made him one of the most famous men in history. In 1583 he sailed to Newfoundland, and took possession in the name of the Virgin Queen, "and signified unto al men, that from that time forward, they should take the same land as a territorie appertaining to the Queene of England" [23]. His great action was not allowed to be forgotten; the gallant knight himself never saw England again, but passed to his grave beneath the rough waters of the Atlantic. Hakluyt, however, printed the story of an eye-witness, Edward Hayes, who gave a graphic account of the whole expedition. Gilbert insisted on returning in the Squirrel, a small crazy craft, rather than in the larger vessel, known as the Hinde. The weather became very foul; and on Monday afternoon, the 9th of September, Hayes says, "the frigate was neere cast away oppressed by the waves, yet at that time recovered: and giving foorth signes of joy the Generall, sitting abaft with a booke in his hand cried out unto us in the Hind (so oft as we did approach within hearing) We are as neere to heaven by sea as by land." About twelve that night, the frigate being ahead of the Hinde, she suddenly went out; and after a minute's awful silence, the men of the Hinde exclaimed, "the General was cast away" [24]. Thus the hero, strong in his belief and fear of God, with chivalrous and stainless name, found his last resting-place in the sea. He was a forerunner of the very noblest type, an example to the men of his own generation, and to those fearless adventurers who have helped to create the British Empire in all parts of the world.

Sir Francis Drake. From an engraving by J. Honbraken in the British Museum.

The northern portions of America were for the most part more easily accessible to the English, and the dangers of Spanish and Portuguese attacks were more remote. The West Indies, however, and even South America, were not without their fascination, and many Englishmen made voyages to those parts, not so much for the purposes of discovery as for trade, buccaneering, and booty. The earliest of these West Indian trading voyages was that of Thomas Tison, who, it is known, sailed to the West, some time previous to the year 1526. He dwelt on one of the West Indian Islands as a secret factor for some English merchants; and "it is probable that some of our marchants had a kinde of trade to the West Indies even in those ancient times and before also: neither doe I see," says Hakluyt, "any reason why the Spaniards should debarre us from it at this present" [25]. As a trader, pirate, and slave-dealer, Sir John Hawkins made three celebrated voyages in 1562, 1564, and 1568, between Guinea and the West Indies. On one of these he was accompanied by Francis Drake, who was destined for far greater things than slave-dealing. After many adventures off the Spanish main, Drake, in the spirit of a Crusader, started on his momentous voyage round the world. In a small vessel called the Golden Hinde or Pelican, with a still smaller ship, the Elizabeth, the great seaman sailed from Plymouth in February 1577. Sailing down the South American coast, he at last arrived at the Straits of Magellan, where one of his company, Master Thomas Doughty, mutinied and was executed. After being deserted by the Elizabeth, the voyage proceeded along the shores of Chili and Peru; and passing still farther north, it is probable that Drake discovered "that portion of North America now known as Oregon, and anticipated by centuries the progress of English colonisation: the New Albion, which he took over from the Indians, being probably the British Columbia of to-day" [26]. Drake's return was made without any very serious mishaps, and he dropped anchor in Plymouth Sound in November 1580. It was a fine exploit, and roundly applauded throughout the country. No one, however, realised at that time, nor indeed for generations to come, that Drake had discovered and annexed what was afterwards to become so large a portion of the British dominions beyond the seas.

One man in particular could not fail to be moved to enthusiasm by these voyages of discovery. The dream of a great country in the far West, peopled by the Anglo-Saxon race, was ever before the eyes of Sir Walter Raleigh. The character of this great man of action was not without many faults, for it was composed of much fine gold tempered with clay. His endeavours, however, to extend the limits of Britain's rule excite the imagination and entrance the mind of the reader. The mantle of Gilbert fell upon the shoulders of Raleigh, who at once attempted to carry on the work of colonisation which had been started by his half-brother in Newfoundland; and the road to which was about to be pointed out by Richard Hakluyt in his Discourse of Western Planting . Raleigh must have appreciated the appeal made by Sir George Peckham, friend of Gilbert, when he said, "Behold heere, good countreymen, the manifold benefits, commodities and pleasures heretofore unknowen, by Gods especiall blessing not onely reveiled unto us, but also as it were infused into our bosomes, who though hitherto like dormice have slumbered in ignorance thereof, being like the cats that are loth for their prey to wet their feet: yet if now therefore at the last we would awake, and with willing mindes (setting frivolous imaginations aside) become industrious instruments to ourselves, questionlesse we should not only hereby set forth the glory of our heavenly father, but also easily attaine to the end of all good purposes that may be wished or desired" [27]. Up to this time, by a curious chance, the coastline of the modern United States, from the St Lawrence to the Savannah River, had scarcely been visited and was, in fact, very little known. Here then was an opportunity for Raleigh; and a land, where, if effort was made, the greatest success might be achieved. The land had been unspoilt and untouched by the Spaniards; those few hardy seamen who had entered harbour or creek had found no signs of gold, and had sailed away again. But it was a land of excellent climate, freed from the ice and fogs of the more northern latitudes in which the Elizabethan seamen had shown such pluck and powers of endurance. Captain Carlile, the son-in-law of Francis Walsingham, had already in 1583 issued his encouraging report concerning American trade. Raleigh could not fail to be struck by the sentence, "that whereas one adventureth in the great enterprise, an hundred for that one will of themselves bee willing and desirous to adventure in the next" [28]. Gilbert's patent for the colonisation of North America had been transferred to Raleigh, who, with great caution, in 1584 dispatched two sea- captains, Amidas and Barlow, to spy out this land of promise. The narrative of these adventurers as given in Hakluyt's Voyages is extremely picturesque. They steered a more southerly course than that of any previous British explorer, and finally reached the island of Roanoke, now within the limits of North Carolina. They described it as a land flowing with milk and honey. "The second of July, we found shole water, wher we smelt so sweet and so strong a smel, as if we had been in the midst of some delicate garden abounding with all kinde of odoriferous flowers.... We found the people most gentle, loving, and faithfull, voide of all guile and treason, and such as live after the maner of the golden age" [29]. Amidas and Barlow thus brought back to their patron Raleigh a story full of hope and wondrous possibilities. They had found a land worthy of colonisation and well suited to the English; and this land of promise and of future greatness was christened by the Virgin Queen—Virginia.

The days of exploration and discovery by sea in the West had practically come to an end; the great epoch of colonisation was about to begin. When Elizabeth came to the throne, English ships had seldom sailed further than Iceland in the north and the Levant in the south-east, where a lucrative trade had sprung up as early as 1511. But by the end of the sixteenth century, owing to the encouragement of the Tudor sovereigns, the religious persecutions, and the "peculiar" policy of Elizabeth, the English flag had been proudly borne into all the seas of the world. The globe had been circumnavigated by Drake and Cavendish; trade through Archangel had been established with Russia; spices had been brought from the Indies by the East India Company; "the commodious and gainful voyage to Brazil" [30] was regularly undertaken by the merchants of Southampton; while a vast fishing trade had steadily grown up off the coasts of Newfoundland. Above all the "navigations, voyages, traffiques, and discoveries of the English nation" had laid the foundation for greater things. Raleigh's dreams were to be accomplished, though not by himself. Like so many others he was attracted by gold; his thoughts lay too readily in the discovery of an El Dorado in South America, of which the Elizabethan poet wrote:—

"Guiana whose rich feet are mines of gold."

The grain of mustard seed had, however, been planted; the idea had been put forth to the world; a new nation was to rise in the Western hemisphere; and, although no definite results were to be seen by the eyes of the Elizabethans, yet their wild adventures, their acts of knight-errantry, their perils and their sufferings had paved the way for the industrious, sober, steady, and more prudent enterprises of Stuart Cavaliers and of Puritan Pilgrims.

Chapter 2

VIRGINIA: THE FIRST GREAT COLONY OF THE BRITISH

The English settlers in America may be less romantic and less interesting figures than their Elizabethan predecessors, but they were undoubtedly fitter instruments for the specific work. The Elizabethan seamen had played their part, and men now arose who were to fulfil a greater destiny. The Gilberts and the Drakes were of a race which had ceased to be, and Fuller justly remarks "how God set up a generation of military men both by sea and land which began and expired with the reign of Queen Elizabeth, like a suit of clothes made for her and worn out by her; for providence so ordered the matter that they almost all attended their mistress before or after, within some short distance, unto her grave" [31]. Although the adventurous spirit of the Golden Age had passed away, men were still left who could echo the words of Sir Humphrey Gilbert and say, "and therefore to give me leave without offence always to live and die in this mind, that he is not worthy to live at all that for fear or danger of death shunneth his country's service and his own honour, seeing death is inevitable and the fame of virtue immortal" [32]. The one great figure who appears to connect the old period with the new was Sir Walter Raleigh. As has already been mentioned, he had sent out an expedition in 1584 to see what possibility there was of establishing a colony in America. The glowing accounts brought back by his two captains made Raleigh decide upon an undertaking which, though it proved a failure, must ever be regarded as memorable in the world's history.

In 1585 Raleigh sent seven ships and one hundred and eight settlers to the land which had been granted to him by patent. The territory had already been named Virginia, in honour of the Queen, and it was here that he hoped to establish a little colony composed of sturdy Englishmen. In June the settlers, having landed in Roanoke, were left under the leadership of Ralph Lane; the other generals, Grenville, Cavendish, and Amidas, returning to the mother country. From the outset it was certain that Raleigh's colony must fail. The man chosen as leader had no special aptitude for the post, being possessed with the mania for discovery rather than the desire to teach the settlers to form a self-supporting community. But even worse than this, Lane made the fatal error of estranging the natives by the severity and brutality of his punishments. Exactly a year after the settlers had landed, Sir Francis Drake put in to see how his friend Raleigh's Utopian schemes progressed. He found the colony in a miserable plight and, yielding to the earnest entreaties of the settlers, took them on board and sailed to England. Raleigh, however, had not forgotten his colony, and had dispatched Sir Richard Grenville with supplies; but when he reached the settlement he found it deserted. Sir Walter Raleigh's buoyant nature was not depressed by this first failure, and in 1587 a fresh attempt to settle Virginia was made. Under the command of White, one hundred and thirty-three men and seventeen women were sent out. White soon returned to England for supplies, leaving his daughter Eleanor Dare, who gave birth to the first white child born in the New World. The unhappy emigrants received but little assistance from the home authorities. Certainly two expeditions were sent out to help them, but they failed because their captains found it more lucrative and exciting to go privateering. The stirring times in Europe and the coming of the Armada were sufficient to absorb the minds of such men as Raleigh and Drake, and the colony in Virginia was left to its fate. What that fate was can only be imagined, for, when White at last reached Virginia in 1589, not a trace of the colony was to be found, while another expedition in 1602 proved equally unsuccessful in the search. Hunger and the Indians had done their cruel work, and the hand of destiny seemed turned against the foundation of an Anglo-Saxon colony in the mysterious West.

There were, however, dominant motives for colonisation at the beginning of the seventeenth century, and these, together with the intrepidity of certain of the Elizabethan school, changed the aspect of the whole question. The previous incentives for discovery and adventure upon the high seas had been the tricks of imagination, the more glorious scheme of spreading Christianity and the race for gold. But now there was a fear amongst the more intellectual thinkers in England that the country was suffering from a surplus population. This purely imaginary danger gave birth to the idea that America might provide new homes for this surplus, and, at the same time, bring new markets into existence which in the future would very materially help to develop the naval resources of the English.

One of the most able and energetic of the new patrons of colonisation was Shakespere's friend, the Earl of Southampton, who in March 1602 dispatched to the West, Bartholomew Gosnold with thirty-two companions. This little band of adventurers landed further north than Raleigh's ill-fated colonists, probably at a spot where in later years the Puritan settlers established themselves. The chief feature of Gosnold's venture was the discovery of a new route to the West by way of the Azores, and thus a week was saved in future voyages. In the following year the Discovery and Speedwell were sent out under Martin Pring, the patrons of the expedition having first obtained formal permission from Sir Walter Raleigh, whose patent rights were still regarded as valid. It is interesting to notice that with this concession on Raleigh's part his connection with Virginia ceased for ever.

One of Pring's patrons was Richard Hakluyt, to whom all Englishmen are indebted for his great prose epic and for the stimulus he gave to the early founders of the British Empire. Hakluyt was born in London about the year 1552. He was educated at Westminster School and Christ Church, Oxford, where he took his degree in 1574. His interest in geography and discovery had been aroused when quite a boy by seeing a map in the possession of a relative, and from that moment, he writes, "I constantly resolved, if ever I was preferred to the University, where better time and more convenient place might be ministred for those studies, I would, by God's assistance, prosecute that knowledge and kinde of literature, the doores whereof (after a sort) were so happily opened before me" [33]. Hakluyt's first book was published in 1582, under the title, Divers Voyages touching the discoverie of America and the Ilands adjacent unto the same, made first of all by Englishmen and afterwards by the Frenchmen and Britons. This work consisted of a collection of documents to support England's claim to the prior discovery of America. In the autumn of 1584 he presented to Queen Elizabeth his Discourse of Western Planting, the writing of which was largely due to the inspiration of Sir Walter Raleigh. The subject matter had been supplied by the two voyagers to Virginia, Captains Amidas and Barlow. The first edition of his great work saw light in the year after the Armada; but Hakluyt was not satisfied, and for nine more years laboured on, until in 1598 he produced the second edition in three volumes, and the world was infinitely the richer for the Principal Navigations, Voyages, Traffiques, and Discoveries of the English Nation.

The year that Hakluyt sent out Pring to make discoveries is ever famous for the death of Queen Elizabeth. The great queen, whatever her faults may have been, had indeed bound her subjects to her by affection and admiration, and created amongst them a remarkable spirit of both patriotism and gallantry. It was therefore a fitting and happy circumstance that associated the last of the Tudors with the first of our American colonies. Virginia, named from Elizabeth, the child, so to speak, of a queen, came in time to be the mother of Presidents. It is not, however, until the accession of the pedantic James that a stern resolve to accomplish the establishment of a colony seems to have been taken. The irony of history is better illustrated in this fact than perhaps elsewhere. The mean mind and timid heart of James I. could never arouse or inspire enthusiasm as Elizabeth's actions had done. And yet the appreciation of the importance of a great Empire was reserved for the reign of the first Stuart rather than during the rule of the greatest of the Tudors.

The pressing question of surplus population which had reached a climax at the accession of James I., together with the prosperity and success of the newly formed East India Company may have had something to do with the momentous decision that was taken in 1606. In that year two companies were formed: the first was the London Company, which was given permission by the Crown to plant in North America between 45° and 38° north latitude; the second division was the Plymouth Company, whose rights of plantation overlapped those of the London Company, their district being between 41° and 34° north latitude. With the history of this second company we shall deal later.

The London Company consisted of various members, such as Richard Hakluyt, the recorder of voyages; Sir George Somers, "a lamb on shore, a lion at sea"; [34] and Sir Thomas Gates. The Council was nominated by the King, and included many well-known men of the day; in particular, Sir Ferdinando Gorges, who played an important part in colonial history for many years, [35] and Sir Edwin Sandys, who, in the perilous time which came upon the Company, fought manfully for the right. The system of administration was of considerable complexity, as the control of affairs was both divided and qualified. In return for finding the capital for the proper working of the scheme, the Company was to receive certain trading privileges. The actual government was vested in two councils, both of which were nominated by James I., the one to be resident in England and supreme in all political and legislative affairs, the other to be established in the colony and liable for the proper administration of all local matters. The orders given to those in office, when the first settlement was made, were to a certain extent harsh, but in no way contrary to the spirit of the times. The Church of England was to be supported and the supremacy of the King to be acknowledged. All serious crimes were to be tried by jury and punished with death, but the penalty for minor offences was left to the discretion of the resident council. The Company took care that no trade was carried on by private individuals, and it was insisted that magazines should be erected for the produce of the colony and for supplying necessities to the colonists. It may be stated finally that the old ideas of enterprise and adventure were not lost sight of, and what had stirred Columbus and many another voyager was now definitely mentioned in the commands. The settlers were told "to show kindness to the savages and heathen people in those parts, and use all proper means to draw them to the true knowledge and service of God" [36].

By the middle of December 1606, one hundred and forty-three colonists [37] were on board three ships ready to sail for their new home in the West. On the morning of New Year's Day, 1607, the little fleet sailed down the Thames. All praise be to them for showing so brave a spirit in launching out into an unknown world at the very dawn of England's expansion. And yet it must be acknowledged that they were the very worst type of settlers that could have been chosen for such an undertaking. They were idle, discontented, impatient, and incapable. Many of them were gentlemen, who had no idea of manual labour; some were goldsmiths and jewellers, who were without knowledge of agriculture, building, or even protecting themselves from savages. But even worse than this was the fact that they had no leader with natural gifts for so important a position. At their head, to begin with, was Christopher Newport, famous as a raider off the Spanish main. In council with him were Gosnold, the intrepid voyager, and Captain John Ratcliffe, a discontented man, as proved by his later actions, although a contemporary describes him as "a very valiant, honest, and painful soldier" [38]. From the very outset there were quarrels, and Captain John Smith, whom we shall meet again, was kept in confinement during the greater part of the voyage. On the 16th April 1607, the storm-tossed adventurers sighted the southernmost extremity of Chesapeake Bay, and called it Cape Henry in honour of the Prince of Wales. On the 13th May they selected a place for settlement, and Jamestown, the first permanent plantation, was established in Virginia on the James River. Almost immediately Edward Maria Wingfield was elected president, which proved to be one of the many mistakes made by the settlers. Nobody can question Wingfield's bravery, honesty, and desire to act justly, but it is very evident from the records that he was formal and pompous in manner, and filled with a too conscious sense of his own dignity. No sooner had the president been elected than the colony was weakened by a division of their party. Captain John Smith with a few followers preferred to accompany

Newport on an exploring expedition, and reached a spot where now stands Richmond City. The Indians, under their leader Powhattan, appeared friendly to this party, but native friendship could only bear a slight strain, and trouble was only too likely to arise from the careless conduct of the settlers who had remained at Jamestown. The time was passed in a series of petty squabbles, and the infant colony struggled through a period of the gravest vicissitudes. Gosnold, one of the best of the party, died, and this was followed by the deposition of Wingfield, Captain Ratcliffe being made governor in his place. His period of office was marked by troubles with the Indians, and dire sickness which broke out amongst the settlers, owing to bad water, want of food, and the unhealthy situation of Jamestown.

At last the dominant character of Captain John Smith manifested itself, and he was chosen chief by common consent. This man's remarkable adventures read like fiction, but there is little doubt that there is a great deal of truth in all that he has left on record. Some of the most romantic episodes that he lays before the reader may perhaps be regarded as exaggerations or even untrustworthy, but it would be entirely erroneous to look upon him as a mere Baron Munchausen or a foolish braggart. He was brave beyond words, robust in person and self-reliant in mind. In all his actions he was public-spirited, and, at the same time, for his age and for his training, tolerant, kindly, and humane. He was one of the most romantic figures of the period, and as such appeals in his narrative to the sympathy of his readers and captures their affection. As a soldier in the wars in the Netherlands he had passed through many a danger. As a traveller in France, Italy, and the near East he had learnt to understand and command men. As a hardy crusader and captain in the Turkish wars he had fought manfully against the infidel in Hungary. He had suffered all the horrors of slavery, from which he had escaped through the forests of Transylvania. This man of many adventures may be regarded by posterity as the chief promoter of the colonisation of Virginia, and, if not her founder, at least her saviour.

The early settlers in Virginia would have suffered the fate of Raleigh's colony of 1587 had it not been for Captain John Smith's perseverance, steady courage, and determination. He struggled hard to teach the colonists the necessity of making themselves a self-sufficing community. Most of the men thought that gold was to be picked up anywhere, failing to see that if they did not strive manfully they must inevitably starve. Smith himself says, "our diet is a little meal and water, and not sufficient of that;" [39] and his words are proved by the fact that within the past six months fifty of the colonists died, and to use the words of the chronicler, "for the most part they died of famine." Smith determined that this should not continue, and he took for his motto, "Nothing is to be expected except by labour." Excellent as was the motto, the material from which he had to build up a colony was of the very worst, and it is only natural that he should write home and ask for "thirty carpenters, blacksmiths, masons, and diggers up of trees' roots, rather than a thousand of such as we have" [40]. His past experiences now stood him in good stead, and he proved himself a capable leader by succeeding in forcing the colony into a small, settled community. When he felt that the colony was for the time being fairly secure he went on exploring expeditions among the Indians. This was part of the purpose and duty of the colony, for men were eager to find a short passage to India, and no one imagined that America was of the gigantic size that later discovery proved it to be. Whilst on these expeditions the adventures of Smith were most extraordinary, and may possibly have been coloured by lapse of time and a brilliant imagination. Once he saved his life by the marvels of his compass and by the writing of notes to his friends in Jamestown; and once indeed, according to his own record, he was saved by the lovely Pocahontas, who pleaded with her father Powhattan for his life. This latter story is, however, extremely unlikely, for the Indian princess could have been only a child at the time, and it is probable that Smith added the account when the fame of Pocahontas had spread to Europe.

Smith spent the whole of the spring of 1609 in Jamestown endeavouring to make the settlers industrious by prosecuting the manufacture of tar, pitch, and soap ashes. Up to this time, with absurd carelessness, the Jamestown fortification had been left without a well, and Smith now remedied this obvious defect. With equal energy he turned to building, and during the months of February, March, and April, he erected twenty houses, besides a blockhouse, and re-roofed the church. Agriculture and the fishing industry were no longer neglected, and while some of the settlers under Smith's guidance brought forty acres under cultivation, others undertook to supply the colony with fish. Struggle as he did, Smith continually suffered reverses, and many disasters overtook the colonists, the most serious being the destruction of their corn by rats. Starvation stared them in the face, but Smith's firmness and activity overcame the horrors of famine, and instead of allowing the settlers to mass together, the men were quartered in different localities where they had to seek food for themselves. When this remarkable man at last left the colony, it can scarcely be said to have been in a prosperous state, but there were four hundred and ninety strong colonists who had been put on the right road towards progress, partly by Smith's example and partly by his doctrine "that he who would not work might not eat."

Captain John Smith from his "Generall Historie of Virginia."

About the time that Smith was preparing to return to England there was in that country a reawakening of interest in what Drayton called, "Virginia, earth's only Paradise." The keener interest that was now being shown was largely due to a number of pamphlets that had been published, and also to the enthusiastic sermons of many of the clergy of the day. In a pamphlet named the Nova Britannia it was pointed out that Virginia was a valuable opening as a new market for English cloth, and, in addition, that trade between the two countries would stimulate the merchant navy. "We shall not still betake ourselves to small and little shipping as we daily do beginne, but we shall rear againe such Marchants Shippes, both tall and stout, as no forreine sayle that swimmes shall make them vayle or stoop; whereby to make this little northern corner of the world to be in a short time the richest storehouse and staple for marchandise in all Europe" [41]. With this idea of making England "the richest storehouse," a new charter was granted to the Company in May 1609. The London Company was now put under a number of influential men, including Robert Cecil, Earl of Salisbury, and Sir Francis Bacon, while at the same time the old directors remained upon the board. Under the new charter the dual control of the two councils disappeared, and the government was to be in the hands of one council nominated in the first case by the King, and afterwards, as vacancies occurred, they were to be filled by men elected by the Company. The powers of the Company were also extended, for besides the right of levying duties, it was conceded that defensive war might be waged if it were thought expedient. By these means the Company practically became an independent body.

The outcome of the change was immediately seen in an expedition which set out under Sir George Somers and Sir Thomas Gates. In July 1609 these adventurers were wrecked upon the uninhabited Bermudas, but in the following spring they succeeded in reaching Virginia. The attractive picture of the settlement as drawn in pamphlet and sermon in England was scarcely true to life. As a matter of fact no sooner had Smith left the colony than its inhabitants dropped back into their slothful ways, which were at once taken advantage of by the cunning Redskins, who, peaceful while the great captain was present, had now become most hostile. Thus Sir Thomas

Gates in this year records, "the state of the Colony ... began to find a sensible declyning: which Powhattan (as a greedy Vulture) obseruing, and boyling with desire of reuenge, he inuited Captaine Ratclife and about thirty others to trade for Corne, and vnder the colour of fairest friendship he brought them within the compasse of his ambush, whereby they were cruelly murthered and massacred" [42].

The fate of the colony once more hung in the balance; starvation was once again at the door. Very fortunately for the settlers, Lord Delawarr arrived as Captain-General and Governor, with, what was most important, supplies. The Company, however was becoming disheartened. The colony had now been in existence for three years and the returns to the shareholders were meagre indeed. Something had to be done and strong measures seemed appropriate. In June 1611, Delawarr embarked for England, but Sir Thomas Dale had already been dispatched with the title of High Marshal of Virginia. He was armed with a military and civil code of the greatest severity, for he was confronted with the arduous task of governing a people made up of "the scourings of London." The military code was from the first practically a dead letter; but the civil enactments were so extremely harsh and so peculiar to modern ideas that they deserve some attention. Daily worship according to the service of the Church of England was enforced by a penalty of six months in the galleys. To refrain from attending Sunday service meant death. If any man "unworthily demean himself unto any preacher or minister of God's word" he was to be openly whipped three times, and after each whipping he was to confess his crime. But these laws were almost mild in comparison with the vague and brutal enactment that "no man shall give disgraceful words or commit any act to the disgrace of any person in this colony, or any part thereof, upon pain of being tied head and feet together upon the ground every night for the space of one month" [43].

These harsh laws continued, but did not affect the tide of emigration from England. In August 1611, Sir Thomas Gates returned as Governor with three hundred fresh settlers [44]. From this moment a much better class of colonists began to come out, bringing with them their own servants, and forming the nucleus of a sound colonial population. There were, of course, other reasons for the improved state of affairs, not the least important being the fact that Gates worked hard for the benefit of the colony. An excellent change was carried out when the settlers deserted unhealthy Jamestown for the more salubrious Henrico. Here a church, a hospital, and good houses of brick were erected, and a palisade was raised as a protection from the Indians. Industries, too, began to thrive, for the records show that both silk and iron were manufactured, while vines were cultivated with success by some Frenchmen introduced by Lord Delawarr. Even in England the affairs of the Company had changed for the better, as in 1612 a fresh charter had been obtained, by which the Bermudas or Somers Islands were added to its dominions.

Prosperous as the colony appeared there was ever the menace of the Indian tribes with whom an intermittent war had been waged for some time, and during which Powhattan had taken captive several of the settlers. Peace, however, existed between the English and Japazaus, the Indian chief of the district along the Potomac, to whom Samuel Argall was sent by the Governor to trade for corn. This was not Argall's first visit to Japazaus, and a certain friendship existed between the two, the Indian chief regarding himself as indebted to the Englishman. With the King of the Potomac district, as wife of one of his captains, was the romantic Pocahontas, daughter of Powhattan. To the unscrupulous and ready-witted Argall this appeared a glorious opportunity of demanding the Princess as a hostage, and paying off old scores against Powhattan. Argall broached the subject to Japazaus, who readily accepted the plan. The story is told with strict truth by Ralph Hamor, the secretary of the colony, who says, "Capt. Argall, having secretly well rewarded him, with a small copper kettle, and som other les valuable toies so highly by him esteemed, that doubtlesse he would have betraied his owne father for them, permitted both him and his wife to returne," [45] but Pocahontas remained a captive. Hearing of his daughter's plight Powhattan immediately restored some of his prisoners and demanded her surrender, but the English not being satisfied, asked for more. By this time other influences were at work, and Pocahontas exhibited no desire to return to her people. In the spring of 1613, she was baptised by the name of Rebecca, and married to one of the most influential settlers, John Rolfe, "a gentleman of approved behaviour and honest cariage" [46]. The marriage was welcomed by the Indian chief, and peace was restored for the time being. Pocahontas and her husband went to England in 1616, where she was fêted and presented at court, but the English climate did not suit the Indian beauty, and she died in the spring of the following year at Gravesend.

The year 1614 is memorable in Virginian history for the first hostile action between the English and their French rivals. Samuel Argall, who has been classified as "a sea-captain with piratical tastes," attacked a French settlement on the coast of Maine and sacked Port Royal, the capital of Acadia or Nova Scotia. These acts were contrary to all the principles of international law, but France, under the weak rule of Marie de' Medici, was in no state to avenge her wrongs, and the matter dropped after a formal complaint by the French ambassador. This and other weighty questions caused an animated discussion in Parliament concerning the rights and privileges of Virginia. Martin, the advocate of the Company, told the House to look to the advantages to be gained in Virginia, and not to waste their time on the trifles that generally engaged their attention. In fact, his speech was so heated that he was forced to confess his errors on bended knee, and with that the House of Commons was satisfied, and dropped the subject.

After the retirement of Gates, Sir Thomas Dale continued the government of Virginia under the merciless code; and yet the colony prospered, private industry and private property being allowed. Dale's second period of office was for two years only, and he departed at a time when a greedy and unprincipled set of men began to administer the affairs of the Company. In 1617 they selected as their Deputy Governor in Virginia the most unsuitable Samuel Argall. Certainly he was a man endowed with ability and resolute courage, but he was one of the few unscrupulous villains who have disgraced colonial history. Immediately on coming into power he issued a series of edicts of arbitrary character. Trade with the Indians was forbidden, but this was not for the advantage of the shareholders of the Company, but for the benefit of their deputy. The settlers were made to work as slaves for Argall, for whom the constitution of the colony afforded splendid opportunities. Such a state of affairs was not to last for long; the despotic conduct of the Governor leaked out at identically the moment the Company passed into the hands of a more honest and capable set of directors [47]. Sir Edwin Sandys, a leader of that party which was soon to turn boldly against the King, together with the brilliantly versatile Southampton and the skilled John Ferrars, were now at the head of Virginian affairs in England.

The history of Virginia changed for the better in 1619, when Sir George Yeardley superseded the piratical Argall. The new Governor was not a particularly strong man, and in many of his actions he proved himself a weak successor of the stern Sir Thomas Dale. On the other hand there was beneath the somewhat too gentle exterior a man of considerable worth, for he succeeded in governing peaceably a turbulent people without falling back upon unnecessary severity. Yeardley's first year of administration is ever famous for the establishment of the earliest representative assembly in the New World. It is only natural that a fully developed scheme was not evolved at once. There is some uncertainty as to what classes actually obtained the franchise, but it is probable that every freeman possessed a vote. Certain it is, however, that each plantation and each county returned two members, and it is equally well-known that the assembly took upon itself both legislative rights and judicial powers. Thus the year 1619 witnessed the creation of Virginia as an almost independent power heralding a revolutionary change in the near future.

The colony seemed prosperous in every way, but there were dark clouds overshadowing the Company on all sides. It was rumoured, and with some truth, that five thousand emigrants had landed in Virginia, and yet only one thousand were actually resident. Men asked themselves the question, "had the settlers returned, or had they died in this so-called land of promise"? The new board of directors, if they had been left to themselves, would have put the Company upon an assured footing, and success would most certainly have attended their efforts. But this was not to be; the Company was attacked from within and without. Lord Warwick's party, a clique within the Company, showed every sign of hostility to Southampton and Sandys. The external attacks came from three sources, not the least important being that of the Crown. James I. was jealous of the power of that Company which he himself had created. His fears were increased by the insidious attacks of the Spanish ambassador, Gondomar, who informed the King that "a seditious Company was but the seminary to a seditious Parliament" [48]. Even the English people, little realising the work that the Company was painfully accomplishing for Imperial purposes, now turned against the men whom, for sentimental reasons, they ought to have supported, and used the popular cry against monopolies to bring about the downfall of the founders of a new nation. The dangers of the Company were increased by the perils of the colony itself. The old Indian hostility had for a few years slumbered, but after the death of Powhattan and the succession of Opechancanough in 1618 the horrors of Indian warfare once more threatened the colony. In the following year the death of a famous Indian, Jack the Feather, was a sufficient pretext, and Opechancanough attacked Virginia. The English proved successful in the end, but not before they had lost three hundred and seventy of their number. It is not to be wondered at that the Assembly issued a severe order that "the inhabitants of every plantation should fall upon their adjoining savages;" [49] this the planters readily obeyed; and the steps taken, though harsh, appear to have been effectual.

The news of the Indian massacres, the action of Spain and the absurd desire of a Spanish marriage, worked upon the mind of James I. to such an extent that he determined to abolish the Company [50]. In 1623 the King demanded the surrender of the charter, which Sandys and his party stoutly refused. A writ of quo warranto was then issued to decide whether the privileges of the Company were purely a monopoly, or whether they were exercised for the public good. The Law Courts gave a verdict against the Company, and the charter was declared null and void. The storm cloud, which had long hung over the Company, had now burst upon the heads of the devoted directors. They were forced to succumb to the most pernicious of all influences, for they had been crushed by greed and covetousness, together with the intrigues of disgraceful courtiers and disappointed speculators who showed a lack of public spirit that too often marked the early years of the Stuart period. In reviewing the actions of the Company it is universally agreed that they had in almost every case been for good; it is, however, acknowledged with similar unanimity that for the actual benefit of the colony in the future it was as well that the Company's powers should pass to the Crown. Had the actions of the Company been disliked in the colony itself, it is inexplicable that the colony should have supported the Company at the time of its trial. The settlers could not foresee what might be the outcome of a continuance of the Company's rule. At the time they merely realised with disgust that James had acted as he had done, solely to gain the fickle and grudging favour of the decadent Spain; but they did not understand that the Company must inevitably in the future, if it had not already done so in the past, act as a trammelling influence upon the progress and prosperity of the little settlement. Unwittingly James, by his action, had removed the fetters, and had given an opportunity of free growth to the colony. It was no longer possible for the welfare of the individual planter to be sacrificed to the merely temporary advantage of the English trader and shareholder. "Morally and politically, indeed, the abrogation of the Virginian charter was a crime;" but "the colony, happily for its future, passed under the control of the Crown while it was yet plastic, undeveloped and insignificant" [51]. Henceforth the constitution of Virginia was of the normal type; the administration was carried on by a governor and two chambers, the one nominated, the other popularly elected.

The first chapter of Virginian history may be said to have closed when the Company ceased to exist, and at the same time the romantic and heroic aspect of the colony was concluded. Although perhaps no individual connected with the foundation of the colony can be compared with the glorious figures of the Elizabethan epoch, yet in the characters of Hakluyt, Southampton, Sandys, and Captain John Smith there was something of the old order. The heroism of the first actors upon the Virginian stage was probably as great as that of their predecessors, but the new order of things did not call upon them to exhibit such feats of strength or of bravery. By the abrogation of the Company's charter a revolution had indeed been effected. From this moment the history of Virginia can only be dealt with in a brief and hasty sketch, for happy is the country that has no history, and such is the case with regard to the later years of England's first great colony. The interests of the settlers are in the future mainly confined to the growth of tobacco, as will be shown in a later chapter, and from 1623 the chroniclers cease to record the story of the terrible struggle for bare existence, but tell rather the tale of a steady but unheroic prosperity amongst a rich class of planters employing negro labour.

The first Governor under the Crown was Sir Francis Wyatt, who was of good character and inspired the colonists with a self-reliant temper. He was succeeded in 1626 by Sir George Yeardley, who had already won the affection of many of the settlers in the days of the Company's rule. The following year, however, Yeardley died; and the Crown appointed a creature of its own, Governor Harvey, who quarrelled with the Assembly on every possible occasion. In fact so bitter did these quarrels become that a settler, Mathews by name, as leader of the popular party, seized Harvey in 1635, and placed him upon a vessel where he was kept in honourable confinement until the old country was reached. It is hardly likely that the colonists imagined that the Crown would take their part against the Governor, but their action was probably due to a general desire to impress the Crown with their power. Charles I., who had previously shown good feeling towards the colony, now behaved foolishly in sending Harvey back to Virginia, where he remained for four years, filling up his time by sending numerous petty and querulous complaints to the home country of the misdoings of the settlers. During Harvey's administration the old proprietors made several attempts to obtain a fresh grant of the charter and the reinstitution of the Company. But with the same ardent spirit as the colonists had supported the Company in 1623, so now they opposed its re-establishment and for the same reason. The change that they had imagined must inevitably take place by the abolition of the Company was a loss of their titles; but having been firmly settled under the Crown they were frightened that if the Company should be again created their titles would be again endangered. The advocate of the colonists was the pliant and pliable Sandys, who, when he reached England, deserted his constituents, and pleaded for the restoration of the old rule. The colony immediately on hearing of this sent word to the King that their representative was acting contrary to their wishes, and in 1639 they received the satisfactory reply that Charles had no intention of restoring the Company.

From this time the settlers appear from contemporary records to have been contented. The writers point out how nature gave freely, how beautiful was the land, and how peaceful were the natives. There can be no doubt that this was the content and boastfulness of a young people, and that it was unduly exaggerated. On the other hand it must also be allowed that though Virginia was not quite the paradise represented in some of the letters written by the settlers, yet it was, when the Civil War broke out in England, a land of comparative peace and plenty.

Sir Francis Wyatt was again sent out to succeed Governor Harvey in 1639, but his period of office was short and uneventful. More stirring times came when the colony passed under the rule of Sir William Berkeley. He was a typical cavalier, bluff in speech, hot in temper, brave in danger, and contemptuous of learning. He may, in later years, have exercised a merciless tyranny, but it was the hardship of his fortunes together with something closely akin to lunacy that drove him to such actions. On his appointment, his instructions were more carefully formulated than had hitherto been the case. This was only natural as the Court party at home were beginning to see the dangers that were looming ahead, and so they trusted that in Virginia trouble might be checked by the exaction of the strictest oaths of allegiance and supremacy, and by the insistence on the service of the Church of England. This latter was hardly necessary as speaking widely the Church of England was the Church of the Virginians. There were, however, three parishes, the members of which were almost entirely nonconformists until dispersed and scattered by a conformity act between the years 1642 and 1644.

Sir William Berkeley had hardly taken up the reins of government when the history of the colony was marked by a great calamity. Opechancanough was now an old man, enfeebled in body and physically incapable of leading his people; but his mind was still as active as ever, his savage cunning was in no way dimmed by years, and he had ever nursed the hatred he had felt for the settlers since the failure of his attack in the days of the Company. The rumours of the outbreak of the Civil War in

England soon reached the ears of the Indians, some of whom had actually seen two ships of the white settlers bombarding each other in the Bay. Opechancanough seized this opportunity of division and strife among the Virginians, and fell upon the colony. Before the settlers were ready to resist, three hundred men, women and children had been slain. The local militia at last made headway against the savages, and after the capture and death of the old chief in 1646 a treaty was made as to the boundary between the English and the Indians, under which peace reigned for thirty years.

It has been the fashion to regard Virginia as a purely Cavalier colony; this is probably due to an attempt to accentuate the difference between the Southern colony and the New England group. It is, however, an exaggeration to say that Virginia was entirely composed of those supporting cavalier principles. Certainly there were large landowners who sympathised with Charles and his party, but there was a very large and prosperous middle class, composed of small landowners and well-to-do tradesmen, amongst whom it was only natural to find various opinions and sympathies. As a whole, however, Virginia may be said to have been Royalist, not from any rooted objection to the Commonwealth, but rather because the Royalist party was temporarily predominant in the settlement. Sir William Berkeley, as a loyal Governor, forbade the showing of any sympathy to the Parliamentary rebels, and he was supported in his action by Charles II., who, in 1650, before he left Breda, despatched a commission empowering Berkeley to act in his name. The far-reaching power of Cromwell was not to be stayed by any such commission, for the Commonwealth was determined "to grasp the whole of the inheritance of the Stuart Kings," [52] and so Ayscue was sent in 1651 to reduce the colonies to submission. On March 12 of the following year, Virginia acknowledged the new power in England, much to the rage and discontent of the Governor. Berkeley had indeed done his best, and had issued a stirring declaration which concluded with these words, "But, gentlemen, by the Grace of God we will not so tamely part with our King and all those blessings we enjoy under him, and if they oppose us, do but follow me, I will either lead you to victory or lose a life which I cannot more gloriously sacrifice than for my loyalty and your security" [53]. The settlers, however, were not stirred, and though a thousand men had been collected at Jamestown, the Assembly refused their support, not so much for the love of Cromwell as because they feared material loss if they resisted him. Had the great Protector lived longer the history of the American colonies might have been very different. He was the first Englishman who can really be said to have understood in its fullest sense the word Empire. But the gods were not generous to this imperialist, and they did not grant to him the necessary time for the achievement of a policy which Cromwell himself classed as similar to that of "Queen Elizabeth of famous memory" [54]. As it was, the rule of the Commonwealth had little definite effect upon Virginia, except that it necessitated a change in governors. The first was Richard Bennet, who was elected by the Assembly in 1652, and ruled for three years. His successor, Edward Digges, was a worthy and sensible man, under whose administration the colony continued a calm and happy existence for one year. In 1656 Samuel Mathews was chosen, but during his rule Virginian history was unimportant, and the only cloud upon the horizon was an Indian panic which came to nothing.

The submission of Virginia was for the time only, and at the restoration of Charles II. once more the royalist party became supreme. The King was accepted with perfect quiescence, and it is probable that the Virginians, like the English, rejoiced at the change, looking forward to the return of more mirthful and joyous days. As England learnt to repent the return of the Stuarts, so also Virginia found that she had fallen upon evil times, a fact which is partially shown in Berkeley's report in 1671. "As for the boundaries of our land, it was once great, ten degrees in latitude, but now it has pleased his Majesty to confine us to halfe a degree. Knowingly I speak this. Pray God it may be for his Majesty's service, but I much fear the contrary.... I thank God, there are no free schools, nor printing , and I hope we shall not have these hundred years; for learning has brought disobedience, and heresy, and sects into the world, and printing has divulged them, and libels against the best government. God keep us from both" [55].

The greed of the cavaliers under Charles II. is notorious, and it affected Virginia just as much as it did England. Lord Arlington and Lord Culpeper obtained in 1672 the most monstrous rights, together with a grant by which the whole soil of the colony passed into their hands. An agency was at once sent to England to oppose this discreditable action, at the same time taking with them a charter for which they hoped to obtain ratification from the King. Needless to say in this they were unsuccessful; but the charter is historically important, because it contained a clause stating that the colonists could not be taxed without the consent of their own legislature. The work of the agency partly failed owing to the supineness of Governor Berkeley; chiefly, however, because the people of Virginia were unable to see that agencies could not be sent without expenditure. When a poll-tax was enacted to cover the necessary expenses of their agents, there was a popular outburst.

The inhabitants of Virginia at this time were much divided, and composed of distinct classes, the well-to-do planter, the tradesman, the "mean whites," the negro and the criminal. The last class had been growing steadily for some years as the colony had been used as a dumping-ground for gaol-birds, and indeed the criminal section would have increased still more had it not been for the better class of settlers who determined to stop it. In April 1670, the General Court held at Jamestown issued a notice "because by the great numbers of felons and other desperate villains being sent over from the prisons in England, the horror yet remaining of the barbarous designs of those villains in September 1663, who attempted at once the subversion of our religion, laws, liberties, rights and privileges," we do now prohibit "the landing of any jail-birds from and after the 20th of January next upon pain of being forced to carry them to some other country" [56]. Although this law tended to exclude a cheap form of labour, nevertheless between 1669 and 1674 Virginia, commercially, was in a most flourishing condition, raising a greater revenue for the Crown than any other settlement. Sir John Knight informed Lord Shaftesbury that £150,000 in customs on tobacco alone had been paid, "so that Virginia is as of great importance to his Majesty as the Spanish Indies to Spain, and employs more ships and breeds more seamen for his Majesty's service than any other trade" [57].

Commercial success was not the only thing that went to make up Virginian history, for there were signs of external danger only too plainly exhibited by numerous outrages on the part of the Indians. Had Berkeley shown any skill or energy in suppressing these disorders all might have gone well; as it was he did nothing, with dire results. The incapacity of the Governor at last aroused the wrath of a young, honest, courageous, but indiscreet, member of the Assembly, named Nathaniel Bacon. He took up arms and was at first pardoned, but when he once again attempted to seize Jamestown he was taken, and died in so mysterious a manner as to give rise to rumours of poison and treachery, though it was also reported, "that, he dyed by inbibing or taking in two (sic) much Brandy" [58]. Bacon's rising had the effect desired in so far as it brought about the recall of Berkeley. So vindictively and cruelly did the Governor punish Bacon's followers that in 1677 the Crown sent three Commissioners, Sir John Berry, Colonel Francis Moryson, and Colonel Herbert Jeffreys to look into the grievances of either side. They almost immediately quarrelled with the Governor, who was anxious to carry on his severe punishments. The King, however, had commanded the Commissioners to show, if possible, the greatest lenience. As a matter of fact out of a population of 15,000, only 500 were on the side of the Governor, and this small party who claimed to be the loyalists, very naturally advocated confiscations and fines. Berkeley obstructed the Commissioners as well as he was able, showing himself reckless of all consequences, and exhibiting gross discourtesy to the King's representatives. The truth was that Berkeley was growing old, and had possessed unlimited power far too long, supported as he had been by a most corrupt Assembly. The end of the quarrel came when the Governor, or more probably, Lady Berkeley, insulted the officials beyond forgiveness. After a consultation at the Governor's house the Commissioners were sent away in his carriage with "the common hangman" for postillion [59]. This outrage upon the laws of hospitality was too much; and Jeffreys immediately assumed the reins of government. Sir William Berkeley gave one more snarl, informing the new Governor that he was "utterly unacquainted" [60] with the laws, customs, and nature of the people; he then sailed for England, which he reached just alive, but "so unlikely to live that it had been very inhuman to have troubled him with any interrogations; so he died without any account given of his government" [61].

Sir Herbert Jeffreys had a difficult task before him in trying to purge the Assembly. Within a year of taking up office he died, leaving no lasting memorial of his skill as Governor, but he is "to be remembered as the first of a long series of officers of the standing army who have held the governorship of a colony" [62]. Jeffreys' successor, Sir Henry Chicheley, only held office for a few months, and at his departure the old type of governor disappears. The year 1679 is remarkable for the new method of administration, a method which proved injurious to the colony. Thomas, Lord Culpeper, was the first of the new scheme, and though he resided in the colony for four years he did nothing for its inhabitants. The appointment of Culpeper was most ill-advised, as he was already detested owing to the grant of 1672. He took up his office at identically the same time as the burgesses acquired the right of sitting as a separate chamber, and he found the council refractory, the colony unprosperous, and the Company of his Majesty's Guards in "mutinous humours" [63]. His tenure of office expired in 1684, and he was succeeded by Lord Howard of Effingham. It cannot be said that the new Governor was idle, but whatever he did was to the disadvantage of Virginia and the Virginians. By a scandalous system of jobbery he inflicted grievous financial injury upon individuals, and at the same time retarded the progress of the colony by a system of new imposts. By his skill he obtained for the Governor and the Council the right of appointing the Secretary to the Assembly, which ought not to have been allowed by a free representative body. From this time the evils of the English colonial system became apparent, and it is now that absentee governors enrich themselves at the expense of their settlements, the actual administration being left to lieutenant governors in the confidence of their chiefs, who remained at home.

The great stumbling-block to colonial prosperity was the lack of unity between the different settlements on the eastern coast of North America. In

1684 an attempt was made to bring about united action against Indians, who had desolated the western borders of the English colonies. A conference was called at Albany, and Virginia, like all the other colonies, sent delegates to discuss the possibility of creating the United States under the British Crown. Nothing, however, came of it, for the jealousies and wranglings of the delegates only too well illustrated the feelings of the different settlements for each other. The Revolution of 1688 was accepted with tranquillity in Virginia, and two years later Francis Nicholson was appointed King William's lieutenant governor. Nicholson was a man of much colonial experience, of violent temper, and scandalous private life. He strongly opposed the desire for political freedom, but at the same time he made an excellent governor, and during his rule, which lasted until 1704 (except for a period of six years, 1692-1698), the colony prospered. A desire for education evinced itself at this period, and in 1691 Commissary Blair was sent to England to obtain a patent for the creation of a college. He returned within two years, his labours having been crowned with success, and in 1693 the second university [64] in America was established under the title of William and Mary College.

As the seventeenth century drew to a close, Virginian progress was stimulated by the settlement, on the upper waters of the James River, of De Richebourg's colony of Huguenots, which is said to have "infused a stream of pure and rich blood into Virginian society." If the test of a colony is its population, Virginia at this time must have been most flourishing. Less than a century had passed since Newport and his one hundred and forty-three settlers had sailed into the James River; the colony had suffered privations, had witnessed many a fluctuation of fortune, but at the dawn of the eighteenth century about one hundred thousand souls were living there in peace, plenty and happiness. During the century that had passed, the settlers had won for themselves political rights, and practically, political freedom. They were to a certain extent restricted by the Navigation Acts, but the influence of the Crown or of the English Parliament was hardly felt. Their interest in English political life was meagre; the importance of getting trustworthy lieutenant governors was far greater to the Virginian than whether Whig or Tory was in power at home. Sometimes the colony was fortunate, sometimes the reverse, but in every case the lieutenant governor was opposed to any extension of political rights. The difficulty of united effort on the part of the planters was, to a certain extent, intensified by a want of towns. Hampton was Virginia's chief port, and was composed of a hundred poor houses, while Williamsburg cannot be regarded as a true centre of either economic or intellectual activity. This lack of town life is pointed out by Commissary Blair, who informed the Bishop of London, "even when attempts have been made by the Assembly to erect towns they have been frustrated. Everyone wants the town near his own house, and the majority of the burgesses have never seen a town, and have no notion of any but a country life" [65]. The lieutenant governors during the eighteenth century had not only to contend with the supineness of the settlers, but also with intercolonial discord. Thus Alexander Spotswood, in 1711, attempted to assist North Carolina against the Tuscarora Indians, but he received no support from either the Council or Assembly of Virginia. Five years later Spotswood was met with similar bickerings and squabbles when South Carolina was invaded by the Yamassees. In 1741 Oglethorpe begged assistance to protect the newly established Georgia; instead of sending their best we are told that his officer brought back "all the scum of Virginia" [66].

The worst feature of Virginian life was the omnipresent and omnipotent slave system, but from the mere commercial aspect this was in favour of the colony at the time. The planters, however, were never ready to leave the colony for imperial purposes owing to the fear of a negro rising at home. This was one of the chief difficulties with which the Governor, Robert Dinwiddie, had to contend, during that trying period of French and Indian attack, which prepared the way for the Seven Years' war. With this period it is not proposed to deal now, but to leave it to a later chapter concerning the struggle between the French colonists in the north and west, and the English settlers upon the eastern seaboard during that period which is peculiarly connected with Britain's imperial story.

Chapter 3

THE COLONISATION OF MARYLAND AND THE CAROLINAS

"Maryland is a province not commonly knowne in England, because the name of Virginia includes or clouds it, it is a Country wholy belonging to that honorable Gentleman the Lord Baltamore" [67]. Such is the description of the colony that now comes before us, and at the time it was penned John Hammond, the writer, told the truth. The colony had arisen under rather peculiar circumstances, which neither resembled the foundation of Virginia nor the settlement of the Pilgrim Fathers. In 1632 Charles I. granted to George Calvert, first Lord Baltimore, an ill-defined tract of territory to the north of Virginia. Baltimore was an old hand at colonisation, for he had some years previous attempted to form a settlement in Newfoundland which had not been successful. David Kirke, who took over the Baltimore lands there, said that Newfoundland agreed with all God's creatures except Jesuits and schismatics, and that a great mortality among the former tribe had driven Baltimore away. Whether this was the true reason, or whether, as it has been proposed, Baltimore was practically driven out by the Presbyterians, it is hard to decide. His next trial as a colony founder was made in the more southern lands of Virginia, but here his Roman Catholicism was sternly opposed by the English Church party. Under these circumstances his Maryland colony seemed likely to flourish, for there were neither schismatics nor churchmen, nor Presbyterians, but only Indians to contend against. Before the first Lord Baltimore could accomplish anything he died, but the grant was transferred to his son Cecil. The charter is an important one, for by it the Proprietors gained both territorial and political rights; the freemen or representative assembly were to be consulted, and with their advice the Proprietor could enact laws. All places of worship were to be consecrated according to the Church of England, and so the Roman Catholic faith had only a subordinate position in a colony which owed its foundation to a true upholder of that belief. From the very first Maryland was better off than several of the other colonies, as the Crown divested itself of the right of levying taxes within the province; but in other respects the constitution was normal, consisting of a governor and two chambers, the proprietor possessing the privilege of creating councillors.

Leonard Calvert, brother of the second Lord Baltimore, sailed to take possession in 1633, accompanied by two Jesuit priests and three hundred emigrants. These colonists were neither gaol-birds nor religious fanatics; they had been selected with great care and were well provided. One of the Jesuits, Father White, has left on record his Impressions in which he says that the colony was founded with a definite religious and educational purpose. "We had not come thither for the purpose of war, but for the sake of benevolence, that we might imbue a rude race with the precepts of civilisation, and open up a way to heaven, as well as impart to them the advantages of remote regions" [68]. When the settlers came to the place of landing they "beheld the natives armed. That night fires were kindled through the whole region, and since so large a ship had never been seen by them messengers were sent everywhere to announce 'that a canoe as large as an island had brought as many men as there was trees in the woods'" [69]. From this moment and onwards the relations with the natives were always friendly. The small independent landowners being free from this danger, at first, lived happy and contented lives, but they were gradually crushed out of existence by large estate-holders working with gangs of indentured labourers.

The people of Virginia looked with some scorn upon their modern neighbours, and it was not long before a quarrel took place. The Isle of Kent lay in such a position off the coast that under Baltimore's patent it ought to have been included in the province of Maryland. But in 1625 the Virginians had settled there for trading purposes, and were determined not to be brought under the yoke of Baltimore's proprietorship. Two years after the establishment of Maryland, the Isle of Kent was under the rule of William Clayborne, a strong Protestant, a contentious man, who was described by his enemies as "a pestilent enemy to the wel-faire of that province and the Lord Proprietor" [70].

Calvert, anxious to establish the rights of his brother, sent two ships to the Isle of Kent, and these were attacked by the crew of a pinnace belonging to Clayborne, lives being lost on both sides. The quarrel continued with so much fervour that it became merged in the greater struggle of the Civil War. Calvert was granted by the King letters of marque for privateering purposes, and he took good care to prey upon his enemy, Clayborne, whose friend Ingle had been furnished with similar letters from Parliament. Thus having placed the quarrel which was really personal under the banners of King and Parliament, the two rivals contended with each other.

The Parliamentary forces were, at first, successful; Ingle and Clayborne invaded Maryland, seized St Mary's, and Calvert was obliged to fly. But with assistance from Governor Berkeley of Virginia, he returned and drove out the Clayborne faction which had disgusted the people by its incapacity and greed. The quarrel ceased for a short time, owing to Calvert's death; but it was not long before it was renewed. Lord Baltimore appointed as his deputy William Stone, an ardent nonconformist and Parliamentarian, who repaid the Proprietor's generosity by leaguing with the people of the Isle of Kent. Traitor though he was, it is to be remembered that during his period of rule one good act was passed. Maryland was already celebrated for its toleration, but in 1649 it was still further enacted that a Christian was not to be "in any ways molested or discountenanced for or in respect of his or her religion, nor in the free exercise thereof" [71].

For the peace of their minds and the preservation of their property Stone and the settlers acknowledged the Parliamentary commissioners, including Clayborne, who landed in 1652. They first displaced Stone, but realising that he was popular, and thinking that it would be advantageous for them, reinstated him. Stone, however, once more proved a trimmer, and sided with the Proprietor; his late followers deserted him and turned to Clayborne. On the establishment of the Protectorate in 1654 Lord Baltimore asserted his rights, claiming that he now held from the Protector Cromwell, and declaring that the commissioners' privileges had ceased. Clayborne and his companions were not the men to take such a rebuff as this. "It was not religion, it was not punctilios they stood upon, it was that sweete, that rich, that large country they aimed at" [72]. With this desire, according to a contemporary, Clayborne asserted his authority by disfranchising the Roman Catholics and forbidding the oath of loyalty to the Proprietor. William Stone, stung to resistance and filled with importance as the representative of Lord Baltimore, took up arms and was defeated by the Protestant party at Providence in 1655. Many of Stone's followers were executed, and their property confiscated; Stone himself was sentenced to death, but was reprieved. Clayborne's party now seemed triumphant, but the home authorities refused to bestow upon him the Isle of Kent, and within two years the Protector restored to Baltimore his proprietorship of Maryland. Trouble still continued, and in 1659 Josias Fendall, the Proprietor's Governor, so worked upon the members of Assembly that they claimed full legislative rights and complete independence of the Baltimore family.

At the Restoration the quarrel came to an end, and Lord Baltimore re-established his rights with nothing more than a mere show of force. Philip Carteret was appointed Governor, and during his term of office a mint was set up in the colony. He was succeeded in 1662 by Charles Calvert to the alarm of the Protestant inhabitants, who sent an extraordinary document to the Lord Mayor and London merchants entitled, "Complaint from heaven with a hue and cry and a petition out of Virginia and Maryland, to the King and his Parliament against the Barklian and Baltimore parties. The platform is Pope Jesuit determined to overthrow England with fire and sword and destructions, and the Maryland Papists to drive us Protestants to purgatory" [73]. These, however, were purely imaginary troubles, and a more real one fell upon both Virginia and Maryland on August 27, 1667, when a terrific gale destroyed in two hours four-fifths of their tobacco and corn, and blew down 15,000 houses. On the whole Virginia suffered perhaps more than Maryland, but neither colony was really subject to such perils; and both, during the first fifteen years of Charles II.'s reign, enriched themselves as well as the Proprietor or the Crown by the fertility of their soil. This period of prosperity, however, gave way to one of unrest.

By the death of Cecil, Lord Baltimore in 1675, Charles Calvert, the late Governor, succeeded as heir to the family titles, estates and proprietorship of Maryland, the latter being placed under his deputy, Thomas Notley. The Proprietor was not at first upon the best of terms with the home government. He was severely reprimanded by the Privy Council for the imprisonment and assassination of a collector of customs. It is not hinted that Baltimore had any actual hand in this crime, but it is thought that he connived "at least ex post facto in his murder." No sooner had the Proprietor got over this difficulty, than he fell out with the settlers, who were caused much uneasiness in 1681 by the limitation of the franchise to those freeholders of 50 acres or those owners of other property of the value of £40. A spirit of unrest was therefore abroad, and there were not wanting those who were ready to snatch the opportunity and pose as patriots against the aggression of the Proprietor. Josias Fendall, who had already tried to deprive the Baltimore family of their rights, and who had now become an unworthy demagogue, leagued with John Coode, a clergyman, and revolted. The insurrection, as such, was short-lived. But exciting events were taking place in England, and Coode again seized his chance when news of the Revolution of 1688 drifted across the Atlantic. He placed himself at the head of the Association for the Defence of the Protestant Religion, and in 1689, pretending that he was serving William III., seized in the King's name the government of Maryland. The King bestowed some signs of favour upon this clever rebel, but his designs were soon discovered, and the government of Maryland was radically changed. In 1691 the colony was placed under the direct control of the Crown; the political rights of the Proprietor were annulled; the Church of England was established, and the Roman Catholics were persecuted.

The first royal Governor was Francis Nicholson, who had served elsewhere successfully, but was regarded with suspicion and dislike by many of the inhabitants of Maryland. Gerald Slye's accusations against Nicholson, in May 1698, give some idea of this dislike, and are of some interest as an indication of the means used by an ignorant colonist to discredit the Governor in England. A few of the accusations will show how utterly foolish these complaints were. Slye began by asserting that "all thinking men are amazed that such a man should have twisted himself into any post in the government, for besides his incapacity and illiteracy, he is a man who first in New York, then in Virginia, and at last in Maryland, has always professed himself an enemy to the present King and government." The next charge was that the Governor "makes his chaplain walk bareheaded before him from home to church." This is further extended by the fact that he "usually makes his chaplain wait ten or twelve hours for service so that often morning prayer is said in the evening." But there are more charges concerning Nicholson's treatment of his chaplain, for he, "a pious and good gentleman, the credit of the clergy in this province, happening one day by the Governor's means [to be] a little disguised in drink" [74] was suddenly summoned to conduct Divine Service. And so charge after charge of the same absurd character were brought against Nicholson not so much because of his ill-doing, but because he had the misfortune to be Governor.

The people of Maryland were not content until in 1715 the fourth Lord Baltimore became a Protestant, and by his conversion it was held that his full rights had revived. Fourteen years later the Proprietor's title obtained an everlasting memorial in the foundation of the city of Baltimore as a port for the planters. The restoration of the Calverts to their former rights was by no means advantageous to the religious life of the colony. The fourth lord was a hanger-on of Frederick, Prince of Wales, while the fifth to hold the title was a notorious profligate. These men insisted on exercising their right of clerical patronage without any regard to the welfare of the Church. Thus George Whitefield, who visited the colony in 1739, failed to arouse religious fervour. His preaching in Maryland was far less successful than it had been in Virginia. The former colony he found in "a dead sleep," and to use his own words, he "spoke home to some ladies concerning the vanity of their false politeness, but, alas! they are wedded to their quadrille and ombre" [75].

If the Marylanders were conspicuous for their irreligion, they were equally noticeable for their industry. A large number of German emigrants had come to the colony, and had started a continuous movement of extension towards the West. To these Germans is entirely due the improved state of the country, and the better means of communication even beyond the mountains. But the rolling westward of the Maryland population brought the colony into close touch with the power of France; and like the other colonies it was destined, about the middle of the eighteenth century, to contend against the policy of the French King, by which, if it had been successful, the seaboard colonies would have been deprived of the possibility of further expansion towards the Pacific.

The history of the Carolinas only resembles that of Maryland in the fact that they were both proprietary colonies. The swampy and low-lying coast to the south of Virginia had, in the early years of colonisation, offered little temptation to settlers, and long remained uninhabited by Englishmen or Spaniards. Certainly in 1564, Laudonnière, a Huguenot gentleman and naval officer, attempted a plantation at Port Royal in South Carolina, and named his fortress Caroline, "in honour of our Prince, King Charles"; [76] but it was an absolute failure, and the history of the fate of these Huguenots at the hands of the brutal Spaniard, Menendez, is as well-known as the tremendous retribution which followed his barbarous cruelty. Captains Amidas and Barlow, in 1584, at the charge and direction of Sir Walter Raleigh, visited this portion of the North American continent, but nothing came of it, and "Caroline" was left strictly alone as if a curse were upon the land. Adventurers from Virginia at last broke down the old prejudices, and by the year 1625 landseekers and discoverers had penetrated as far south as the Chowan. By a strange chance the country named by Laudonnière was destined in 1629 to receive much the same name from an Englishman for much the same reason. In that year Sir

Robert Heath obtained from Charles I. a grant of land to the south of Virginia, which was called after the King "the province of Carolina." No practical result, however, came from this grant, and Carolina, as it may now be called, still remained uninhabited except for the natives.

The first real charter to the Lords Proprietor of Carolina was dated the 24th March 1663, but owing to the previous grant of Charles I. numerous legal steps had to be taken before matters were satisfactorily arranged. The land between Virginia and Florida was now granted to eight patentees, amongst whom were the Duke of Albemarle, the Earl of Clarendon, Sir William Berkeley, but above all the Earl of Shaftesbury. These Proprietors had political and territorial authority, but there was also to be an assembly of freeholders with legislative powers. Twenty thousand acres of land were reserved for the original Proprietors, but at the same time a notice was issued inviting planters to settle in the colony, promising one hundred acres to each settler within five years, together with the privilege of residing in a land blest with the doctrine of freedom of conscience. This notice was published not only in England, but also in Barbadoes, the Bermudas, Virginia and New England, so that the colonisation of the Carolinas was not only, nor even mainly, undertaken by adventurers from the home country. On Albemarle River a settlement was made from Virginia, which formed the nucleus of North Carolina. Near Cape Fear the New Englanders also had a little colony which was absorbed by a more prosperous settlement from Virginia. Settlers soon came from Barbadoes, for there the news had been welcomed, and hundreds of experienced planters showed themselves willing to accept the offer of the Proprietors, and expressed a desire to come with their negroes and servants. They had, no doubt, been tempted by the extra inducements published in August 1663, when the Carolinas were advertised as wonderfully healthy and a land capable of bearing commodities not yet produced in other plantations as wine, oil, currants, raisins, silks, etc. Most of the Barbadoes planters were afterwards absorbed in the colony sent out from England forming the nucleus of South Carolina. The history of the first year in the Carolinas is practically unknown, except that in September the province was divided into two, and the northern section seems to have been already settled. The growth of the colony must have been steady, for in June 1665, Thomas Woodward, surveyor for the Proprietors in Albemarle county, shows that the population has increased, and that "the bounds of the county of Albemarle, fortie miles square, will not comprehend the inhabitants there already seated" [77]. He continues to give the Proprietors excellent advice, and recommends that they should show generosity if they wish to encourage settlers; "so if your Lordships please to give large Incouragement for some time till the country be more fully Peopled your Honore may contract for the future upon what condition you please. But for the present, To thenke that any men will remove from Virginia upon harder Conditione then they can live there will prove (I feare) a vaine Imagination, It bein Land only that they come for" [78]. There were however, others who continued to praise the colony, and one writer in 1670 says of Ashley River, "it is like a bowling alley, full of dainty brooks and rivers of running water; full of large and stately timber" [79]. The reader can hardly refrain from wondering where the resemblance to a bowling alley is to be found. Again the panegyrist says in a somewhat peculiar sentence, "as of the land of Canaan, it may be said it is a land flowing with milk and honey, and it lies in the same latitude" [80]. The Proprietors were very anxious to preserve this lovely land for the "better folk," and in December 1671 Lord Ashley wrote to Captain Holstead not to invite the poorer sort to Carolina, "for we find ourselves mightily mistaken in endeavouring to get a great number of poor people there, it being substantial men and their families that must make the plantation which will stock the country with negroes, cattle, and other necessaries, whereas others rely and eat upon us" [81].

Carolina's presiding genius and champion was Lord Shaftesbury's medical adviser, secretary, and personal friend, John Locke. He is supposed in 1667 to have drawn up the Fundamental Constitutions which contained an elaborate scheme of feudal government. Whether he did produce this astounding document has never been conclusively proved, nor is it of much value, since the principles contained in it were never enforced as a working system, for they were neither adapted to the times nor the conditions of a colony of freemen. By the year 1670 the elective Assembly possessed the definite powers of appointing officers, establishing law courts, and superintending the military defences of the colony. These privileges did not prevent them committing a great blunder by which the colony was converted into a paradise for the bankrupt and the pauper, but a hell for the honest and willing settler. It was now enacted that no colonist for the first five years after the true foundation of the colony should be liable for any exterior debts; that no newcomer need pay any taxes for his first year; and that marriage should be regarded as valid if mutual consent should be declared before the governor.

The northern section of the colony suffered most, and for fifty years this part of Carolina was wearied by ever recurring disputes and insurrections. "The colony indeed seems to have reached that chronic state of anarchy when the imprisonment and deposition of a governor is a passing incident which hardly influences the life of the community" [82]. Thus during the government of Thomas Eastchurch, who was sent out by the Proprietors to Albemarle in 1677, there was much trouble. Eastchurch appointed as his deputy the immoral Thomas Miller of the King's Customs. "Now Miller had a failing, not as the Proprietors point out, the common one of religious bigotry which had bred such dissension in New England, but a weakness for strong liquor" [83]. On his arrival he undertook to model the Parliament, "no doubt with alcoholic readiness and assurance, which proceeding we learn without surprise gave the people occasion to oppose and imprison him" [84]. Thereupon certain unscrupulous men took Miller's place and began at once to collect the Customs and so defrauded the Crown. For some short time angry words passed between the home Government and the colony, but the storm was calmed by the restoration of the King's duties. Eastchurch was succeeded by Culpeper, who controlled affairs until Seth Sothel came out as governor in 1683. The new ruler's rapacity and arbitrary conduct caused the Assembly to depose and banish him, paying no attention to the feeble remonstrance of the Proprietors. Meanwhile the southern portion of Carolina, particularly the settlements of Yeamans at Cape Fear and Sayle at Charleston, proved themselves more orderly and promising than the anarchic Albemarle; and probably for this reason the Proprietors displayed towards them more consideration. The constitution which was granted to

Charleston in 1670 was most liberal in character, for not only were the freemen allowed to elect the members of the House of Representatives, but they also possessed the privilege of nominating ten out of the twenty councillors. As so many of the settlers had come from Antiqua, "weary of the hurricane," [85] or from Barbadoes, they naturally reproduced their old methods of life, and having been accustomed to slaves, they tried to force the Indians into servility; but they found the Red Indian very different from the African negro, for he was possessed of a proud spirit and remarkable cunning that saved him from serfdom. The community of the South was one of wealthy traders who generally lived in the capital, partly because of the fine harbour and the insalubrious swamps inland, and partly because of the scheme of the Proprietors by which every freeholder had a town lot one-twentieth the extent of his whole domain.

The first governor was William Sayle, of Barbadoes, described in 1670 as "a man of no great sufficiency" [86]. It is very difficult at this distance of time to deduce the character of this governor, for Henry Brayne wrote, "Sayle is one of the unfittest men in the world for his place"; and he then proceeded to call him "crazy" [87]. On the other hand, when Sayle died in 1671, being at least eighty years of age, he is called "the good aged governor"; [88] and the Council of Ashley River, on March 4, 1671, recorded that he was "very much lamented by our people, whose life was as dear to them as the hopes of their prosperity" [89]. Sayle's chief work during his short period of office was an attempt to inculcate godly ways amongst the somewhat ungodly colonists. He urged the Proprietors to send out an orthodox minister, and proposed the man "which I and many others have lived under as the greatest of our mercies" [90]. He knew very well that some special inducement would have to be held out to the Proprietors, and so uses the scriptural words, "for where the Ark of God is, there is peace and tranquillity" [91].

Sayle was succeeded by Joseph West as governor in 1671, but his appointment was only temporary, as Lord Shaftesbury in the autumn of that year sent a commission to Sir John Yeamans. His unpopularity, however, caused his deposition; and Joseph West was again nominated as governor in 1674, a post which he filled with conspicuous satisfaction and success for eleven years. While West was still in office, the Lords Proprietor issued an order in December 1679 for the proper establishment of Charlestown. "Wherefore we think fit to let you know that the Oyster Point is the place we do appoint for the port-town, of which you are to take notice and call it Charlestown, and order the meetings of the Council to be there held, and the Secretary's, Registrar's, and Surveyor's offices to be kept within that town. And you are to take care to lay out the streets broad and in straight lines, and that in your grant of town-lots you do bound everyone's land towards the streets in an even line, and suffer no one to encroach with his buildings upon the streets, whereby to make them narrower than they were first designed" [92]. Such was the town to which West welcomed the Huguenots who were excluded from the colonies of their own country. The Proprietors, too, appreciating the wisdom of their governor, afforded the unhappy French means of cultivating their native produce of wine, oil, and silk, so that they soon established new homes for their distressed brethren, "who return daily into Babylon for want of such a haven" [93]. By the end of West's administration the Clarendon settlements centering round Charlestown had become extremely well-to-do, and the town government, which was of excellent character, administered the affairs of about three thousand people. But the southern territory fell into the evil ways of North Carolina; and after West's retirement, which finally took place in 1685, a series of unsatisfactory governors caused a continual bickering, ill-feeling, and well nigh insurrection. Sothel, whose bad government in Albemarle was already known in the south, was appointed governor in 1690; but after a year the southern settlers, taking example from their northern brethren, drove him out.

The Proprietors at last found that they had had enough of this disgusting incompetence and anarchy. The Locke Constitutions had failed in every way; a change must be made; and it appeared that an amalgamation of North and South under one governor might have the effect desired. Their first choice of an administrator was most unsuccessful; Philip Ludwell of Virginia found he had a hard task before him in restoring peace out of chaos and anarchy. The task was too much for him, and having proved himself incapable was succeeded by a Carolina planter, Thomas Smith, in 1692. Bickering and quarrels continued; Indian attacks were occasionally met and dealt with; but the southern Spaniards were an ever present danger that made Smith's rule no sinecure. After three years Joseph Archdale, a quaker, and one of the Proprietors, came out as governor, but after a few months in the colony he was succeeded by his nephew, Joseph Blake. The benign rule of both these governors gave at last to the Carolinas a peace which they had not known for twenty years. The Huguenots were once again welcomed by Blake, and although they had been steadily settling in the Carolinas, particularly since the Revocation of the Edict of Nantes in 1685, yet they now obtained a more hearty welcome and complete toleration. So much had Blake's government done for the Carolinas that the royal special agent in 1699 records, "if this place were duly encouraged, it would be the most useful to the Crown of all the Plantations upon the continent of America."

There were, however, two external dangers to which the Carolinas were exposed at the very moment they seemed to have obtained internal peace. The first was the new French settlement on the Mississippi; the second was the fear of Spanish aggression from Florida. The French danger was never really very extreme, and the Carolinas escaped many of the horrors of New England history. But the Spanish peril was true enough, for as early as 1680 a party of Scotch Presbyterians were routed from their little settlement at Port Royal, and this was regarded by the Carolina settlers as a just cause of complaint and an insult to his Majesty King Charles. To their great disappointment in 1699, when Edward Randolph was sent out to make investigations concerning Spanish intrusions, he brought with him no troops for their protection. At the beginning of the eighteenth century, therefore, it appeared best to the settlers that for their own defence they should take offensive action.

The war of the Spanish Succession, or, as it was called in the colonies, Queen Anne's war, had broken out, and rumours had reached the settlers of a coming Spanish onslaught. To meet this, James Moore, a political adventurer, but a very brave and capable man, led 500 English and 800 Indian allies into Spanish territory and took the unprotected town of St

Augustine; but the fort, which was used as a last stronghold, resisted him for three months, and as he was unprovided with siege guns, he was obliged to retire on the appearance of a Spanish man-of-war. Nothing daunted, but rather elated with their previous success, a larger raid was made in 1704. Sir Nathaniel Johnstone was now governor, and he commissioned Colonel Moore to attack Apalachee, eighty miles to the west of St Augustine. In this action Moore was again successful, as Colonel Brewton records that "by this conquest of Apalachee the Province was freed from any danger from that part during the whole war" [94]. The Spaniards, however, did not remain idle, and in 1706, in alliance with the French from Martinique, with a fleet of ten sail and a force of 800 men attacked Charlestown. The inhabitants were terrified, and their anguish was intensified by the horror of a severe outbreak of yellow fever. Many of them, therefore, fled from the town, but Sir Nathaniel Johnstone routed the combined forces of France and Spain and captured no fewer than 230 prisoners.

Factious quarrels within the Province itself now threatened the safety of the settlers. Since 1691 North and South Carolina had been united under one governor, but the custom had been established that the northern portion of the colony was always under the administration of a deputy. In 1711 Thomas Cary disputed with Edward Hyde as to which held the office; it was decided in favour of the latter. The purely personal quarrel drove Cary to forget his feelings of patriotism, and flying from Carolina he stirred up the Tuscarora Indians, who, with fiendish delight, attacked a small settlement of Germans from the Palatinate. South Carolina, where the supreme governor dwelt, immediately dispatched an army to the assistance of the North, with the effect that apparent peace was gained and the army was no longer required. Immediately upon its withdrawal, however, the Tuscaroras again fell upon the helpless people; this was too much, vengeance must be taken; and this fierce Indian tribe was practically decimated and forced to migrate north.

Although the Treaty of Utrecht was signed in 1713, and the Spanish War of Succession came to an end, yet there was little hope of peace in the West as long as either side allied with the Indians. The fate of the

Tuscaroras may have stimulated the Yamassee Indians to revenge in 1716. In April, headed by Spaniards, they massacred about eighty inhabitants of Granville County, South Carolina. Charles Craven, the governor, proved himself a man of vigour, activity, and stern resolve, and by his efforts within a few months the colony was assured of safety, and there was apparent peace between the settlers of Carolina and the Spaniards of Florida.

In the winter of 1719 that perpetual love of dissension, and dislike of any federal action, was once more manifested by the Assembly of South Carolina. The governor was a son of Sir Nathaniel Johnstone, and he had done his best for the Proprietors, but unlike the northern portions the South now disowned all proprietary rule and elected a governor under the Crown. The home authorities immediately sent out Francis Nicholson, a capable colonial official who had already had experience in New York, Virginia, and Maryland. Ten years later the Proprietors accepted the inevitable, and being compensated financially, handed over the Carolinas to the Crown. They probably never regretted the bargain, as in 1739 the war against Spain once more jeopardised the existence of the English settlements in the south, the inhabitants of which were in chronic fear of murder and rapine. The chief Spanish attack was made in 1742, when an army of 5000 landed at St Simon's, owing to the failure of Captain Hardy to intercept the enemy's fleet. The expedition was unsuccessful; the colonists held their own; eighty prisoners were brought into Charlestown; and the Spaniards retired.

The share taken by the two Carolinas in American history during the next few years was far less than that of other colonies, but will be dealt with in another chapter. The great interest of the early history of the Carolinas is that the colony won for itself against very considerable odds the rights of local government and freedom from the shackles of the Proprietors. The settlers exhibited from first to last that full determination which is peculiarly associated with those of English stock to control their own destiny without the leading-strings of a few, perhaps benevolent, but generally misguided, human beings, whose powers have been conferred upon them by chance. The settlers of the Carolinas were a dogged type of men who faced external dangers with courage and good sense, distinctly contradictory of their pig-headed, factious, anarchic spirit in all internal affairs.

Chapter 4

THE PURITANS IN PLYMOUTH AND MASSACHUSETTS

It has been customary to regard the members of the colony of Virginia as Cavaliers of the most ardent type, but, as has been shown, this is scarcely correct, and amongst the Virginians there were many who did not approve of either the actions of Laud or the dissimulation of Charles. In much the same way it would be erroneous to ascribe to the New England group a plebeian origin. The Virginian gentleman found his counterpart in the New England colonies of Plymouth and Massachusetts. It is, however, more true to describe these two colonies as the offspring and embodiment of Puritanism, than to describe Virginia as purely monarchical. In the northern colonies, congregationalism was the chief form of religious worship, and this, as was natural, determined their political form; it was no insurmountable step from a belief in congregations to a belief in republics. The men who found this step so easy were a very different pattern to the early ne'er-do-wells of Virginian colonisation. The northern colonies were founded by the yeoman and the trader, both of whom were patient, watchful, and ready to assert with an Englishman's doggedness all political rights. These men formed small organic communities filled with the very strongest sense of corporate life. Not that these forms took an absolutely exact line, for in some cases the community was a pure democracy with limitations and restrictions; in others there was a very wide and modified oligarchy. The men were the very best of settlers; they knew what they wanted, and were ready to work and even sacrifice their lives to gain that object. It is not surprising that in the New England colonies prosperity raised its head long before it had come to Virginia, though the soil of the latter was far more fertile than the sterile lands of the northern group.

The Plymouth Company had been formed at the same time as the London Company, but it had accomplished very little [95]. In 1607 it dispatched an expedition under George Popham and Raleigh Gilbert to the River Kennebec, in the territory afterwards called Maine. The climate, however, did not suit the adventurers, and owing to the mismanagement of the leaders and the indifference of the Company nothing came of the undertaking. For thirteen years the Plymouth Company made no further effort, but in 1620 it was entirely reorganised, placed upon a new footing, and renamed the New England Company. This may have been caused by two things. In the first place Captain John Smith had made a voyage to New England in 1614; it was indeed that resourceful but perhaps boastful adventurer who either gave the name by which the country was afterwards known, or gave currency to an already existing though not generally accepted title. "In the moneth of Aprill, 1614 ... I chanced to arrive in New-England, a parte of Ameryca at the Ile of Monahiggin, in 43½ of Northerly Latitude" [96]. But even this voyage and the several others that followed would not have been sufficient to arouse the Plymouth Company. It was in truth a second and deeper cause that started the reorganisation of a corporation that had so long lain dormant. A new force had now entered into colonisation that was to do much for the establishment of the Anglo-Saxon race in America. Religion had sent men to convert the savages, but now religious persecution sent men to make homes amongst those barbarians.

It is unnecessary here to discuss the rise of the Puritans as an important sect in English history. They were those "whose minds had derived a peculiar character from the daily contemplation of superior beings and eternal interests" [97]. They differed in nearly every respect from the ordinary Englishman of the Elizabethan period, and yet they were in many instances intellectual and well- bred. They saw, however, that "they could not have the Word freely preached and the sacraments administered without idolatrous gear," and so they concluded to break away from the Church. It was this separation that gained for them the name of Separatists, and brought upon them the punishment of the State. To avoid this some sought leave from Elizabeth to settle in the land "which lieth to the west," their object being to "settle in Canada and greatly annoy the bloody and persecuting Spaniard in the Bay of Mexico" [98]. Such was the knowledge of geography about 1591, and it was very fortunate for the would-be-colonists that nothing came of the scheme. Two years later some Independents of London fled to Amsterdam, where they hoped to exercise their religion unmolested. Soon after the beginning of the seventeenth century the Nonconformists of Gainsborough took refuge in the Low Countries, to be followed in 1606 by the Congregationalists from Scrooby. They first found shelter in Amsterdam, and later, some, choosing John Robinson as their minister, moved to Leyden.

The laws of England had driven these men abroad, but they never forgot the fact that they were Englishmen. They found their families growing up around them and naturally imbibing foreign ideas. This fact deeply pained the parents, who looked back upon their own happy youths in Tudor England. They determined, therefore, to leave the Netherlands, and William Bradford, their faithful chronicler, tells in quaint but honest words why they were driven to this decision. "In ye agitation of their thoughts, and much discours of things hear aboute; at length they began to incline to this new conclusion, of remooual to some other place. Not out of any new fanglednes, or other such like giddie humor, by which men are oftentimes transported to their great hurt & danger. But for sundrie weightie & solid reasons" [99]. The most serious of these reasons "and of all sorowes most heauie to be borne; was that many of their children, by these occasions (and ye great licentiousnes of youth in y^t countrie) and ye manifold Temptations of the place, were drawne away by euill examples into extrauagante & dangerous courses, getting ye raines off their neks & departing from their parents. Some became souldjers, others took vpon them farr viages by Sea; and other some worse courses ... so that they saw their posteritie would be in danger to degenerate & be corrupted" [100]. It was for this reason, then, in particular, that the people of the congregation of Leyden turned their thoughts to the "countries of America which are frutful & fitt for habitation; being deuoyed of all ciuill Inhabitants; wher ther are only saluage & brutish men which range vp and downe, litle otherwise than ye wild beasts of the same" [101]. And yet though they sought a home for themselves where they might worship as they pleased, they were at the same time filled with that missionary spirit which had encouraged Columbus and many another adventurer to persevere. Their great aim was to lay "some good foundation or at least make some way thereunto, for ye propagating & advancing ye gospell of ye Kingdom of Christ in those remote parts of ye world; yea, though they should be but even as stepping stones unto others for ye performing of so great a work" [102].

With these intentions the ever famous Pilgrim Fathers came to England, bringing with them a document admitting the supremacy of the State in religious matters. The wording of the clauses, however, was so artful that these Puritans proved that though gentle as doves they were not without the wisdom of the serpent. They obtained leave from James I. to set out on their voyage; but they were financed by certain London traders who were to receive all the profits for the first seven years, when the partnership was to be dissolved. Until this dissolution the whole band was to live as a community with joint property, trade, and labour. A few labourers were sent out by the London partners, but the group to which the term of Pilgrim Fathers strictly applies was composed of forty-one Puritan emigrants and their families, who had, as a friend said, "been instrumental to break the ice for others; the honours shall be yours to the world's end" [103]. The voyage of the Mayflower is now one of the most familiar events in the history of the British Empire. The little vessel, accompanied by the Speedwell, which had to return, sailed from Plymouth in August 1620. The original intention of the emigrants had been to land on part of the shores of Virginia; but owing to storms, the fragile character of the vessel, and the obstinacy of the captain, they reached Cape Cod, "which is onely a headland of high hils of sand ouergrowne with shrubbie pines hurts and such trash" [104]. While lying off this inhospitable promontory the emigrants with forethought bound themselves together by a social compact, thus forming a true body politic.

The Pilgrims landed at a spot "fit for habitation" in Cape Cod Harbour on the 22nd of December. Exploring expeditions were undertaken by the more adventurous under Miles Standish, a man after the type of Captain John Smith, but less boastful and of sterner religious character. No definite settlement was fixed upon and the people were therefore forced to remain in the neighbourhood of Cape Cod, where they faced the winter unprepared. Although their minister, John Robinson, had described them months before as "well-weaned from the delicate milk of the Mother country and inurred to the difficulties of a strange land," [105] yet their sufferings during those wild and stormy months must have been terrible. Several of the party died, amongst them their first governor, William Carver. His successor was the already mentioned chronicler, William Bradford, who served the colony well and faithfully for twelve years. He was the first American citizen of English birth who was selected as governor by free choice. His strength of character, moral rectitude, and lofty public spirit made him worthy of the high office conferred upon him. Fortunately his first year of government was freed from the burden of Indian attacks. The truth was that the Pilgrim Fathers always preserved friendly relations with the neighbouring Redskins; partly because they had been so reduced in numbers by pestilence that they were never a serious danger, and partly owing to Edward Winslow, one of the ablest and most highly educated of the settlers, who had saved, by his knowledge of medicine, the Indian chief's life, thus establishing from the first amicable relations.

Amidst the most heart-rending adversity the Pilgrim Fathers worked at the communal industry, and struggled through those months of cold and semi-starvation, helped no doubt by the fact that they were religious enthusiasts filled with a sense of a divine mission. In May 1621 Bradford records the first marriage amongst the settlers, which was conducted on somewhat novel lines, for "according to ye laudable custome of ye Low-cuntries, in which they had liued was thought most requisite to be performed, by the magistrate" [106]. In November fifty additional settlers came out from the Leyden congregation, and these not only increased the difficulty of supplying food for everyone, but also introduced a feeling of dissatisfaction with what they found. Bradford had, however, the laugh on his side. On Christmas Day the Governor called them to work as usual, but "the new company ... said it wente against their consciences to work on y^t day." They were therefore allowed to remain at home, the rest of the colony going out to work; but when the governor came home at noon, "he found them in ye streete at play openly; some pitching ye barr & some at stoole-ball and such like sports. So he went to them and took away their Implements and tould them that it was against his conscience, that they should play & others worke" [107].

The settlers had indeed laboured hard and not in vain, for a definite grant of their territory was issued by the New England Company, and there was now no fear of their log-fort, their houses, or their twenty-six acres of cleared ground being seized by the original members to whom the land had been granted by James I. The little plot of ground thus carefully tended seems to have been a real oasis in the wilderness. An eye-witness, Edward Winslow, has drawn an ideal picture of the settlement. "Here are grapes, white and red, and very sweet and strong also; strawberries, gooseberries, raspas, etc.; plums of three sorts, white, black and red, being almost as good as a damson; abundance of roses, white, red and damask; single but very sweet indeed. The country wanted only industrious men to employ" [108]. With such a tempting account it is not surprising that thirty-five new settlers went out in 1622.

The communal principle gradually began to break down. The younger men did not care to work so hard and find that they gained no more than the weak and aged; nor were the married men pleased with the idea of their wives cooking, washing, and sewing for the bachelors. As early as 1623, signs of the disappearance of the system were beginning to show themselves; and by 1627 its break up was completed when the interests of the London partners were transferred to six of the chief settlers with a general division of land and live stock. The government of the settlement was now placed on an assured footing; the laws were passed by the whole body of freemen, who had also the double right of electing the governor and a committee of seven assistants. Under the new methods the colony throve apace, and three years after the change, two new townships were formed and these sent delegates to an assembly which was primarily composed of the whole body of freemen, but which, owing to the existence of these delegates, gradually developed, until in New Plymouth there was a proper bicameral legislature with a governor at its head.

The Plymouth colonists set "the example of a compact religious brotherhood" [109]. In 1636 they passed a code of laws which in no way clashed with those of England, but applied more especially to the style of life which they had adopted. The brotherhood extended its bounds year by year, and hardly a score of years had passed since their first landing before eight prim, clean, and comfortable towns had been built, containing a population of about 3000 inhabitants. By this time the Civil War had broken out in England, but the settlers were little affected by it, for they lived their own quiet lives and went on their way, filled with religious fervour and working hard to support themselves.

After the Restoration, however, they felt bound to bestir themselves in political affairs, and in June 1661 their general court sent a petition to Charles II., asking him to confirm their liberties, explaining to him that they were his faithful subjects "who did hither transport ourselves to serve our God with a pure conscience, according to His will revealed, not a three days' journey as Moses, but near three thousand miles into a vast howling wilderness, inhabited only by barbarians." They concluded their petition in the quaintest words, saying that if only the King will grant their wishes, "we say with him, it is enough, our Joseph (or rather) our Charles is yet alive" [110]. The poverty of the Plymouth brethren about this time is evidenced by their lack of funds necessary for the renewal of their charter in 1665; and also in the fact that the people were not able to maintain scholars for their ministers, "but are necessitated to make use of a gifted brother in some places" [111]. Nevertheless in this same year they are computed to have had a fighting force of 2500 men; and on two later occasions (1676 and 1690) they were strong enough to make strenuous but ineffectual attempts to obtain a charter from the Crown. The little colony that has perhaps the proudest of all positions in American history was finally, in 1691, merged in its more arrogant and pushing neighbour Massachusetts, and the land of the Pilgrim Fathers lost its identity.

Just as Puritanism had been the cause of the foundation of New Plymouth, so it was in the case of Massachusetts. Lord Macaulay has pointed out that "the Puritan was made up of two different men, the one all self-abasement, penitent gratitude, passion; the other proud, calm, inflexible, sagacious" [112]. The first type represented New Plymouth, where Puritanism was distressed, and where its followers struggled manfully but were self-abased. Massachusetts, on the other hand, resembled the second type; here Puritanism was vigorous; the upholders of the belief were aggressive, strong, determined, and pushing. Thus the two colonies were not only different in character, but for that very reason were destined to differ in prosperity.

As early as 1620, Sir Ferdinando Gorges and others had been interested in the colonisation of New England; and in a document issued in the following year, strict injunctions were laid down for the carrying out of material fit for the foundation of a settlement. Thus, every "shipp of three score tons shall carry with them twoe Piggs, two Calves, twoe couple of tame Rabbetts, two couple of Hens and a cocke" [113]. Nothing, however, seems to have been permanently established, and within two years this New England Company is said to have been "in a moribund condition" [114]. In 1623 some Dorchester traders started a fishing station at Cape Ann, Massachusetts Bay. The manager was Roger Conant, who had disagreed with his brethren in New Plymouth and had separated from them. Three years later the scheme was abandoned; most of the settlers returned except Conant and a small band who "squatted" at Naumkeag, better known in later years as Salem. The failure of the merchants did not discourage John White, incumbent of Dorchester, and he determined to form a settlement for Puritans, from which there sprang the colony of Massachusetts. Matters were at once hurried on, and in 1629 six Puritan partners obtained a grant of land from the New England Company, which was to extend westward as far as the Pacific Ocean, then believed to be but a short distance. One of the partners, John Endecott, was selected to toleration; but to the Puritan toleration was only significant of indifference, and was therefore an abhorrent principle at the very time he so sorely needed it. The religious dissensions during the early years of the colony of Massachusetts illustrate the fanatical and bigoted character of the Puritan quite as clearly as any particular event or series of events in English history. It is painful to find even in the first few months of the settlement, when Endecott was still in command, many evidences of intolerance. John and Samuel Browne collected a congregation and conducted the service according to the Book of Common Prayer; but so horrible did this appear to Endecott that these luckless men were expelled from the colony. Two years later political and social rights were intimately connected with religious privileges by an ordinance that no one was to be a freeman unless he belonged to a church; and this was still further extended in 1635, so that no man could vote at a town meeting unless he possessed the ecclesiastical qualification.

Religious troubles were fomented, after 1631, by the able but bigoted Roger Williams. He was a man of very considerable gifts, being both an energetic and attractive preacher, but at the same time filled with an intense hatred of Erastianism. As soon as he arrived he was chosen minister of Salem, where he exhibited his imperfect sense of proportion and gained for himself the title of "a haberdasher of small questions" [118]. His energy and impulsiveness led him astray, and the more intellectual could hardly fail to see that his mind was incapable of distinguishing the vital from the trifle. His political doctrines forced him into extraordinary actions, such as that of persuading Endecott to cut the cross out of the royal ensign; while at the same time he not only denied the English sovereign's right to grant territory in North America, but also with equal vehemence repudiated all secular control in religious affairs. For four years the freemen of Massachusetts quietly suffered Roger Williams' whimsicalities, but in October 1635 their patience had come to an end, and the General Court of the Colony banished him with twenty of his disciples, as his sympathetic chronicler says, "and that in the extremity of winter, forcing him to betake himselfe into the vast wilderness to sit down amongst the Indians" [119]. The kindly governor, John Winthrop, does not seem to have approved of the verdict, for many years afterwards Roger Williams wrote "that ever honoured Governour Mr Winthrop privately wrote to me to steer my course to Nahigonset Bay.... I took his prudent motion as an hint and voice from God, and waving all other thoughts and motions, I steered my course from Salem (though in winter snow which I feel yet) unto these parts, wherein I may say Peniel, that is, I have seene the face of God" [120]. During the year 1635 three notable personages came to the colony. The first was Henry Vane, the younger, "who," wrote Winthrop, "being a young gentleman of excellent parts, and had been employed by his father (when he was ambassador) in foreign affairs; yet, being called to the obedience of the gospel, forsook the honors and preferments of the court, to enjoy the ordinances of Christ in their purity here" [121]. The other two recruits were, John Wheelwright, a clergyman, and his sister Mrs Anne Hutchinson, who was a woman of great learning and brilliance, but by instinct an agitator of a most indiscreet and impetuous character; although both acute and resolute, she allowed herself to be carried away by her passion for theological controversy. Her religious views were Antinomian and were strongly opposed to the doctrines of the Puritans, who believed in justification by faith, strengthened by sanctified works. To Governor Winthrop the distinction between the two doctrines appeared to be a mere jargon of words, and he was not very far wrong when he said "no man could tell, except some few who knew the bottom of the matter, where any difference was" [122]. Mrs Hutchinson soon had a large following, including Wheelwright, Thomas Hooker, and John Cotton, but the latter deserted her and refused to follow her in all her heresies. In 1636 she was strongly supported by Harry Vane, who was for a short time the governor; but in the following year both she and her brother were tried before the General Court and were banished as heretics.

Meantime the education of Massachusetts was not neglected, as is proved by the foundation in 1636 of Harvard College at Cambridge, for "it pleased God to stir up the heart of one Mr Harvard (a godly gentleman and a lover of learning, then living amongst us) to give the one halfe of his Estate (it being in all about 1700 l.) towards the erecting of a Colledge, and all his Library" [123]. The building was erected rapidly and was "very faire and comely within and without" [124]. says an anonymous writer in 1641; but Charles II.'s commissioners do not seem to have been so much impressed, as twenty years later they speak of it as a wooden college. The great days of Harvard had not as yet arrived; nor indeed was the learning more advanced even as late as 1680, for the whole place is described by two Dutch visitors as smelling like a tavern. "We inquired," they say, "how many professors there were, and they replied not one, that there was no money to support one" [125]. But out of such small beginnings a great educational establishment rose which has won for itself a famous name and added lustre to the annals of the colony.

It seemed extremely likely that the war-clouds that had arisen in the Old Country might drift across the Atlantic to New England. It was for this reason that some sort of confederation between the colonies was proposed; and in 1643 Massachusetts, New Haven, Plymouth, and Connecticut formed the first New England Confederacy. A distinct desire for religious and political unity had been in the air for some time, not only because of the dread of Dutch and Indian attack, but also because it was hoped that intercolonial quarrels might be checked, and a firm and united attitude might be shown towards any encroachments on the part of the British Government. There were, however, in this confederation two essential weaknesses which sooner or later would inevitably wreck the whole scheme. In the first place Massachusetts was by far the largest, richest, and most prosperous of the colonies; it was therefore called upon to contribute the largest share, but received no more than the weaker and poorer members of the Union. Secondly, although the federal government was exactly what was wanted, it could exercise no direct control over the citizens of any particular colony. This latter was probably the chief cause of the non-success of the confederation. Maine and the settlements along the Narragansett Bay in vain pleaded to be enrolled in the first United States; but they were refused as being neither sufficiently settled nor possessing political order. The four confederate colonies bound themselves by written conditions and were denominated "The United Colonies of New England." It was obvious from the very beginning that disagreement would come, if for no other reason because of the struggle that was taking place in England. Massachusetts was no more for the Parliament than for the King, while the other New England colonies were as a whole sturdy supporters of Pym and his party. Disagreement bred disagreement, as is seen in the proposal to fight the Dutch in America, while Blake was winning fame in European waters. This, however, was prevented by the commissioners of one colony standing out against the opinions of the others. A similar lack of unity was only too apparent in 1654, when Massachusetts consented to make war against the Nyantic Indians, but the indifference and incapacity of their captain caused general dissatisfaction among the rest of the confederation.

The attitude of Massachusetts toward England during the Civil Wars was a most unsatisfactory one; it was as it were prophetic of what was to come. The contemptuous and haughty indifference shown by the colony to Cromwell was not because of any deep-seated loyalty to Charles I.; it was rather the exhibition of an independent spirit and a desire to leave England and English affairs strictly alone, if they were allowed, in turn, to live under the government of a governor and magistrates of their own choosing and under laws of their own making. This feeling does not seem to have been understood in England, and at the time of the Restoration the colony was regarded as having been Parliamentarian in its sympathies, whereas indeed it had been separatist. The Royal Commissioners in 1661 found that Massachusetts "was the last and hardest persuaded to use his Majesty's name in their forms of justice"; [126] and yet in February the King was petitioned to look upon the colonists kindly and "let not the Kinge heare men's wordes: your servants are true men, fearers of God and the Kinge, not given to change, zealous of government and peaceable in Israel, we are not seditious as to the interest of Cæsar nor schismaticks as to the matters of religion" [127].

The religion of Massachusetts was, at this time, of the narrowest and most bigoted type. The colonists were intolerant of any opinion save their own, and their cruel fanaticism was excited particularly against the humble and law-abiding sect of Quakers. The General Court at Boston regarded the Quakers as a positive danger to the State, and as people "who besides their absurd and blasphemous doctrines, do like rogues and vagabonds come in upon us" [128]. In 1656 two Quaker women landed at Boston; they were immediately treated with extreme brutality and finally banished to the Barbadoes. This led to further definite enactments, and at the instigation of some of the most intolerant clergy of Boston, an act was passed imposing the penalty of death in cases of extreme obstinacy. So brutal were the punishments inflicted even where no extreme obstinacy was shown that it is probable that death was preferable and welcomed by the ill-treated wretches who had fallen into the hands of these fanatics. At the Restoration, Edward Burrough, an English Quaker, took up the case of his brethren in Massachusetts, and laid before Charles II. a list of brutalities that were only equalled by the horrors of the Inquisition. We read of men being whipped twenty-three times, receiving 370 stripes from a whip with three knotted cords; two unhappy wretches were cut to bits by 139 blows from pitched ropes, one being "brought near unto death, much of his body being beat like unto a jelly" [129]. Others were put neck and heels in irons, or burnt deeply in the hand; some had their ears cut off by the hangman; while many other free-born subjects of the King were "sold for bondmen and bondwomen to Barbadoes, Virginia, or any of the English Plantations" [130]. Burrough succeeded in persuading the King to take some action, and the Massachusetts Council was severely reprimanded for the treatment it had meted out to the Quakers. As a result of the King's interference the General Court at Boston determined in 1661 to act with as much lenity as possible to the Quakers, but to prevent their intrusion it was recognised that "a sharp law" against them was a necessity.

During the last quarter of the seventeenth century the New England Confederacy, including Massachusetts, was disturbed by all the horrors of Indian warfare. In the year 1670 the Pokanoket Indians under their chief Metacam, or as he was generally known, King Philip, became unfriendly. For some time the warfare was not of a very serious character, but at last in 1674 an Indian convert brought news of a general attack, and paid the penalty of his fidelity to the English by being murdered by Philip or one of his braves. The Indian chief now fell upon the extreme south of New Plymouth, and fire, murder, and rapine were common throughout the land. The Puritans of Boston, under their Governor Leverett, saw in this terrible slaughter the hand of the Lord, and in November the whole city passed a day of humiliation. Within the chapels and homes their sins were openly acknowledged, but the people showed more of the spirit of the Pharisee than of the Publican in this humiliation before God. They penitently confessed that they had neglected divine service, but what was to them still worse, they had shown sinful lenity to the heretical sect of Quakers, and had indeed invited the Almighty's wrath by an extravagance in apparel and in wearing long hair. Pharisaical as this day of humiliation sounds, the greater number of the people were probably genuine in their attitude towards what they regarded as sin; and certainly when the time came they were ready to prove themselves sturdy fighters. It was only natural that the settlers should be successful in the end, for as a civilised people they were better armed and better organised, but their victory was delayed in the coming, and when the war was really over they found that it had cost them dear. Edward Randolph writing at the time sums up the English losses at a high figure. "The losse to the English in the severall colonies in their habitations and stock, is reckoned to amount to 150,000 l., there having been about 1200 houses burned, 8000 head of cattle great and small, killed, and many thousand bushels of wheat, pease and other grain burned ... and upward of 3000 Indians, men, women and children destroyed" [131]. King Philip, who had caused all this destruction, was in 1676 hunted down and shot "with a brace of bullets ... this seasonable prey was soon divided, they cut off his Head and Hands and conveyed them to Rhode Island, and quartered his Body and hung it upon four trees" [132]. With this last act of unnecessary barbarity the Indian power was broken, and Philip's war was at an end.

Meantime the administration of New England had been vested in the hands of special commissioners, whose powers were transferred to the Privy Council. Under this system, revenue officers appointed in England were sent out in 1675 to enforce the Navigation Acts, which were excellent as a stimulus to English shipping, but were nevertheless retrograde with regard to the colonies. Edward Randolph was despatched to America to report upon the working of the colonial system under these famous laws, and he showed, even as early as this, that the revenue acts were openly violated by the people, who, a century later, were to be notorious for their smuggling proclivities. Massachusetts was looked upon by the home authorities with the strongest suspicion, which was still further intensified by Edward Randolph's eight specific charges against the settlers. (1) That they have no right to the land or government in any part of New England, and that they have always been regarded as usurpers; (2) that they have formed themselves into a commonwealth, denying appeals to England, and refusing to take the oath of allegiance; (3) that they have protected the regicides; (4) that they coin their own money with their own impress; (5) that in 1665 they opposed the King's commissioners with armed force; (6) that they have put men to death for matters of religion; (7) that they impose an oath of fidelity to their government; (8) that they have violated all the acts of Trade and Navigation to the annual loss of £100,000 to the King's Customs. After these charges had reached England, the agents of the Massachusetts government, William Stoughton and Peter Bulkeley, were called upon to answer the serious indictment. They pleaded that they were unable to answer any other questions but those concerning the business on which they had come; but they agreed that as private individuals they would make some kind of defence, and at the same time promised, on behalf of the settlers, amendment in the future. This submission only acted as an incentive for further attack, and Randolph now charged the "Bostoners" with denying the right of baptism to those not born in church fellowship; and also with fining certain persons for absenting themselves from the meeting- houses. The Committee of Trade and Plantations next turned to the Charter of the colony, and this was severely criticised; then the Laws of the colony were discussed, and many illegal imposts were discovered. Amongst other things it was seen that three shillings and fourpence was the fine levied for galloping in the streets of Boston; that five shillings was demanded from those who dared to observe Christmas Day, and that no less than £5 was the fine for importing playing cards; with all of which they now found serious fault, though it must be allowed that they tended to create "an ideally holy and unhappy community" [133]. All this time Stoughton and Bulkeley were most anxious to return to America, but they were obliged to stay all through 1678, and it was only in 1679 that they were able to leave, because England was too busy with the Popish Plot to worry about the affairs of the far distant Massachusetts. The matter, however, was by no means finished. Randolph was determined to bring the colony to book; and when he was again sent out in 1680 to supervise the customs he at once renewed his charges. "The Bostoners, after all the protestations by their agents, are acting as high as ever, and the merchants trading as freely; no ship having been seized for irregular trading, although they did in 1677 make a second law to prevent it" [134]. He then says that his life was threatened by these smugglers, and that as he has only life and hope left, he is unwilling to expose himself to the rage of a bewildered multitude. He concludes by beseeching for strong measures, which he considers are essential, and "for his Majesty to write more letters will signify no more than the London Gazette" [135]. This appeal had its effect, and the King practically threatened to land redcoats in Boston "a century before their time, when there should be no Washington to organise resistance, no European coalition to distract their operations, and no French fleet and army to drive them from the Continent" [136]. Even after this thundering declaration the actions of the settlers were not always in accordance with strict loyalty, and in 1684, though their agents loudly protested, the Court of Chancery decreed the Massachusetts Charter to be null and void. James II.'s well-intentioned efforts carried out in the wrong way by the wrong methods, and generally by the wrong men, deprived him of popularity both in his home dominions and in his growing Empire in the West. His great scheme for the colonies was one of union; but his action was far more destructive than anything that George III. ever proposed or imagined. The representative principle was snatched from the youthful colonies; and they were deprived of their legislative, executive and financial rights, which were given to a royal Governor and Council, ruling an united province entitled New England, and bearing a special flag of its own. The Governor appointed by the King was Colonel Sir Edmund Andros, a very active and most capable administrator, but an ardent churchman, and therefore particularly unacceptable to the Puritan colonies of the New England group. He was by no means a young man when he arrived to take over the administration in December 1686, but with surprising energy he set about doing what he could by extending the frontier against the Indians, and establishing a line of garrisoned forts to keep them in awe. Discontent, however, was visible on every side; Connecticut refused to give up its charter, which, according to tradition, was hidden in an oak; while the town of Ipswich, Mass. refused like Watertown many years earlier to pay taxes without representation. When James issued his Declaration of Indulgence some of the best of the Massachusetts colonists imagined that it meant real toleration; Increase Mather was one of these. He had conducted the diplomatic relations of the colony during the struggle over the charter; he was well-beloved as the minister of the old North Church of Boston, and as President of Harvard College. For these reasons he was once again selected as mediator, and was deputed to plead with James on behalf of his colony, but like so many in England he found that he had come on a fruitless errand, and that genuine toleration was very far from the thoughts of the Papist King.

The news of the Revolution in England in November 1688 aroused the people of Massachusetts. Sir Edmund Andros, instead of accepting the inevitable, arrested John Winslow, the bearer of the good tidings. The discontent which had long been simmering beneath the surface now broke out. The covetousness of the rulers, the ruination of trade, the oppression of the people, and that "base drudgerie" to which they had been put stirred them to a state of frenzy. Boston and Charlestown armed; Andros was unable to quell the fury, and he was captured by his subordinates, who claimed that "the exercise of Sir Edmund's commission, so contrarie to the Magna Charta, is surely enough to call him to account by his superiors" [137]. In this the people of New England made a mistake, for although Andros was sent over to England with a party of his accusers, he was only examined by the Lords of the Committee for Trade and Plantations, and was almost immediately released without being finally tried.

The rule of William and Mary in England was acknowledged willingly in Massachusetts. A new charter was granted to the colony, in which it was stated that the Governor, Lieutenant-Governor and Secretary were to be appointed by the Crown. The franchise was now based upon a property qualification, and the religious oligarchy was swept away. The first

Council was nominated by the Crown, but in the future the members were to be selected by the General Court. The little colony that owed its origin to the Pilgrim Fathers was incorporated within the prosperous bounds of Massachusetts, which from this date to the great schism remained a Crown colony with distinct tendencies towards, and sometimes clearly expressed desires of, emancipation and independence. "It was not as though the colony complained of grievances which could be enquired into and put right; it simply adopted towards England now openly and now by equivocation an attitude of 'hands off'" [138].

The first Governor of the new Crown colony was that romantic character, Sir William Phipps. He was born in 1650 on a small plantation on the banks of the Kennebec; he was one of twenty-six children, and until eighteen years of age kept "sheep in the wilderness." There is little doubt that from early times he was determined to succeed, and he always prophesied that one day he would be the owner of a fair brick house in Green Lane, North Boston. According to his earliest biographer he was one of the most remarkable men of his day, being "of an Enterprising Genius and naturally disclaimed Littleness: But in his Disposition for Business was of the Dutch Mould, where with a little show of Wit, there is much Wisdom demonstrated, as can be shewn by any Nation. His Talent lay not in the Airs that serve chiefly for the pleasant and sudden Turns of Conversation; but he might say as Themistocles, though he could not play the Fiddle, yet he knew how to make a little City become a great One. He would prudently contrive a weighty Undertaking, and then patiently pursue it unto the End. He was of an Inclination, cutting rather like a Hatchet than like a Razor" [139]. Such was the character of this man, who, in 1683, found himself the Captain of a King's ship. In 1687 he was fortunate enough to discover a wrecked vessel filled with treasure, and after being entertained and knighted by James II. he returned to New England to build the "fair brick house" of which he had foretold. After the resettlement of Massachusetts, which now practically extended from Rhode Island to New Brunswick, excluding New Hampshire, Phipps was appointed Governor. He owed his appointment to the favour of Increase Mather, but it seems to have been welcomed generally, for Phipps was at first popular, generous, and well-meaning. At the outset he was confronted by difficulties that would have baffled a man of far greater capacity. The taxation of the colony had not been specifically mentioned in the charter, and the colonists seized upon the opportunity to enact that no taxes were to be levied without the consent of the Assembly. The home government immediately rejected this, and so opened the door for the squabbles and recriminations eighty years afterwards, which led to the separation of the American colonies from the mother country. Gradually Phipps lost his popularity, which had to a certain extent been founded upon his romantic history. He became brutal, covetous and violent, and so in 1694 the Bostonians turned against him. His temper had never been calm, and it is said that by the end of his period of office he was engaged in violent quarrels with every man of importance in the province.

The governorship of the colony between 1698 and 1701 was amalgamated with those of New York, New Jersey, and New Hampshire. The Earl of Bellomont was given supreme control, and won the goodwill of the people by favouring the Democratic Party and recommending many reforms. His special title to Fame is his suppression of the pirates along the coasts, who according to Bellomont's complaint in 1698 had been protected and encouraged by Benjamin Fletcher, Governor of New York. "I have likewise discovered that protections were publickly exposed to sale at the said rates to Pyrats that were of other companies ... and made discovery of the bonds the Pyrates entered into to Coll: Fletcher when he granted them Commissions" [140]. Bellomont was determined to save the colonies from these sea-wolves, and in 1701 he had the satisfaction, just before he died, of bringing the infamous Captain Kidd to the gallows.

The later history of Massachusetts must be left to the chapter on French Aggression. The colony founded first as a trading Company by a few adventurous Puritans had in seventy years become not only one of the most prosperous, but also one of the largest of the thirteen States. It had embraced several of the smaller and weaker settlements, the history of one of which has already been traced; the story of the others has yet to be told.

Chapter 5

CONNECTICUT; RHODE ISLAND AND PROVIDENCE PLANTATION; NEW HAVEN; MAINE; NEW HAMPSHIRE

The early history of the group of colonies which is now to engage the attention is less interesting than that of either Virginia or Massachusetts. There is not the glamour of a first colony as in the case of Virginia; the men were not Pilgrim Fathers in the true sense as in Plymouth; the prosperity of Massachusetts, the rivalries of Maryland, and the Spanish danger in the Carolinas, are all wanting in this portion of New England. There is therefore not only a lack of romance, but there is too a pettiness in the quarrels which continually occurred in these colonies.

The New England Company, when once it had started an active existence, made every effort to extract some advantage from the land which had been granted to it. In 1631 Lord Saye and Sele, Lord Brooke and others obtained from the Company a tract of land in the rich valley of the Connecticut River. Very little, however, came of this scheme; and the first true settlement was made against the strenuous opposition of the Dutch, by a party from New Plymouth. A fresh influx of settlers came from the already rising colony of Massachusetts, for they had found that the land was somewhat sterile, at any rate not sufficiently fertile to support them all. The settlers on the Connecticut came from the town of Dorchester, and planted themselves at Windsor, to the disgust of the New Plymouth settlers, who were at last forced to retire. This proved, as often enough in future years, that the unscrupulous and overbearing temper of the men of Massachusetts earned for them a reward which they did not deserve. The patentees, seeing their rights invaded by these Dorchester filibusters, sent out a small party to establish their privileges, but these in turn were routed, and the men of Massachusetts were left in possession, though contrary to the wishes of their mother-settlement. When, however, the versatile John Winthrop, son of the more statesmanlike Governor, arrived with a commission as Governor of the new colony on behalf of the patentees, Massachusetts ceased to complain, and allowed the secession to become complete. Within two years the new colony of Connecticut had a population of eight hundred men, women and children, grouped in three towns, Hartford, Wethersfield, and Windsor. The freemen of these towns declared in 1638 that their constitution was the same as that of Massachusetts; but there was one great dissimilarity, for no religious test was imposed. This constitution occupies a famous place in the world's history, for not only was it the first written constitution that actually created a government, but it has also been characterised as "the oldest political constitution in America" [141]. By means of this important document, issued in January 1639, all possible claims to sovereignty on the part of Massachusetts were placed on one side for ever; or was there any reference to the sovereignty of Charles I. or the home parliament. The document was merely an agreement amongst the colonists themselves, and by abstaining from any religious tests, or intolerance, they earned the gratitude and admiration of mankind, and throughout the whole colonial period bravely sustained this liberal spirit which had distinguished them so early in their history.

Before accomplishing this great work the colonists had a hard fight for existence against the Pequod Indians. As early as 1633 a Virginian ship's captain, Stone, was killed by this tribe near the mouth of the Connecticut River; two years later John Oldham, a trader, was also murdered by a party of Narragansetts inhabiting Block Island. It was evident that the redskins must be taught a severe lesson if Englishmen were to live in peace. Endecott, with a small force from Massachusetts, was despatched to punish the Narragansetts, but he utterly failed in his attack upon the island tribe. In retaliation the settlers in Connecticut were surrounded by the murderous Pequods, and cut off from the sea; fortunately, Roger Williams, having the confidence and goodwill of the redskins, managed, at this time of trial, to obtain the neutrality of the Narragansetts. This was a great advantage, as Massachusetts deserted the new settlement, leaving it to fight its own battles. Leaders with plenty of courage were not wanting, and Captains Mason and Underhill, with ninety men, marched against the Pequods. Two hundred of these tribesmen had attacked Wethersfield, and "having put poles in their Conoos, as we put Masts in our boats, and upon them hung our English mens and womens shirts and smocks in stead of sayles, and in way of bravado came along in sight of us as we stood upon Seybrooke Fort" [142]. Captain John Mason was not the man to be discouraged by such warlike displays, and with considerable strategy attacked them on the flank and assaulted their chief stronghold. The action was a hot one, for although only two Englishmen were slain, many were wounded, and six hundred Pequods are reported to have fallen. The men of Connecticut were desperate, and fighting for their lives. They were determined to annihilate the Pequod tribe once for all, and to establish peace by means of a sanguinary slaughter. Their actions may appear brutal, but they were necessary as Captain John Underhill took care to explain. "Great and dolefull was the bloudy sight to the view of young souldiers that never had beene in Warre, to see so many soules lie gasping on the ground so thicke in some places, that you could hardly passe along. It may be demanded, Why should you be so furious (as some have said), should not christians have more mercy and compassion? But I would refer you to David's warre, when a people is growne to such a height of bloud and sinne against God and man, and all confederates in the action, there hee hath no respect to persons, but harrowes them and sawes them and puts them to the sword" [143]. This massacre and total destruction of the Pequods had the important effect of reversing the territorial relations between the English and the Indians; direct communication between the mouth of the

Connecticut and Boston was now made possible, and some form of union could only be a matter of time.

As has already been shown Connecticut did join in such a union when it entered into the Confederation of New England in 1643, and it was as a member of that group that it passed through the period of the civil wars. With the Restoration the ambitions of the settlers increased, and in 1661 John Winthrop went to England to obtain a charter which would define the boundaries of the colony, and include within it the smaller settlement of New Haven, the members of which protested in vain. The patent of incorporation was granted in 1662, and the document concludes with the words which illustrate the interesting but absurd legal fiction under which the King granted land in America. The Governor and Company of the English colonists of Connecticut are to hold "the same of his Majesty, his heirs and successors as of the manor of East Greenwich in free and common soccage, yielding the fifth part of all gold or silver ore" [144]. So ridiculous was this fiction that the colonists were actually supposed to be represented in the home parliament by the member of the borough containing the manor of East Greenwich. It is not surprising that even as early as this period these rigid Presbyterians felt that if the actions of the home government endangered their welfare they would be justified in ignoring that authority, and relying only upon the common weal as supreme law in the colony. But though they regarded with jealousy any attempt to limit their rights, they were too weak, owing to internal dissension, to throw off the yoke of the home authorities. They had in no way added to their strength by the incorporation of New Haven, but rather increased their weakness. This unstable condition is illustrated in particular, first by the emigration of the people of the town of Branford, who, armed with their civil and ecclesiastical records, preferred to occupy lands near the Delaware rather than stay under the jurisdiction of Connecticut; and secondly by the description of Connecticut itself, as recorded by the Governor, William Leete, in 1680. He shows that for the last seven years the popularity of the colony had evidently declined in England, for only one or two settlers had come from the home country each year. The population had certainly increased by about five hundred in eight years; from 2050 in 1671 to 2507 in 1679; but there was very little unity of feeling or purpose owing to the religious sects being peculiarly mixed, some being Presbyterians, some "strict congregational men," some "more large congregational men," some Quakers, and four or five are classified by the Governor as "seven-day men" [145].

For twenty-three years the people of Connecticut imagined that they enjoyed the benefits of the charter gained by Winthrop in 1662, "ye advantages and priviledges whereof made us indeed a very happy people; and by ye blessing of God upon our endeavours we have made a considerable improvement of your dominions here, which with ye defense of ourselves from ye force of both forraign and intestine enemies has cost us much expence of treasure & blood" [146]. James II., however, cared for none of these things; the charter was forfeited in 1685; and like Massachusetts, Connecticut felt the heavy hand of the too zealous Sir Edmund Andros. Being "commissionated by his Majesty," [147] Andros appeared with sixty grenadiers in 1687 at Hartford, and took over the government. On his capture, as already recorded, the people of Connecticut in May 1689 joyfully fell back upon their old form of government under the late charter, the forfeiture of which had been declared illegal in England.

Owing to King William's War, Connecticut was within an ace of losing its government, and for purposes of defence being united, in 1690, with its stronger neighbour New York; the proposals fell through, and the fears of the citizens were set at rest by a legal confirmation of their constitution. The colony from this time undoubtedly advanced. Its system of government was active and vigorous; each township controlled its own affairs, and in the early years of the eighteenth century local government lay entirely in the hands of the Select-men, to the exclusion of English officials. At the same time education was encouraged; a college was established by the clergy in 1698, which found its final home at Newhaven in 1717. Before this printing had been undertaken, the first press being erected in 1709 at New London; the immediate work done was not of a first-rate character, but it was the beginning of better things. At the same time it is only fair to point out that the colony was cursed by the presence of turbulent and quarrelsome negro and mulatto slaves; it was regarded with suspicion by the English governors as a protector of pirates; and it certainly must be blamed for its niggardly contributions of both men and money in the great expeditions against the French.

Connecticut was not the only settlement that was partly formed by a secession from the parent colony of Massachusetts; nor was it an isolated example of colonial establishments, for during the same period several other colonies grew up along the Eastern seaboard. The Reverend Roger Williams, after his banishment from Massachusetts in October 1635, purchased land from the Indians, and with twelve other householders settled at Providence, by the advice of Mr Winslow, the Governor of New Plymouth. Thus Williams was able to describe himself many years later as "by God's mercy the first beginner of the mother town of Providence and of the Colony of Rhode Island" [148]. Williams' settlers immediately started a simple form of government, by which all freemen were to hold quarterly meetings and settle judicial questions, while five Select-men were to transact all executive business. Following Williams' example, Mrs Anne Hutchinson, as another refugee from the intolerance of Massachusetts, came to much the same district in 1637. She purchased from the Indians the island of Aquedneck, or, as it was afterwards known, Rhode Island. Her heretical followers soon founded the town of Portsmouth, and here the government was carried on by William Coddington as judge. Mrs Hutchinson, having now time for inventing new heresies, almost immediately caused a fresh secession, and some of her hitherto ardent admirers, finding her new doctrines intolerable, left Portsmouth, and under Coddington established themselves at Newport. The colonies were reunited in 1640, with Coddington as Governor, and a regular government was instituted composed of two "assistants" from each township.

Providence and Rhode Island were regarded with dislike and suspicion by all the other colonies, being classified as the asylum for sectaries, the hot-bed of anarchy, and the true home of extreme democracy. This attitude is not surprising when it is remembered that both colonies owed their existence to parties of religious outcasts. Rhode Island nevertheless prospered, although throughout the first few years of its existence it was the centre of disorder, bickerings, and factious quarrels. At the bottom of most of the trouble was Samuel Gorton, a contentious and troublesome man, leader of a band of fanatics, who had forced themselves upon a party of Williams' settlers at Pawtuxet. The settlers appealed to Massachusetts to remove him as "a proud and pestilent seducer"; [149] and had indeed placed themselves under the jurisdiction of that colony for this very purpose. In 1643, Gorton, of "insolent and riotous carriage," with nine of his followers, was imprisoned for some months at Boston, for blasphemy. The quarrel, however, did not end here. It was carried by Gorton to England, where he appealed to the Parliamentary Commissioners, who commanded the General Court to allow Gorton and his band to dwell in peace. This, at last, the Massachusetts' government consented to do with contemptuous indifference, but when Gorton pleaded for their protection against the Indians he pleaded in vain.

In the same year as the conclusion of the Gorton controversy, Providence, Portsmouth and Newport, combined into a properly constituted community. This was the outcome of a visit paid to England in 1643 by Roger Williams, who asked for a definite charter of incorporation. In 1647, therefore, a general assembly of freemen, governor and assistants, with a court of commissioners, was established for the "Colony of Rhode Island and Providence Plantation." At first the assembly met in the different towns by rotation, and the method of voting was most complicated and non- progressive; every matter had to be voted on in each town, and was to be considered as lost unless it was carried by a majority in every town. So complex a system proved inadequate, and in 1664 an ordinary representative assembly was created. What was equally important and showed Rhode Island to be more enlightened than most of the other colonies, was the clear announcement of the doctrine of freedom of conscience to all who "live civilly." To the annoyance of Massachusetts the Rhode Island authorities consistently adhered to this doctrine, and refused to join in the barbarous persecutions of the Quakers.

The settlers expressly thanked Charles II. for sending Commissioners, and made great demonstration of their loyalty and obedience in 1665. Such actions are rather surprising in a Puritan colony, but they may have been due to the King's grant of a charter, two years before, in which they obtained a definition of their boundaries. The colony of this period was described with some minuteness by the Commissioners, who called attention to the fact that Quakers and Generalists were admitted, and that owing to the variety of sects there were no places for the worship of God, "but they sometimes associate in one house, and sometimes in another" [150]. The colony certainly did not advance with the strides that had been made by Massachusetts, and the people were still extremely unpopular with the other colonists, being denounced on one occasion as "scum and dregs." Nevertheless under the government of Peleg Sandford in 1680, Rhode Island was a small, happy, self-sufficing colony. The chief town was Newport, built almost entirely of timber. As to exterior commerce it seems to have been non-existent; "wee have no shippinge belonginge to our Colloney, but only a few sloopes," and "as for Merchants wee have none, but the most of our Colloney live comfortably by improvinge the wildernesse" [151].

This happy state of affairs was somewhat rudely disturbed by James II.'s action in depriving Rhode Island and Providence Plantation of that charter of which they were so proud, and which gave "full liberty of conscience provided that the pretence of liberty extend not to licentiousnesse" [152]. James' harsh treatment did not last for long, and to the joy of the inhabitants after the Revolution the action of the Papist King was declared illegal. A time of peace and prosperity now followed. From 1696 to 1726 Rhode Island increased in wealth and population, under the annually elected Governor, Samuel Cranston, who, during these thirty years of office, proved himself a firm, popular, and successful administrator.

During the year in which Rhode Island was established, another colony, New Haven, was founded to the South. In 1637 Theophilus Eaton, a leader in the Baltic Company, and "of great esteem for religion," [153] together with a party of settlers who were wealthier men than most colonists, settled at the mouth of the Quinipiac River, facing Long Island. The religious beliefs of the settlers were of the most bigoted kind; their freemen were strictly limited to Church members; and their minister, "the reverend, judicious and godly Mr John Davenport," [154] asserted that the scripture was sufficient guide for all civil affairs. They soon found "a fit place to erect a Toune, which they built in very little time, and with very faire houses and compleat streets; but in a little time they over-stockt it with Chattell, although many of them did follow merchandizing and Maritime affairs, but their remoteness from Mattachusets Bay, where the chiefe traffique lay, hindered them much" [155]. Ten years after its foundation, the colony was seen to be commercially on the decline, although other towns had grown up such as Guildford, Milford, and Stamford. They were all governed as one town without representation, and the executive was placed in the hands of an elected Governor and four assistants. The commercial depression did not last for long; trade began to increase again, and Newhaven became a flourishing state, the inhabitants of which were noted for the magnificence of their buildings and their astonishing opulence.

After the Restoration the colony fell under the displeasure of the Crown. Two of the regicides, William Goffe and Edward Whalley had, first, come to Boston, then to Connecticut, and finally to New Haven. The home government ordered their arrest, and Winthrop was very active in sending these orders to the Governors of the different colonies, including the Governor of New Haven, who knew that these men had come within his rights of jurisdiction but took no steps to effect their arrest. For some time the King had had strong doubts as to the loyalty of New England as a whole; here, in any case, was a colony that needed watching; and so, in 1662, as has already been shown, New Haven was absorbed by Connecticut. There can be no doubt that Charles had now struck two hearty blows against the much vaunted New England Confederation. His refusal to allow the ill-treatment of the Quakers, and his punishment of New Haven, were sufficient to make the Confederation nothing more important than a triennial meeting of federal commissioners, who sat till 1684, but whose powers were nil, whose mutual beliefs were non-existent, and who were only in complete concord in resistance to the Indian raids.

Maine was yet another colony of New England, which had a purely independent foundation, but which was destined to be absorbed by its more prosperous neighbour. As early as 1623, Levitt established a settlement on Casco Bay; [156] while at the same time, Sir Ferdinando Gorges, "the Father of English Colonisation in North America," [157] made a plantation at Saco. He followed this up by the formation of a company in 1631, but four years later the whole territory then called New Somersetshire was granted to Gorges. Five years later he received from Charles I. a charter granting to him "all that part and portion of New England lying and between the River Pascataway ... to Kenebeck even as far as the head thereof" [158]. Sir Ferdinando very soon drew up a most grotesque constitution for his colony, creating almost more officials than there were citizens, and whose titles were very magnificent, but quite meaningless. In exactly the same district the New England Company claimed to have proprietary rights, and it was not long before many semi- independent settlements were made in the neighbourhood of Gorges Colony.

The Civil War having broken out in 1642 Sir Ferdinando Gorges was too much engaged at home to pay any attention to Maine, "for when he was between three and four score years of age did personally engage in our Royal Martyr's service; and particularly in the siege of Bristow, and was plundered and imprisoned several times, by reason whereof he was discountenanced by the pretended Commissioners for foreign plantations" [159]. Soon after his exploits at Bristol, Gorges died after proving himself a man of resolute purpose, but endowed with narrow ideas. He had certainly taken an active part in the struggle for gain and position amongst a large number of the most worthless and servile courtiers, but still around him and his memory there is a halo of grandeur, borrowed perhaps from the generation to which he really belonged, nevertheless reflecting upon his person something of that glory that ought to belong to him who was the last figure of that grand procession of giants which numbered amongst its train, Gilbert and Drake, Smith and Raleigh.

No sooner had Gorges passed away than Edward Rigby claimed the whole of Maine under a grant from the New England Company. Against this the heirs of Sir Ferdinando put in a strong counter-claim; the decision between the disputants was left to the authorities in Massachusetts, who divided the towns into equal halves, three being allotted to Rigby, and three to the Gorges claimant. The inhabitants of the colony were not consulted, and in 1649 they took the matter into their own hands and declared themselves a body politic with an elective governor and council. But this was not to last. In the early days of the settlement the colonists showed no signs of religious bigotry or of any religious views at all, but gradually they came to sympathise with both the religion and the political opinions of Massachusetts, so that between 1651 and 1658 the townships of Maine readily accepted the authority of the greater colony.

Soon after the Restoration, Ferdinando Gorges, the grandson of the original patentee, sought to assert his authority over Maine, but his exertions were not supported by the Crown, and he was unsuccessful. In 1665 the home authorities set up a provisional government in the colony, but concerning its history very little is known. According to the Commissioners of that year the inhabitants themselves petitioned that they might continue under his Majesty's immediate government. They expressed their gratitude to Charles II. for his "fatherly care of them after so long a death inflicted on their minds and fortunes by the usurpation of the Massachusetts power," [160] and they ask that the insults of others towards them may be prevented for the future by the appointment of Sir Robert Carr as their governor. But this statement seems very improbable and can hardly have expressed the general wishes of the people.

It is not surprising that Sir Robert Carr was anxious to obtain the government of the colony, as from contemporary descriptions it appears to have been a fertile and productive territory. "In these Provinces are great store of wild ducks, geese, and deer, strawberries, raspberries, gooseberries, barberries, bilberries, several sorts of oaks and pines, chestnuts and walnuts, sometimes four or five miles together; the more northerly the country, the better the timber is accounted" [161]. The true value of Maine was realised by William Dyre, who pointed out to Charles II. the manifold advantages that he would gain if he purchased Maine for himself. By such an action the King would have absolute dominion over those seas and might settle a duty on all fisheries there; at the same time he might very easily reduce the turbulent spirits in Massachusetts "to a ready subjection," while enriching himself with masts, tar, timber, etc., and thus "conduce to the safety of his maritime affairs" [162]. There were, however, other very different views on Maine, and John Josselyn, an Englishman of good family, does not speak well of either the country or its inhabitants, but there are reasons for supposing that he may have been maliciously inclined. The people of Maine in 1675 "may be divided," he writes, "into Magistrates, Husbandmen or Planters, and fishermen; of the magistrates some be Royalists, the rest perverse Spirits, the like are the planters and fishers.... The planters are or should be restless pains takers, providing for their Cattle, planting and sowing of Corn ... but if they be of a droanish disposition as some are, they become wretchedly poor and miserable.... They have a custom of taking Tobacco, sleeping at noon, sitting long at meals sometimes four times in a day, and now and then drinking a dram of the bottle extraordinarily" [163].

The people of Maine may have been all that Josselyn said, but it is far from likely. They were sufficiently alert to resent the government of the Crown, and in 1668 the majority of the settlers acquiesced in the reassertion of authority by Massachusetts. For ten years the quarrel between Ferdinando Gorges and Massachusetts continued, but in 1678, although his grandfather is reported to have spent £20,000 on the colony, the grandson's claims were extinguished by the purchase of his rights for £1250. From this moment Maine ceased to exist as a separate colony, and continued incorporated with Massachusetts for many years.

The last of this early group of colonies was New Hampshire, which, in turn, like its weaker brethren, became amalgamated with the colony of Massachusetts. Early in the reign of Charles I., Captain John Mason, with Sir Ferdinando Gorges and others, formed for colonial purposes the Laconia Company. When Gorges was granted rights in Maine in 1635, Captain John Mason also received a grant of territory to the south, where a settlement was formed, and though by no means a true political community, was called New Hampshire. Mason died soon after the naming of his colony and received no benefits from his grant, which had embraced two earlier settlements: the first founded by David Thompson near the

Piscataqua; the second fifteen miles up the Cocheco, founded by Bristol and Shrewsbury merchants, who had transferred their rights to Lord Saye and Sele and Lord Brooke. It was in this latter stretch of territory that purely independent settlements were made, such as Dover, Exeter, and Hampton. The latter town, realising its weakness as an independent community, soon chose to be regarded as within the jurisdiction of Massachusetts. The authorities of Massachusetts undoubtedly suffered from "earth hunger," and the transfer of Hampton was merely the first of a series of aggressions, for between 1642 and 1643 the other towns of New Hampshire were swallowed within the greedy maw of the stronger colony. No remonstrance came from England, for the people of the home country had enough difficulties to contend with; while the Mason family appear to have made no serious attempts to recover their rights. After the Restoration, however, following the example of Ferdinando Gorges, the heirs of Mason petitioned the Privy Council to restore to them the rights and privileges contained in the grant of 1635. The law officers of the Crown took the matter into serious consideration, and although their verdict was against the Mason family, they declared at the same time that the colony of New Hampshire was outside the jurisdiction of Massachusetts, which had annexed it and wrongfully renamed it Norfolk. This was one more blow for the New England Confederation and for Massachusetts in particular. The King and his ministers were only too pleased to have had such an opportunity, for the Royal Commissioners had but recently accused Massachusetts of disloyalty. They had, in fact, declared that unless the King punished the authorities, the well-affected inhabitants would never dare to own themselves loyal subjects. To better effect the total subjugation of the colony, one of the Commissioners, Sir Robert Carr, proposed that he should be made governor of New Hampshire, a proposal which shows only too clearly the selfish aims of the Crown officials. The actual state of New Hampshire did not seem to trouble the Commissioners, and whilst the bickering between the home country and Massachusetts continued, the unfortunate inhabitants of New Hampshire were suffering all the horrors of the already mentioned King Philip's Indian war. For this reason the settlers took the matter into their own hands and turned to the more powerful colony of Massachusetts for assistance and protection. In 1678 the inhabitants of Portsmouth and Dover supplicated the Crown to be kept under the jurisdiction of the stronger colony. The petition from Dover is particularly noteworthy because of its tawdry character. The petitioners speak of the favour of his Majesty, "which like the sweet influences of superior or heavenly bodies to the tender plants have cherished us in our weaker beginnings, having been continued through your special grace, under your Majesty's protection and government of the Massachusetts, to which we voluntarily subjected ourselves many years ago, yet not without some necessity in part felt for want of government and in part feared upon the account of protection" [164]. In spite of this petition the Crown created New Hampshire a separate province, with a council and representative assembly. The first governor selected was John Cutts, "a very just and honest but ancient and infirm man," [165] and with his appointment the people of Massachusetts revoked all former commissions.

The colony did not forget its old guardian, and looked upon it always with loyal affection, a feeling which was intensified during the tyrannical governorship of Edward Cranfield. From 1682 to 1685 this man's disgraceful conduct was tolerated, but at last the men of New Hampshire could bear his despotism no longer, broke into open rebellion, and Cranfield fled for refuge to the West Indies. The desired result was immediately obtained, for New Hampshire was reunited to Massachusetts. This, however, was not to last for long, for after the Revolution in England the proprietorship of New Hampshire was again debated. Samuel Allen had purchased from the heirs of Captain Mason any rights which they continued to imagine they possessed; and by the corrupt connivance of an English official, Allen succeeded in obtaining a proprietary governorship with a council partly nominated by the Crown and partly by himself. It is a remarkable fact that, unlike the other colonies at this time, New Hampshire obtained no charter. The only freedom allowed to its inhabitants was the exercise of a few independent rights by means of the representative assembly elected by the freeholders.

The acceptance of the Revolution in America marks an epoch of American history. All the New England colonies had been established, and had either proved themselves sturdy enough to stand alone, or had been forced to find shelter beneath the wing of the more powerful Connecticut or Massachusetts. The New England Confederation had been tried and found wanting. The time for union was evidently not ripe, but this embryo of the United States ceased to exist at identically the hour it was most wanted. A union of all the colonies was what might have been expected when French aggression and Canadian pluck taxed all the resources of the colonists; the scheme of union, however, failed, and the French had to be met in that haphazard and unprepared way in which, it would appear from history, Englishmen are accustomed not only to meet supreme danger, but to come through it with success.

Chapter 6

THE FIGHT WITH THE DUTCH FOR THEIR SETTLEMENT OF NEW NETHERLAND

A new epoch in colonial history was reached when England adopted a warlike policy to obtain mastery in the West. During the Protectorate, England and Holland were for the first time engaged in desperate warfare. The numerous common interests that existed in the two countries, such as religion and republicanism, were of no avail to keep the peace. The war that brought such honour to Admiral Blake was not a war against a "natural enemy," but rather a contest between trade rivals using the same methods and having the same opinions. The spirit which animated Cromwell in naval affairs was not Puritanic; it was rather that of the Elizabethan epoch. The old naval enthusiasm which had so long slept in the stagnant days of the first Stuarts had now awakened with renewed vigour, as if its long years of drowsiness had afforded true refreshment. The celebrated Navigation Act, "the legislative monument of the Commonwealth," [166] was the outward and visible sign of this change in 1651. "It was the first manifestation of the newly awakened consciousness of the community, the act which laid the foundation of the English commercial empire.... It consummated the work which had been commenced by Drake, discussed and expounded by Raleigh, continued by Roe, Smith, Winthrop, and Calvert" [167]. The Dutch, "the Phœnicians of the modern world, the waggoners of all seas," [168] were severely injured by the new law, for goods were no longer to be imported into England save in English vessels or those vessels belonging to the country of which the goods were the natural product or manufacture. This important protective enactment was reissued in the reign of Charles II., and, as on the former occasion, it was one of the main causes of embroiling England and Holland.

For the proper enforcement of the Navigation Act, the English colonies in the West required a geographical compactness which in the central period of the seventeenth century they did not possess. A formidable foreign rival held a valuable commercial settlement between the northern and southern colonies, for the Dutch possessed in New Amsterdam the very best harbour along the coast. By the reign of Charles II. the hatred of the Dutch had become a passion amongst Englishmen, and it had not only been fostered by the Cromwellian war, but by trade-jealousy both in the East and in the West. In America the rising colonies of New England, in particular, looked with greedy eyes upon the splendid waterway of the River Hudson, which was the finest route for Indian trade. They had, too, suffered at the hands of their rivals; both the settlements in Connecticut and Long Island had for many years engaged in innumerable land disputes with the Dutch, nor did the people of New Haven forget that some of their brethren had been driven out of New Sweden, which the Dutch now held.

The Dutch had made their first settlement in 1626 as an outcome of the foundation of the Dutch West India Company five years before. In its functions this corporation very closely resembled the English East India Company, for it made a special combination of naval and commercial affairs, and almost its first work was the establishment of the New Netherland settlement on Long Island and along the River Hudson. Their chief town was planted on Manhattan Island and called New Amsterdam, the population of which soon after its foundation was 270 souls. A contemporary narrative speaks cheerfully of the probable success of the colony, and states that they had a prosperous beginning and that "the natives of New Netherland are very well disposed so long as no injury is done them" [169]. But from the very first the governors were bad; it was in fact irregularities in administration and want of enterprise and courage that caused the recall of Van Twiller in 1637. His successor Kieft proved himself equally incapable, for he was arbitrary and ill- advised, earning the detestation of both Dutch patroons and English settlers. The colonists themselves were few and poor, and the methods employed by the Company lacked any trace of liberality or real knowledge of colonial affairs. Peter Stuyvesant, "that resolute soldier," came into office in 1647; he was the best governor who up to that time had been sent out, but he was nothing more than a martinet, without either sympathy or flexibility. Van der Douch in 1650 described the colony as sadly decayed, and gave as the reasons that "the Managers of the Company adopted a wrong course at first, and as we think had more regard for their own interests than for the welfare of the country.... It seems as if from the first the Company have sought to stock this land with their own employés, which was a great mistake, for when their time was out, they returned home.... Trade, without which, when it is legitimate, no country is prosperous, is by their acts so decayed that the like is nowhere else. It is more suited for slaves than freemen in consequence of the restrictions upon it ... we would speak well of the government ... under Director Stuyvesant, which still stands, if indeed that may be called standing, which lies completely under foot" [170].

It may have been this complaint or feelings similar to those stated therein that forced Stuyvesant to do something that would show that his rule over the colony had a stimulating effect. He had regarded for some time with jealousy the little settlement of New Sweden, or as it was known in later years, Delaware. This colony had been established by one Minuit, who had been formerly employed by the Dutch West India Company. He was a friend of William Usselinx or Ussling, who had as early as 1624 obtained a charter from Gustavus Adolphus for a trading company "to Asia, Africa, America, and Magellanica." [171] But it was not until 1638 that Minuit's Swedish following arrived in America and erected Fort Christina, named after that extraordinary royal tomboy, the Queen of Sweden. They soon had so far settled themselves as to be strong enough to drive out a party from New Haven, but they had not calculated on the hostility of the Dutch. Stuyvesant was determined to seize New Sweden, and set out in 1651 to exert Dutch rights, and for their protection established Fort Casimir on the site of what is now Newcastle, Del. This was merely the beginning of a larger policy of annexation, which was accomplished in 1655 when the Swedish settlement passed into the hands of the Dutch without bloodshed on the appearance of the Governor with an army of 700 men. The conquered territory was immediately sold to the city of Amsterdam and a colony was established there under the name of New Amstel. On the surface this energetic policy had much to recommend it from the Dutch point of view; but in reality the people of the New Netherlands gained but little, as in that colony there were no popular institutions, no true self-government, and not even the advantage of a really efficient despotism to give interior strength or possibilities of exterior advance. The fact was that Stuyvesant's action resulted only in harm to his colony, for in carrying out the extirpation of the Swedish settlement in Delaware he absolutely drained his own resources and left himself unprepared and incapable of resisting the onslaught of the English.

The crushing blow fell in August 1664. In the March of that year Charles II. granted to his brother James, Duke of York, all the territory then held by the Dutch, on the plea that it was really British soil by right of discovery. This was the mere reassertion of an old claim, for James I. had demanded the territory by right of "occupancy" as early as 1621, and Charles I. did the same by "first discovery, occupation, and possession"; Cromwell too had attempted to make possession a real thing in 1654, but the first Dutch War ended too soon. The action of Charles II. may well be regarded as a very practical declaration of war. Colonel Richard Nicolls was appointed to seize the New Netherlands. He was the most important of the Commissioners sent out to report on the state of the colonies, and was a good soldier, a man of great courage, but at the same time forbearing and lenient. The colony which he was ordered to attack contained a population of about 1500 souls, 600 of whom were of English stock, dwelling for the most part on Long Island, which was partially Anglicised by an influx of settlers from Connecticut and New Haven. At the end of August Nicolls arrived off New Amsterdam with four ships, and 450 soldiers and Connecticut volunteers. On September 4 he sent terms to Stuyvesant, stating that "His Majesty, being tender of the effusion of Christian blood, confirms and secures estates, life and liberty to every Dutch inhabitant who shall readily submit to his Government, but those who shall oppose his Majesty's gracious intention must expect all the miseries of a war which they bring on themselves" [172]. Stuyvesant offered very little resistance, and Nicolls soon found himself in possession of New Amsterdam. The Dutch West India Company failed to see that they had been largely to blame for leaving their colony inadequately defended, and preferred to pour out the vials of their wrath upon the unfortunate Stuyvesant, who, according to the Company, "first following the example of heedless interested parties, gave himself no other concern than about the prosperity of his bouweries, and, when the pinch came, allowed himself to be rode over by Clergymen, women and cowards, in order to surrender to the English what he could defend with reputation, for the sake of thus saving their private properties" [173].

The conquest of the main city did not leave Colonel Nicolls idle. The rest of the province had to be subdued, and by his commands the Assistant Commissioner, Cartwright, went forward, took Fort Orange, better known as Albany, and above all laid the foundations of that friendship between the English and the Iroquois which was to prove of such importance in future years. Sir Robert Carr was also sent to take the settlements along the Delaware; but his violence and rapacity in this work contrasted very strongly with the calm and firm rule of Nicolls, and Carr earned for himself unenviable notoriety for his severity, which, it has been said, was "the one exception to the humanity and moderation shown by the English" [174]. There were other difficulties which presented themselves to the Governor of New York, not the least being the foundation of New Jersey. James, Duke of York, immediately after the capture of the Dutch settlements, granted all the territory from the Hudson to the Delaware to Sir George Carteret and Lord Berkeley. The district was named New Jersey, and Philip Carteret was sent out by his kinsman to supervise his interests. Nicolls strongly disapproved of this measure; he was a man with a keen political insight, and he saw in this mangling of the province the seed of much commercial and political dispute. His warning was, of course, unheeded, but that he was right was amply proved by the later history of New Jersey. Nicolls had also to undo the ill done in Albany by his second in command, Brodhead, who had shown an extraordinary lack of administrative ability, treating the Dutch colonists as an inferior and conquered people, and making numerous arbitrary arrests upon the most trifling charges. Fortunately for the safety of the colony, news of Brodhead's action reached Nicolls and the despotic deputy was suspended.

The government of New York was no sinecure. It was probably the most cosmopolitan town in North America, and though perhaps it is an exaggeration, it has been asserted that eighteen languages could be heard in the streets of the late Dutch capital. Before its capture it had become more Anglicised, as Stuyvesant had not feared but favoured the English. The first thing done by Nicolls was to put the town in a state of defence so as to resist any attempt on the part of the Dutch to regain possession, which was essayed by De Ruyter in 1665, but without success. A far more oppressive burden to a man who really had his heart in his work was the difficulty of obtaining supplies for the soldiers. The English Governor wrote a most pathetic appeal to the Duke of York, telling him how he was paying what he could out of his own pocket, but that the people were starving. He describes how the inhabitants of Long Island were in terrible poverty, and how New York was in "a mean condition ... not one soldier has lain in a pair of sheets or on any bed but canvas and straw" since the capture of the town. He said very pluckily that he did not mind the ruin of his own fortune, but that he could not bear the loss of his reputation; and then, probably to gain his way, he concluded with a delightful sentence of praise that ought to have won the Duke's heart, and which Nicolls no doubt intended that it should. The colony, he writes, exhibited general joy and thanksgiving for the signal victory of the Duke over the Dutch off Lowestoft in June, and for the preservation of His Royal Highness's person, "the very news whereof has revived their spirits and is antidote both against hunger and cold" [175].

Meantime representatives from the English-speaking towns met in February 1665 on Long Island; here, acting in accordance with the wishes of the Governor, a scheme of administration was drawn up; a code of laws was promulgated, and no attempt was made to interfere with the Dutch language. Every town was granted powers of assessment, and the right of choosing a church was given to the freemen who were to declare its denomination. In the cases of the two main Dutch towns of New York and Albany, Nicolls was careful not to arouse ill-feeling, and he allowed them to keep their own mayors. When the first governor retired in 1668, a tribute to his excellent work was paid him by his fellow commissioner Maverick; "he has done his Majesty very considerable service in these parts," he says, "having kept persons of different judgments and divers nations in peace, when a great part of the world was in wars: and as to the Indians, they were never brought into such a peaceable posture and fair correspondence as by his means they now are" [176]. Richard Nicolls was succeeded by Francis Lovelace, who had already acted for three years as deputy governor of Long Island. He had before him as governor of New York a far harder task. He followed a man of wonderful power, and it was now his duty to carry on Nicolls' policy and bring the preponderant Dutch population surely but quietly under the recently established British authority. To accomplish this he adopted a paternal rule; he granted toleration to all religions; he attempted to gain the goodwill of the Indians by purchasing their lands and refraining from any action which might be regarded as aggressive. At the same time he helped the colony very considerably by opening up intercourse between New York and Massachusetts, and by the establishment of a regular post between the two capitals. On the other hand, however, Lovelace was not really suited to his post. He was a courtier of the conventional type, and regarded his stay in New York as a form of exile. He speaks of being in "Egyptian darkness," and asks in one of his letters what is stirring on the stage in "Brittang." In writing to Sir Joseph Williamson he tries to arouse his sympathy and says, "we had as well crossed Lethal as the Athlantiq Ocean." The news from home came to him far too seldom, for the conveyance of letters was as slow "as the production of ellephats, once almost in two years" [177].

Lovelace's rule soon became unpopular for he was determined to carry out his plan of paternal despotism and resisted very firmly every attempt to create popular representation, which was continually demanded. He angered the settlers by what they regarded a severe tax for defensive purposes, and he showed his contempt for the freeholders of Long Island by ordering their protest against his actions to be burnt. It was unfortunate that this man should have so alienated both Dutch and English alike, for his period of government coincided with a most critical epoch in the world's history. In 1670 Charles had allied with Louis XIV. against the Dutch, and one of the first acts of retaliation on the part of the authorities in Holland was to retake their colony of the New Netherlands. In July 1673 the Dutch Admiral Cornelius Eversen appeared off Fort James when Francis Lovelace was away at New Haven. The settlers, instead of resisting the Dutch, remembered their hatred of the Governor, and Captain Manning, second in command, having fired one gun, surrendered, an action which was called at the time "a shame and derision to their English nation as hath not been heard of" [178]. Lovelace on his return found the Dutch flag flying over the settlement, and, having no supporters, fled to Long Island, where the English towns had refused to give way, not because of goodwill towards the Governor, but because of patriotism. Here Lovelace met with a scanty welcome and within a few days was arrested, ostensibly on account of a debt owing to the Duke of York, and was sent back to England on the 30th July 1673, where he died soon after.

Weary of a war which was solely for the advantage of the French, Charles II. came to terms with the Dutch at the Treaty of Westminster, 1674. The New Netherlands once more became New York, but the English ministers made a great error in also restoring to Carteret and Berkeley their rights in New Jersey. The advice of Nicolls was again neglected, and instead of making New York a compact province, the chance of unity was lost by severing from its jurisdiction the territory of New Jersey. Sir Edmund Andros, who was now appointed governor, did his best to neutralise the effect of this by contending that New Jersey was still tributary to New York, asserting his rights with considerable vigour. But the partners in New Jersey were too great favourites at court to suffer any loss, and before the question was settled Andros was recalled in 1680. His rule was particularly wise and moderate, and during his governorship New York experienced a healthy expansion. One thing, however, he would never grant, though the settlers were always clamouring for it, and that was a clearly defined constitution with political rights and privileges similar to those in the New England colonies.

The exceptionally able Thomas Dongan succeeded Andros, but did not arrive until 1683. He was forced to contend, as will be shown later, with French aggression in the valley of the Hudson; his method being a firm alliance with the Five Nations or Iroquois. They were a wild and dangerous people, and as such have been described by one who knew them well. "They likewise paint their Faces, red, blue, &c., and then they look like the Devil himself ... they treat their Enemies with great Cruelty in Time of War, for they first bite off the Nails of the Fingers of their Captives, and cut off some Joints, and sometimes the whole of the Fingers; after that the Captives are obliged to sing and dance before them ... and finally they roast them before a slow Fire for some Days, and eat them." It is interesting to note that the writer records what must have been a great relief to his readers in the colonies, that "they are very friendly to us" [179]. This amicable relationship between the English and the Five Nations was largely due to Dongan's good sense and administrative genius. He persuaded them to become so much subjects of Great Britain as to set up the arms of James II. upon their wigwams. The English king, when he heard of his governor's action, informed Louis XIV. that, as the Iroquois were now true British subjects, he expected them to be treated as such. Dongan's work did not stop here. He was well aware that the Iroquois' friendship was an uncertain prop on which to depend, and therefore palisaded the towns of Albany and Schenectady, thus beginning the famous system of frontier forts. By his actions he gained the goodwill of the New Yorkers, to whom, on behalf of the Proprietors, he granted a charter of incorporation in 1685. But this acceptance of the views of the people was only very temporary, as it was reversed in the next year, while at the same time all rights of legislation were vested in a Council appointed by the Crown.

As has already been shown, James II. amalgamated the colonies in 1685 under Sir Edmund Andros and New York became part of New England. The Governor was kept far too busy in Massachusetts to pay any attention to New York, which was placed under a deputy-governor, Colonel Francis Nicholson, with three Dutch councillors. Nicholson was a clearheaded, observant man, who had had colonial experience, and would have been a success except for the fact that he lacked moral force. His position soon became a very awkward one, for in 1689 he heard that William III. was all-powerful in England, while he held his commission from Andros, the Stuart governor, who was in captivity at Boston. At the same time France had declared war and the Canadians might invade the colony at any moment. Unfortunately for Nicholson, although he summoned the authorities, he quarrelled with his subordinate Cuyler, and things were at a deadlock. At this point the people, seething under the restraints and burdens which had been placed upon them during the reign of James II., rose in open revolt, led by a German brewer, Jacob Leisler. Nicholson was immediately deposed; a convention met, and ten out of the eighteen representatives invested Leisler with dictatorial authority. He was a man of some cunning, and under the pretence of possessing a commission, by intercepting letters and by maltreating their writers, he succeeded in keeping himself in office for very nearly three years. His period of government was distinguished by the first Colonial Congress at Albany, to which he summoned representatives from all the colonies to discuss definite and united action against the French. Leisler himself proposed a joint invasion of Canada, and it is probable that it was only his own arrogance that prevented it. His followers soon came to be as much hated as their leader, and one indignant citizen wrote in January 1690, "never was such a pack of ignorant, scandalous, malicious, false, imprudent, impertinent rascals herded together, out of hell" [180]. Careful though Leisler had been to search letters and prevent the news of his usurpation reaching England, he was unsuccessful. In 1690 the English Government dispatched Colonel Slaughter to take Leisler's place. The usurper was first met by a force under Major Ralph Ingoldsby, second in command to the new Governor; a slight resistance was offered, and Leisler "fired a vast number of great and small shot in the City, whereby several of his Majesty's subjects were killed and wounded as they passed in the streets upon their Lawful Occasions" [181]. But Leisler had lost his former following and he was captured and hanged, together with his chief supporter Jacob Millborne.

As James II. had left New York without a constitution, a representative assembly was called in May 1691, and a declaratory act was passed which annulled Leisler's proceedings. It required that all elections in the future should be annual, that the franchise should belong to the 40s. freeholders only, and that the colony itself should be apportioned into constituencies. At the same time it laid down liberty of conscience except for Papists, allowing a declaration instead of an oath to please the Quakers. But above all it declared that no tax was to be imposed unless it was voted by the colony. The act seemed satisfactory enough, except the important reservation with regard to taxation; a reservation which was sufficient to cause the Crown to veto the whole document, and New York was again without a true and defined constitution. Such a state of affairs was particularly bad when the colony in 1692 passed under the rule of the notoriously corrupt Benjamin Fletcher. There are, however, two things to be said for this man, whose work has been spoken of as full of deceit, fraud, and subterfuge. In the first place it has been proved that in military matters he showed considerable skill and activity; while in the second he undoubtedly realised before many men of his day the danger of disunion. In May 1696 he wrote, "The Indians, though monsters, want not sense, but plainly see we are not united, and it is apparent that the stronger these colonies grow in parts, the weaker we are on the whole, every little government setting up for despotic power and allowing no appeal to the Crown, but valuing themselves on their own strength and on a little juggling in defeating all commands and injunctions of the King" [182]. On the other hand it must be allowed that Fletcher's methods were particularly scandalous, for not only did he practically license smuggling and piracy by levying blackmail upon those who carried on these lucrative trades, but he made personal friends of them, as for example Captain Tew, "a most notorious pirate," with whom, to the scandal of the inhabitants, he occasionally dined.

As has been shown in another chapter, the Earl of Bellomont was made governor in 1698 to prevent these nefarious undertakings, and as ruler of

New York, New Jersey, New Hampshire, and Massachusetts he did such good work that he was universally and sincerely regretted when he died in 1701. He was succeeded by Lord Cornbury, who was a profligate in character and overbearing in manner. His rule was one of petty spite and conflict, and having won the especial hatred of the dissenters and generally alienated popular support, his recall in 1708 was as much a cause of rejoicing as Bellomont's death had been of lamentation.

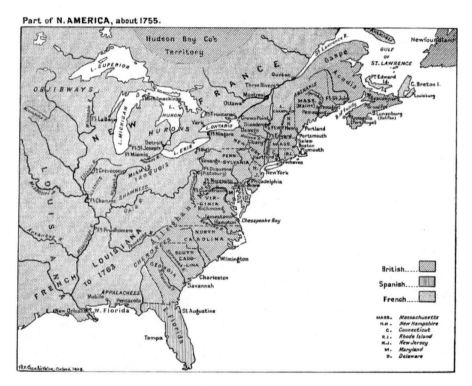

Map of North America, 1755.

The first sixty years of the eighteenth century were to the inhabitants of New York years of anxiety and peril, for there was the ever present danger of the French to the north and west. The story of these years will be told elsewhere, and here only a rapid sketch can be given of the domestic history of the colony. Four governors or deputy-governors attract particular attention during this period. The first was Governor Burnet, [183] son of the celebrated Bishop, who made himself conspicuous in 1724 by writing a pamphlet in defence of paper money. The governorship of William Cosby was not without a constitutional interest, ten years later, in the prosecution of John Peter Zengler, publisher of the New York Weekly Journal, for criticising the government. He was described as a "seditious Person, and a frequent Printer and Publisher of false News and seditious Libels" [184]. The same Governor had also a hard struggle with his people, which caused him to write to the home Government for more power and patronage, for "ye example and spirit of the Boston people begins to spread amongst these Colonys In a most prodigious maner, I have had more trouble to manige these people then I could have imagined, however for this time I have done pritty well with them; I wish I may come off as well with them of ye Jarsys" [185].

It is evident that as late as 1740 the position of governor was one of lucrative importance; in that year George Clarke, junior, offered the Duke of Newcastle £1000 if he would appoint Mr Clarke, senior, governor, instead of lieutenant-governor as he then was. But this must have been almost the last case that the post was financially desirable, for it was clearly the reverse between 1743 and 1753, when George Clinton was governor. He himself writes, "The Govern^t of New York will not be near so valuable to Govr Clinton as it has been to his predecessors.—The Province of New Jersey having always till now been united with New York, and under the same government, and the salary paid by New Jersey has always been £1000 besides other considerable advantages, so that the making New Jersey a separate and distinct govern^t makes New York at least £1000 a year less in value to Govr Clinton than it was to his predecessors" [186]. There were, however, other reasons which in the near future would make the financial position of the Governor still more precarious, and Clinton could hardly be expected to foresee that the advantages gained over the French during his lifetime would in later years be one of the main causes of entire independence of official governors sent from England.

Chapter 7

THE QUAKER SETTLEMENTS AND GEORGIA

There are few examples in history of the possessions of an ardent Roman Catholic passing quietly and amicably into the hands of members of the Society of Friends, but the Quaker colonies stand pre-eminent as one instance of this exceptional circumstance. The Quakers were probably the most persecuted of all religious sects in North America, and yet by the irony of fate, one of the most thriving settlements owed its origin to them; its capital Philadelphia became the most important town of the Thirteen Colonies, and for one hundred and seventeen years was regarded as the commercial, political, and social capital of the bickering and jarring states. In the history of these Quaker settlements the disunited character of the colonies is peculiarly apparent, and in no colony or group of colonies is it better exemplified than in those of New Jersey and Pennsylvania. The high-handed action of Charles II. in claiming Dutch territory and granting it to his brother James, Duke of York, has already been noticed. As soon as his claim had been authenticated by the victory of Richard Nicolls, the Duke lavishly granted to Sir George Carteret and Lord Berkeley the land from the Hudson to the Delaware, and it was renamed East and West New Jersey. From the very first the settlers hated the Proprietors for being pronounced absentees endeavouring to exercise control over those who had already purchased the titles to their lands, and demanding an unearned increment in a most repellent form. For three years Philip Carteret, the Governor, did not call a representative assembly, and at last when he did so, imagining the spirit of the colonists to be broken, he met with a point-blank refusal from two of the towns. The colony was, in fact, in a state of mutiny. It was all very well for those in authority to refrain from claiming quit rents for five years, but this was only a sop to the settlers, who were angered by the demand that all patents of lands must be obtained from the Proprietors. The colonists therefore broke into open revolt; set up their own representative and deposed Carteret. The rebellion was soon crushed by the Proprietors, but with this state of affairs within, New Jersey was not in a condition to resist the attack of the Dutch from without, and in 1673 the old owners took possession.

The Treaty of Westminster in 1674 restored English rule, and the Duke of York claimed that all previous titles were annulled by the Conquest. The new arrangement now made was, that the Duke reserved to himself the left bank of the Delaware; Carteret was granted a tract of land on the southern bank of the Hudson; while Berkeley's share was no longer existent, for he had sold his rights to two Quakers, John Fenwick and "Edward Byllinge, of Westminster, gent, in whom the title thereunto then was" [187]. Fenwick appears to have been a man of energy, for he endeavoured to form a settlement on the right bank of the Delaware, which was strenuously opposed by Sir Edmund Andros, as representative for the Duke of York. Fenwick, however, won in the end, and established the colony of Salem. About the same time Edward Byllinge transferred any rights he might possess to William Penn, the world-famed Quaker. He with others of the Society of Friends began to colonise on the Delaware, and their plans were still further encouraged in 1680 by a grant from the Duke of York including the new colony of Salem. As a balance to this gift to the Quakers, James, in the following year, increased the territories of the Carteret family and restored the government to Philip Carteret, who found, on his return, that his old methods were no longer possible; the proprietary power had already been considerably weakened, and the settlers had learnt to manage their own affairs. Sir George Carteret, recognising that his rights, privileges, and perquisites were practically nil, very sensibly sold this valueless property to William Penn, Gawen Laurie, and other Quakers. With that extraordinary desire for the construction of fantastic constitutions, the new Proprietors at first attempted to foist upon the settlers a scheme of government which was so elaborate that it was useless and unworkable. In a very short time they found that they were obliged to fall back upon the more simple system of a governor, council, and representative assembly.

The results of this action on the part of Carteret and Penn were on the whole satisfactory. It so happened that some of the new Proprietors were Scotsmen, and they stimulated emigration from the North, and New Jersey was all the better for a strong infusion of the vigorous Scottish race. The action, too, had the effect of bringing East and West New Jersey into closer contact, and so paved the way for union. In 1692 another step was taken in this direction, for the Proprietors of both colonies appointed Andrew Hamilton as joint-governor. There were, however, many difficulties to be overcome before union was possible. In the first place there were unending disputes with New York about the levying of duties; while secondly, the Proprietors' rights had now become so complicated by frequent sale and transfer that matters were in dire confusion; besides these very rights appeared to the settlers themselves as injurious to the welfare of the colony. They looked for political privileges for themselves, which would, according to the Proprietors, clash with their interests. To grant to the settlers rights which were on the surface merely political, appeared, and indeed would be, the abnegation of all proprietary territorial claims. The man who might have done so much for the union of the New Jerseys had unfortunately transferred his affections elsewhere. Penn, filled with schemes of pure philanthropy, had left his first settlement to look after itself and had brought all his energies to bear upon his new venture in Pennsylvania. Even without Penn's assistance the union of the two Jerseys was bound to come. In 1701 it was pointed out by the Colonial Office of that day, that "by several letters, memorials, and other papers, as well from the inhabitants as Proprietors of both these provinces, that they are at present in confusion and anarchy; and that it is much to be apprehended lest by the heats of the parties that are amongst them, they should fall into such violences as may endanger the lives of many persons and destroy the colony" [188]. It seemed obvious to those in London that some form of union was necessary to save the colony from this fate, and so New Jersey from the River Hudson to the River Delaware became a united province when the Proprietors surrendered all their political and territorial rights in 1702. For a short time New Jersey with New York suffered under the scandalous administration of the brainless and profligate Lord Cornbury, but his evil work was to a certain extent remedied by Governor Robert Hunter, who proved himself an able colonial administrator.

The tract of land to which Penn had transferred his philanthropic schemes lay to the south of the river Delaware. It had been taken from the Swedes and at one time had been granted to Maryland, but up to the year 1681 it had remained unoccupied. The Quaker Penn, a man of high social position, friend and favourite of James II., readily accepted this piece of territory in liquidation of a debt of £16,000 owed to him by the Crown. The agreement now drawn up between Penn and the Duke of York was remarkable for its utter indifference to all constitutional forms. Penn was appointed Proprietor, but his powers were to a certain extent limited; on all legislative matters the Crown reserved the right of veto, and in all financial affairs the newly formed colony was to be regarded as an integral portion of the realm; while, as a further hold over revenue, an accredited agent of the colony was to reside in England and was to explain any infraction of the revenue laws.

Pennsylvania, as first conceived by the Proprietor, was not a colony for one sect only. He offered no particular inducements to Quakers rather than to others. The early emigrants were a veritable olla podrida, and consisted of English Quakers, Scottish and Irish Presbyterians, German Mennonites, and French Huguenots. It was not long, however, before the Quaker element distinctly preponderated, with two obvious results. In the first place one of the strongest tenets of Quakerism was a horror of war and bloodshed, which belief was steadily upheld by the Pennsylvanians and proved in later years most baneful to the colony when the French began their aggressions. The second result was just as good as the first had been bad. The Quakers taught and believed the equality of all men before God;

to them there was no distinction between settler and savage, and unlike some of the colonists in the Puritan group, offered the best of treatment to the Red Indians.

In the autumn of 1681, William Penn dispatched four commissioners to found the colony that was in later years to become so famous. William Crispen, Nathaniel Allen, John Bezar and William Heage were chosen by the Proprietor to select a site on the Delaware; Crispen, Penn's kinsman, died on the voyage, but the other three faithfully carried out their orders and selected a spot where the river "is most navigable, high dry and healthy; that is where most ships can ride, of deepest draught of water, if possible to load or unload at the bank or key (sic) side without boating or lightering of it" [189]. Thomas Howe had been appointed surveyor-general and at once proceeded to lay out the city of Philadelphia upon a modification of the plans of Penn and covering a surface area of about 1200 to 1300 acres. William Penn stands alone as the founder of a great city of which he was justly proud, and in 1683 he was able to write, "Philadelphia: the expectation of those who are concerned in this province is at last laid out, to the great content of those here who are anyways interested therein. The situation is a neck of land and lieth between two navigable rivers, Delaware and Sculkill, whereby it hath two fronts upon the water, each a mile, and two from river to river" [190].

Penn was quick to foresee a prosperous future for his colony, but he nearly ruined it at the outset by drawing up a well-intentioned but somewhat cumbersome constitution. There were to be two elective chambers: the Upper or council, consisting of 72 members, and the Lower, which was at first to contain 200, and later 500 members. This constitution, however, was impossible to manage; the Lower assembly was obviously far too large and proved superfluous; while the Upper was found to be too bulky for a Cabinet or executive government; for these reasons a few months after its conception it was radically altered. The pruning-knife was called into use and the 72 of the Upper chamber were cut down to 18; at the same time the absurd number of 200 was reduced to 26, and the right of initiating legislation was taken from the representatives. But Penn was not yet satisfied and undertook still further alterations in 1686, when he appointed five Commissioners of State, three of whom were to be a quorum, and to whom the right of veto in all legislative affairs was granted. This scheme was almost as bad as his first constitution, for it gave excessive powers to three or four men; fortunately for the colony it was not perpetuated.

Early in its history troubles came upon Pennsylvania, which had been founded "with the pious wish and desire that its inhabitants might dwell together in brotherly love and unity" [191]. The flight of James II. was the first serious blow to Penn's colonial prosperity; it may be that he was one of the few men who sincerely and deeply regretted the fall of the last male Stuart ruler of England, for in James' misfortune Penn also suffered for a time, and his plans as a colony promoter received a severe check. At the same time Pennsylvania was torn by internal quarrels concerning what were called the "Territories" or Delaware. This district, on the south bank of the Delaware River, had been transferred from the administration of New York and placed under that of Pennsylvania. The dispute that arose had for its cause the appointment of magistrates, and it was only settled by a compromise in which Delaware was for the future to have its own executive, but there was only to be one elective chamber for the whole province. Still worse days came to Pennsylvania when the colony was included in the commission to the pirate-loving Benjamin Fletcher. As in New York, so in the Quaker settlement he proved himself arbitrary in conduct, brutal and unwise in action, immoral and corrupt in his private life. The only comfort to the Pennsylvanian settlers during his rule was that they won their right to initiate legislation.

A promise of the renewal of the good days of the past appeared when Penn succeeded in 1694 in regaining his proprietary rights, now somewhat shorn of their former privileges. The Proprietor immediately set about the restoration of his colony's prosperity, but excellent as his work was, Pennsylvania was still more fortunate in having amongst its members Gabriel Thomas, one of the brightest colonial authors of that period. He has not only left some writings of particular merit, but his name has been handed down to posterity as one who laboured hard for seventeen years to build up, firmly and strongly, the Quaker settlements in the West. Such work was necessarily slow, and Penn, when he again visited his colony, must have been much grieved with its moral condition if Lewis Morris, Governor of New Jersey, wrote the truth. "Pennsylvania is settled by People of all Languages and Religions in Europe, but the people called Quakers are the most numerous of anyone persuasion ... the Church of England gains ground in that Country, and most of the Quakers that came off with Mr Keith are come over to it: the Youth of that country are like those in the neighbouring Provinces very Debaucht and ignorant" [192].

A long series of disputes with the other colonies began in 1701, which intensified the danger already only too obvious, caused by the disunion of the American states and left them the more open to French attack. In addition to their antipathy to war, the Pennsylvanians now pleaded poverty as an excuse for refusing to assist in contributing funds towards the restoration of the fortifications of New York. Penn's common sense forced him to advocate the contribution, but all his eloquence was wasted upon his settlers, and he pleaded and remonstrated in vain. A fresh dispute followed, again arising from the government of Delaware. Since the last quarrel the Assembly had met alternately at Newcastle and Philadelphia. The people of Pennsylvania, as members of the more important state, demanded that in the future any legislation passed at Newcastle should be ratified and confirmed at Philadelphia. This was naturally intolerable to the weaker side, and the outcome of the dispute was the granting of a new charter and the complete separation of Delaware in 1703.

The last official act of William Penn was the incorporation of his beloved city of Philadelphia, which had steadily increased in size and population. A contemporary in 1710, possibly Daniel Defoe, has left on record a description of the town which gives some idea of its character and importance. Philadelphia "is a noble, large and populous city, standing on as much ground as our English City of Bristol.... It is built square in Form of a Chess-Board with each Front facing one of the Rivers. There are several Streets near two Mile long, as wide as Holborn, and better built, after the English Manner. The chief are Broad Street, King-street, High-street, tho' there are several other handsome Streets that take their Names from the Productions of the Country: as Mulberry, Walnut, Beech,

Sassafras, Cedar, Vine, Ash and Chestnut Streets.... The Number of the Inhabitants is generally suppos'd to be upwards of 15,000 besides Slaves.... And if I were oblig'd to live out of my native Country, I should not be long puzzled in finding a Place of Retirement, which should be Philadelphia. There the oppress'd in Fortune or Principles may find a happy Asylum, and drop quietly to their Graves without Fear or Want" [193]. Such was the happy city within thirty years of its foundation, and as a political centre it remained supreme until after the American War of Independence.

Penn retired from the colony in 1701, but continued to take the keenest interest in all that went on. At one time he remonstrated with the assembly for attacking his secretary and staunch supporter, James Logan, who acted as the Proprietor's agent during his long years of absence. As long as Penn lived he was able to exercise some control, but when he died in 1718 he left to his heirs a proprietary claim over a colony torn in pieces by disputes and factions. The brothers John and Thomas Penn were never popular, and up to the resignation of their claims in 1759 there were continual quarrels, sometimes over the Governor's salary, and sometimes because the Proprietors, who possessed three-fourths of the province, refused to allow the taxation of their lands for military operations against the French.

It is a noticeable fact that the two last colonies of the famous Thirteen were founded on philanthropic bases. The excellent William Penn established Pennsylvania as a home of toleration and peace; and the last of the original states, Georgia, was founded, upon motives that were highly creditable to their originator. The colony of Georgia owed its existence to James Oglethorpe, who, after serving a short time in the army, became a Member of Parliament and was placed upon a Parliamentary Committee to inquire into the state of the prisons, at that time conducted on barbarous lines. What he then learnt led Oglethorpe to propose the formation of a colony where men might honestly work and better their position instead of pining away in the horrible debtors' gaols. In addition to this, as he said, "Christianity will be extended by the execution of this design; since the good discipline established by the Society will reform the manners of these miserable objects" [194]. There is, too, in his account of the advantages of the colony, a hint as to the possible pecuniary gain of the individual and of the nation, for "when hereafter it shall be well-peopled and rightly cultivated, England may be supplied from thence with raw Silk, Wine, Oil, Dyes, Drugs, and many other materials for manufactures, which she is obliged to purchase from Southern countries" [195]. Tempted by these proposals, the Government readily fell in with his scheme and granted to Oglethorpe and his associates, including the famous Thomas Coram, a tract of land to the south of the Savannah River and north of the Spanish settlements in Florida, and here the debtors' colony was to serve as a barrier and rampart against Spanish aggression. The Corporation was called "The Trustees for the colonisation of Georgia," and was given full powers of administration for twenty-six years, at the expiration of which all privileges were to pass to the Crown.

In the autumn of 1732, James Oglethorpe embarked with 114 settlers; they were unsatisfactory colonists, for the men who had so hopelessly failed in England had not that grit and sturdy endurance necessary for founders of new homes in the West. The colony, however, started well, for Oglethorpe immediately won the goodwill of the natives, and made a wise selection of a site for the first settlement about twenty miles from the mouth of the Savannah River. The town itself was guarded on the water side by high banks, while impenetrable swamps on the land side served as sufficient barrier to any warlike incursions that might be attempted. Besides these advantages, Oglethorpe had also made friendly overtures to the neighbouring colonies, and in 1733 was able to say with satisfaction that "if the colony is attacked it may be relieved by sea from Port Royal, or the Bahamas; and the militia of South Carolina is ready to support it, by land" [196]. Oglethorpe's satisfaction must have been very short-lived. From the very first the colonists grumbled, quarrelled, and disputed, and their resident minister, the Reverend Samuel Quincy, gives a horrible but exaggerated account of the colony in 1735. "Affairs here are but in an ill-condition, through the discouragements attending the settlement.... The magistrate, to whom the government of the colony was left, proves a most insolent and tyrannical fellow. Several just complaints have been sent home against him, which do not meet with a proper regard, and this has made people very uneasie.... In short, Georgia, which was seemingly intended to be the asylum of the distressed, unless things are greatly altered, is likely to be itself a mere scene of distress.... Notwithstanding the place has been settled nigh three years, I believe, I may venture to say there is not one family which can subsist without further assistance" [197]. Affairs though gloomy were scarcely as black as Quincy depicted them, for in the next few years there was every sign of progress. Already in 1734 there had been a large increase of population by the immigration of Salzburg Germans under their pastor Martin Bolzius, who had fled from the persecution of their Prince Bishop. Two years later the colony had grown sufficiently to found a second settlement, Frederica, seventy miles south of the Savannah, at the mouth of the Alatamaha River; and a party of Highlanders about the same time founded New Inverness. Trade also began to increase and a definite commercial station was established at Augusta.

In the same year as the foundation of Frederica, John Wesley, accompanied by his brother Charles, came out as chaplain to the Georgian flock. He was in residence for a year and nine months, during which period he seems to have quarrelled with many of the inhabitants and particularly with the Moravians, and proved himself both indiscreet and ill-tempered. He himself records in his Journal that he was told by one man, "I will never hear you any more. And all the people are of my mind. For we won't hear ourselves abused. Besides, they say, they are Protestants. But as for you, they can't tell what Religion you are of. They never heard of such a religion before. They do not know what to make of it. And then, your private behaviour—all the quarrels that have been here since you came, have been long of you. Indeed there is neither man nor woman in the Town, who minds a word you say. And so you may preach long enough; but nobody will come to hear you" [198]. Wesley seems to have allowed his own personal feelings to enter into his religious life. He desired to marry a young woman of his congregation, Sophia Hankey by name, but she preferred to marry a Mr Williamson. Thereupon, apparently without any other reason than his own personal feelings, Wesley excluded Mrs Williamson from communion. Her husband very naturally regarded this as a slur upon his wife's character and brought an action against Wesley, who was forbidden to leave the colony while the question was pending. He records in his Journal for December 2nd what then took place. "In the Afternoon the Magistrates publish'd an Order requiring all the Officers and Centinels, to prevent my going out of the Province; and forbidding any person to assist me so to do. Being now only a Prisoner at large, in a Place, where I knew by experience every Day would give fresh opportunity, to procure Evidence of words I never said, and actions I never did; I saw clearly the Hour was come for leaving the Place: And as soon as Evening Prayers were over, about Eight o'clock, the tide then serving, I shook off the dust of my Feet, and left Georgia, after having preach'd the Gospel there (not as I ought but as I was able) one Year and nearly Nine Months" [199]. In regarding Wesley's action at this time, it is to be remembered that he was a self-confident, impulsive young enthusiast, lacking knowledge of human nature, and also that he had not passed through those years of struggle and earnest work which in later times made him a man of tact and forbearance.

Meantime a serious danger threatened the colony. In 1736, the Spaniards, who had long viewed Georgia with suspicion, made an armed reconnaissance, but nothing could be done, for there was at that time no war between the two countries in Europe. It was not until 1739 that Walpole was forced by popular demand to declare war against Spain, an act which he regarded with disgust as contrary to all his principles and desires. Georgia was in a particularly exposed position with regard to Spanish aggression, and Oglethorpe decided to take the offensive as a defensive measure and carry the war into the enemy's country. Reading the signs of the times and knowing what was hatching in Europe, the English Governor collected a force of about 600 volunteers and boldly marched for Florida in October 1738. He had been partly led to this action by the fact that news had been brought that the Spanish troops had been increased in St Augustine, and that the civil inhabitants had been turned out of their houses to give quarters to the royal forces. Oglethorpe's move was an unsatisfactory one, not through want of bravery on his part, but rather because he was a poor judge of men and his soldiers were wanting in the spirit of loyalty; some had even concerted a plot with the Spanish, while others had actually deserted to the enemy.

Nothing daunted, Oglethorpe spent the summer of 1739 securing the alliance of most of the neighbouring Indian tribes, and when war was formally declared against Spain the Georgian Governor was in a better position for whatever fate might have in store.

The home authorities ordered Oglethorpe to attack St Augustine, but before he could do so the Spaniards struck the first blow. Some fifty miles south of the town of Frederica, the Governor had thought it advisable to erect a military station on Amelia Island. This was the first natural object of Spanish attack, but their success was limited to the murder of two invalids. Oglethorpe, on the other hand, was more fortunate in capturing a Spanish outpost, which tempted him to risk an attack on St Augustine itself. He set out in March 1740, with a land force of about 2000 men, composed of Georgian militia and Indian allies; being supported at sea by four King's ships and a small schooner from South Carolina. This latter was practically the only help from the members of the richer colony, the generosity of which was of a very limited character; they ought really to have assisted Oglethorpe as well as they were able, for their danger from the Spaniards was almost as extreme as that of Georgia. Ill-supported as he was, the Governor captured three small fortresses, but soon found that the seizure of the capital of Florida was beyond his slender resources. The few Carolina troops deserted; his own men were struck down by fever; and his Indian allies left him in disgust because he tried to restrain their natural ferocity. In June, having realised that his attempt was hopeless, he retreated. His work, however, was not entirely unsuccessful, for although he had failed to do what he had intended, he succeeded in staving off from Georgia any serious Spanish attack for the next two years.

The year 1742 marks the crisis of Oglethorpe's career, for it was then that he won for himself a reputation for daring and strategy. The Spaniards attacked the colony and, knowing of their approach by means of his Indian allies, Oglethorpe concentrated all his forces upon the town of Frederica. The Spanish vanguard made an impetuous onslaught against which the Governor led with considerable daring his own ill-organised men. He showed that spirit of courage and prowess that fascinated even his wretched followers, who gave him willingly what support they could. He himself captured single-handed two of the Spaniards. But his strategy was yet to be displayed. As the fight continued, he sent through the wood a flank force which fell upon the Spaniards so suddenly and unexpectedly that they were routed with heavy loss, and the panic was sustained by an expedient of Oglethorpe's invention. By means of a deserter he succeeded in hoodwinking the enemy, declaring that he was ready for a second assault, which would be welcomed with the same hearty spirit that had been accorded to the first; at the same time he informed them, in mere bravado, that he was expecting an English fleet. As a matter of fact the desire for a second attack and the arrival of English vessels were mere figments of Oglethorpe's imagination. But as the gods fight on the side of the brave, so Oglethorpe was rewarded by the almost miraculous appearance of a few men-of-war. From that moment Georgia may be said to have earned her safety. She owed her existence to Oglethorpe, and to him and his cunning she owed her salvation. It may be truly said that at last the colony had thoroughly justified its existence and had fulfilled one of the main functions for which it had been created. The aforetime debtors of England had not shown particular courage, but their leader had fulfilled the promise of ten years before, and Georgia had stood firm and strong as a bulwark defending its more prosperous neighbours who lay upon the northern frontier. Those neighbours had much for which to thank the weakly colony, to whom in time of stress they had given little or no assistance. It was only one more example of the lack of unity, and one more instance of that failure to secure really effective co-operation which, had it existed, would have made so great a difference to the advance of the colonies. Georgia's position was, however, all the more exalted, for under Oglethorpe she had stood alone and had not been found wanting.

The colony was now safe from invasion, but there were many internal difficulties that had to be confronted. The debtors of England were not like the hardy and cheerful Salzburgers who managed to flourish and enjoy life. The climate itself was one of the most serious drawbacks to white labour, and an influential party saw that the colony could hardly compete against the other southern states where slave labour was employed. This party was supported in its views by George Whitefield, who had come, to Georgia in 1738 and who strongly advocated negro slavery. When it is remembered that one of the most permanent triumphs of the Evangelical party was the abolition of slavery, it is curious that one of the earliest and greatest of its leaders should have defended and encouraged the slave owners. But his advocacy had no effect upon the Trustees, who were firm in their determination to prevent negro slave traffic. The settlers sent a strong protest to England in 1739, stating that "Timber is the only thing we have here ... yet we cannot manufacture it for a Foreign Market but at double the Expense of other Colonies; as for Instance, the River of May, which is but twenty miles from us, with the Allowance of negroes, load Vessels with that Commodity at one Half of the Price that we can do.... We are very sensible of the Inconveniences and Mischiefs that have already, and do daily arise from an unlimited Use of Negroes; but we are as sensible, that these may be prevented by a due Limitation" [200]. The Trustees replied that the introduction of negroes would be the introduction of a "baneful Commodity, which, it is well known by sad Experience, has brought our Neighbour Colonies to the Brink of Ruin, by driving out their White Inhabitants, who were their Glory and Strength, to make room for Black, who are now become the Terror of their unadvised Masters" [201]. Excellent as the answer of the Trustees was, there can be little doubt that for lack of proper executive both the restrictions on liquor and on slavery were systematically evaded and after 1752 were allowed to lapse.

Oglethorpe, promoted to the rank of General, left Georgia in 1743, never to return. The colony cannot be called an entire success; the very philanthropy upon which it was founded deprived it to a certain extent of those enduring qualities which had made the New England colonies strong and healthy provinces. But though Oglethorpe had not accomplished all that he had wanted to do, a modern writer has paid him a high tribute when he says that he "had attained a far larger measure of success than most men could have won with such material" [202]. That the colony was prospering is shown by Edmund Burke in 1759, when he said, "At present Georgia is beginning to emerge, though slowly, out of the difficulties that attended its first establishment: It is still but indifferently peopled, though it is now twenty-six years since its first settlement. Not one of our colonies was of so slow a growth, though none had so much of the attention of the Government, or of the people in general, or raised so great expectations in the beginning. They export some corn and lumber to the West Indies; they raise some rice, and of late are going with success into indigo.

It is not to be doubted but in time, when their internal divisions are a little better composed, the remaining errors in the government corrected, and the people begin to multiply, that they will become a useful province" [203].

William Pitt, First Earl of Chatham. From the painting by W. Hoare in the National Portrait Gallery.

Some of the "errors in the government" had come up for discussion as early as 1751, when for the first time a representative assembly was called, but it was only granted deliberative functions. The whole character of the government of Georgia was radically altered when, according to the original agreement, the colony passed into the hands of the Crown. The population now consisted of 2380 whites and 1060 negroes, and these came to be governed under a constitution of normal type consisting of a governor, council, and executive officers nominated by the Crown, and a representative assembly elected by the freeholders.

Such, then, was the history of the last colony to be founded, completing the unlucky number thirteen, and it remained the weakest and least efficient of all. From small beginnings the English colonies came into being along the Eastern seaboard of America. Puritans and cavaliers, profligates and mechanics, all helped to create what might have been except for sad misunderstandings part of the British empire of to-day. Behind the Alleghany slopes another great power was attempting to form a colonial empire. North of the St Lawrence, New France had already been established; by the waters of the Gulf of Mexico, Louisiana had already been named. In some places not inaccessible hills, in others not unnavigable rivers divided the Briton from the Gaul. It was inevitable that sooner or later the struggle between the two great powers must come. It might be fought in Europe upon battlefields which are familiar to all, but it was also fought out upon the far distant border line, and the struggles of the colonial militia with the French Canadian backwoodsman presents a story of endurance, courage, and determination equal if not superior to the annals of those English regiments which fought in the Netherlands or on "the plains of Germany."

Chapter 8

THE SOCIAL AND ECONOMIC HISTORY OF NEW ENGLAND

"God sifted a whole nation that he might send choice grain over into this wilderness" [204]. With regard to New England this statement was in part true, for the people of those northern colonies exhibited a remarkable homogeneity, and their leaders were men of a peculiarly lofty character. That this population grew with leaps and bounds during the first century of settlement is well attested by records. As early as 1643, Massachusetts had a population of 20,000; while Plymouth, Connecticut, and Newhaven, taken together, must have numbered between eleven and twelve thousand. At the Restoration the total population is placed at 80,000, of which two-thirds dwelt in Massachusetts. The eighteenth century statistics show a steady increase, 100,000 whites and 4000 negroes being a rough computation for the year 1714.

The people dwelt for the most part in little towns, each one of which was a separate commonwealth possessing representative government. The corporations were the chief landholders and watched with the greatest jealousy any increase of individual possession which might trespass upon their rights. The system was one of antiquity and carries our thoughts back to mediæval methods where police, finance, justice, and agriculture were all concentrated in one manorial district. Just as in England in Plantagenet days there were the division of the land into strips, the rights of common pasture, and the tilling on a communal principle, so in the New England of the seventeenth century these systems were employed with partial success. The houses in which the settlers dwelt were for the most part built of wood, and stretched in orderly rows along trim streets. Each homestead was detached, and like the houses of our Teutonic forefathers, "was surrounded with a clearing," which in America was usually allotted to fruit trees. The comfort of the houses was of a very doubtful character, log huts were extremely draughty, so that houses of brick and stone were most coveted, but only obtainable by the rich. Although in Plymouth as early as 1645 glass seems to have been common in the windows, yet the houses were mainly of wood, which was also the case at Newport as late as 1686. Governor Bradstreet six years before this had recorded that Boston had suffered severely by fire and that the houses were therefore to be rebuilt with brick or stone, "yet hardly to be obtained by reason of the inhabitants' poverty" [205]. Wooden houses continued to be built, and in fact in a few instances exist to this day. In Boston they were still common in 1750, if we are to believe Captain Francis Goelet. "Boston," he writes, "the Metropolis of North America, Is Accounted The Largest Town upon the Continent, Haveing about Three Thousand Houses in it, about two Thirds them Wooden Framed Clap Boarded, &c" [206].

The men of Boston, and of New England in general, were, owing to natural circumstances, traders. They had found themselves in a land of splendid harbours, and so they went down to the sea in ships and trafficked upon its waters. It has of course been urged that this trade of the colonies was sadly restricted by the English people, who as a nation of shopkeepers were determined that "the cultivators of America might be confined to their shop" [207]. For this reason the Navigation Act of 1660, on the lines of the famous Act of 1651, insisted on certain enumerated articles being landed in British ports only; and this was still further extended by two later enactments. But even Adam Smith allows that "though the policy of Great Britain with regard to the trade of her colonies has been dictated by the same mercantile spirit as that of other nations, it has, however, upon the whole, been less illiberal and oppressive than that of any of them" [208].

The colonial system was in truth a mistake, but it never undermined the trade of the British settlements, as was the case in French Canada, owing to the corrupt and negligent methods of Bigot and his gang. The result was that the New England trader flourished. The trade had of course small beginnings; at first merely fish and fur were exported to Virginia. Then corn, cattle, and butter were sent to the West Indies, and exchanged for cotton and fruits. More distant voyages followed, and in 1643, wine, iron, and wool were imported from Spain. In the meantime iron had been discovered in Massachusetts by the younger Winthrop at Lynn and Braintree; and the Commissioners in 1665 certified that there was "good store of iron made in this province" [209]. The Commissioners were, however, too optimistic, for the iron raised proved to be of inferior quality; partly because of this inferiority, but chiefly owing to trade regulations, scarcity of labour, and high wages, all cutlery and farm implements were imported from England well into the eighteenth century. The reported discovery of silver in Rhode Island in 1648 caused a nine days' wonder, and then the excitement subsided for nothing came of it. Lead was also found as early as 1650 in Lynn, but these mineral industries never rose to great importance under British rule.

Minor commercial industries seem to have flourished, as there are frequent references to masons, bricklayers, ropemakers, powder and pitch-makers, and in 1650 Boston had its own goldsmith. Clothmaking was not altogether unknown, as certain clothiers from Yorkshire settled at Rowley in 1639 and established weaving and spinning. The venture was, however, unsatisfactory, and although New England encouraged by bounties the textile industry, yet it took long to mature, and as late as 1700 there was only one small cloth mill in Connecticut. At the same time it is evident that the different colonies varied very much in their prosperity. Plymouth is reported to the Committee of Trade and Plantations to have no trade beyond the sea. About the same time Governor Bradstreet complains of the poverty of Boston, and says "the country in general is very poor, and it is hard for the people to clothe themselves and families" [210]. The general trade of New England, however, in the eighteenth century seems to have been good. Daniel Neale, a very careful writer of the day, records in 1720 that the imports from England were "all sorts of Woollen Drapery, Silks, Stuffs, and Hats; all Sorts of Linnen and printed Callicoes, all sorts of Iron Manufacture ... to the value of 100,000 l. annually and upwards. In Return for these Goods, our Merchants export from thence about 100,000 Quintals of dried Cod-fish Yearly, which they send to Portugal, Spain, and several Ports of Italy, the returns for which are made to London out of the Products of those Countries, and may amount to the value of about 80,000 l. annually" [211]. Governor Wentworth reports in 1730 that New Hampshire manufactured timber "into beams, planks, knees, boards ... and sometimes into house-frames" [212]. But long before this it had been exported to England for naval purposes, and on two occasions at least the Massachusetts Government bought the goodwill of the home authorities by a timely present of masts. In particular, however, this timber was used by the colonies for shipbuilding, which became an industry of importance, and in later years those employed in it actually excelled the English shipwrights. In 1631 Winthrop built a thirty-ton vessel, soon to be followed by others of a hundred and even three hundred tons; and seven years later the first New England vessel sailed safely across the Atlantic into the Thames. Although in 1643 Massachusetts could only boast five ships ranging from one hundred to five hundred tons, yet in 1665 the colony had one hundred and ninety-two ships of all sizes; and in 1708 possessed two hundred, twenty of which were over one hundred tons burthen. Rhode Island ran Massachusetts very close in this shipbuilding race. Between 1690 and 1710 her vessels are said to have increased six-fold, and in 1740 the inhabitants could proudly boast that they owned no fewer than one hundred and twenty ships. Connecticut never competed in this form of industry, and in 1708 she is reported to have had only thirty vessels. New Hampshire too carried on her over-sea traffic by means of strange vessels, possessing only five ships of her own. In 1748, although trade was supposed to be in a very depressed state, five hundred and forty ships sailed from Boston, a fact which showed a considerable export and import commerce.

It would be erroneous to imagine that the colonies in the eighteenth century were in any way struggling, poverty-stricken communities. Their trade had grown with leaps and bounds, and they carried on a profitable commerce with England which Sir Robert Walpole had encouraged on the grounds that "the greater the prosperity of the colonies, the greater would be their demand for English goods" [213]. That this proved true is shown by William Pitt saying in 1766, "the profits to Great Britain from the trade of the colonies are two millions a year. That was the fund that carried you triumphantly through the last war.... And shall a miserable financier come with a boast that he can filch a peppercorn into the exchequer to the loss of millions to the nation?" [214] For the same reason Adam Smith has given a conspicuous place to colonial trade in his Wealth of Nations. "Though the wealth of Great Britain," he writes, "has increased very much since the establishment of the Act of Navigation, it certainly has not increased in the same proportion as that of the colonies.... The industry of Great Britain, instead of being accommodated to a great number of small markets, has been principally suited to one great market.... The expectation of a rupture with the colonies accordingly has struck the people of Great Britain with more terror than they ever felt for a Spanish Armada or a French invasion" [215].

The colonists did not, however, simply depend upon trade for their means of livelihood; many of them engaged in agriculture. During the winter months their beasts suffered as much as those in England, for until the eighteenth century there were no winter roots. In the same way the rotation of crops was much restricted, as the settlers were totally ignorant of artificial grasses. They had still to wait for Lord Townshend to make his agricultural experiments at home before they could grow turnips, cereals, and grasses on scientific principles. On the other hand they seem to have anticipated the discoveries of Mr Jethro Tull of Mount Prosperous, and some years previous to his work on husbandry they had inaugurated deep tillage. Tobacco, the principal commodity of the southern colonies, was not introduced into New England until 1660, but its place as a staple was taken by the cultivation of large quantities of rape, hemp, and flax. The colonists also, after many disappointments, came to be enthusiastic breeders of sheep, horses, goats, and cattle. At first the sheep fared very badly; the wool crop was short, and the climate proved unsuitable to the English stock. By 1642, however, there were one thousand sheep in Massachusetts, and these increased very rapidly. The authorities were most anxious to encourage sheep-farming, and in 1654 the exportation of sheep was forbidden. In Rhode Island and Connecticut they flourished upon the public lands, and by 1670 the latter colony was able to export a fairly large quantity of wool.

During the whole period there was a great lack of specie, which in the early years had not been a very serious drawback, as barter was the ordinary method of exchange, but as the colonies advanced in importance it was a decided check upon foreign commerce. In 1631, Massachusetts declared corn to be legal tender, and four years later it was ordained that public dues were to be paid in this commodity at the rate of 6s. per bushel. This system was employed in the next decade by both Connecticut and Newhaven, with decidedly disadvantageous results, for it brought about the inconvenience of a double price; the monetary payment being about half the actual value of the payment in kind. For many years in the Indian trade the settlers had used Indian shell money or wampum. This medium of exchange was first applied in New Plymouth in 1627, and was afterwards employed by Coddington when he bought Aquedneck. In 1641, wampum was declared legal tender under £10, but within eight years the Massachusetts Assembly refused to accept it for taxes. The fact was that it depended solely upon Indian trade, and when this began to decline, wampum was valueless. Rhode Island was the last colony to discontinue its use for taxes, which it did in 1662; though it acted as small change in Newhaven well into the eighteenth century.

As early as 1642, Massachusetts, by means of its foreign trade, began to obtain coined money in the shape of Dutch ducats and rix-dollars. But the extraordinary mixture of coins was very awkward, so that in 1652 a mint was established in the colony. John Hall, the goldsmith of Boston, was made its master. The coins had stamped upon them the word Massachusetts encircling a tree, which was in early years a willow, later an oak, and finally a pine. Charles II. was furious at this attack upon his coinage, and the story goes that to appease his wrath he was told that the emblem of the oak was in grateful memory of his glorious escape at Boscobel.

Towards the end of the seventeenth century the amount of coin in the country had very largely increased, but in the commercially backward Connecticut, barter was still common. As late as 1698, gold was very scarce, and taxes continued to be paid entirely in silver. The colonists firmly believed in the enriching powers of paper money, which in New England was issued in particularly large quantities by Rhode Island. The real disadvantage was intercolonial, and not internal, so that most of the colonists failed to understand the interference of the home authorities, either in 1740, when the Lords Commissioners for Trade and Plantations forbade the governors to sanction the issue of bills of credit, or again in 1744, when an Act of Parliament was passed forbidding paper money altogether. The fact was that the settlers believed, like Governor Burnet, "that this manner of compulsive credit does in fact keep up its value here, and that it occasions much more trade and business than would be without it, and that more specie is exported to England by reason of these Paper Bills than could be if there was no circulation but of specie" [216].

It is not surprising that the colonists should also labour under the economic delusion that it was necessary to regulate wages and prices. At first Massachusetts left them both free, but after three years, wages were found to have risen to what was then regarded as the monstrous rate of 3s. a day for carpenters and 2s. 6d. a day for common workmen. In 1633, therefore, a scale of wages was proposed by the General Court, and "they made an order that carpenters, masons, etc., should take but two shillings the day, and labourers but eighteenpence, and that no commodity should be sold at above fourpence in the shilling more than it cost for ready money in England" [217]. The enactment, however, proved fruitless, and was repealed two years later. The enormous rise in wages and the extortionate prices still exercised the minds of those in authority, and a committee was appointed in 1637. The outcome of their deliberations was that about 1643 the wages of farm labourers were fixed at 1s. 6d. a day. This remuneration appears to have been ample, and it has been calculated that a careful man could save enough in five years to become the tenant of a small farm. This was not so difficult as it might seem, for small holdings were common, and as succession was by gavelkind and not through primogeniture, holdings tended to be kept limited in extent. The accumulation of land was rather the exception than the rule, though there are occasional examples, as in Newhaven, where some estates contained as many as three thousand acres.

The thriftless man could not, of course, save very much out of such a wage, and there were therefore many paupers. The burden of their support fell upon the towns, and in the case of New Plymouth, it was not long before the township became "the poor law unit" [218]. The decision as to a man's settlement caused as much difficulty in the Puritan colonies as it was doing in England at the time. In 1639, Massachusetts ordained that two magistrates should decide this momentous question. Six years later the power of decision was put in the hands of a committee; while immediately before the Restoration a three months' residence was selected as the period of settlement necessary to denote a man's parish.

The richer inhabitants of the Puritan colonies no doubt had slaves, but throughout the seventeenth and eighteenth centuries negro slavery in New England was never a very flourishing institution. The tenets of Calvinism naturally warred against such a practice, while "the main influence ... was no doubt the unfitness of the climate and soil for servile industry" [219]. The Rhode Island authorities were from the first against perpetual bondage, and in 1646, Massachusetts also raised its voice against slavery. As late as 1680 there were, according to Governor Brodstreet, only one hundred and twenty negro slaves in the colony, and they sold for £10, £15, and £20 apiece. The methods of employment do not seem to have been harsh, and according to Mrs Knight in 1704, the slaves and masters in Connecticut had their meals together: "into the dish goes the black hoof as freely as the white hand" [220]. Towards the end of the seventeenth century slavery slightly increased in New England, and it was found necessary to pass several laws for the better regulation of the negro. In 1703, in Massachusetts, slaves were not to be set free unless their masters guaranteed that they would not become a burden on the poor rate. Two years later the marriage between slaves and whites was forbidden, and a £4 duty was placed upon every imported negro. In 1708 the blacks in Rhode

Island numbered only four hundred and twenty-six, but within twelve years they had risen to one thousand, three hundred. At the same time Connecticut had eight hundred, while Massachusetts was the worst offender with three thousand.

The actions and protestations of the New Englanders were somewhat contradictory. Although negro slavery was preached against, it was nevertheless practised. So too with regard to the Indians. The New Englander treated the savage with contempt, yet several efforts were made, not without some success, to convert the Redskin to the Christian faith. Thomas Mayhew has earned for himself historic fame by being the first who really made definite attempts to bring the natives into touch with the doctrines of Christianity. In 1643, with the ready assistance of his Indian colleague Hiacoomes, he did what he could, and at least succeeded in founding schools in some of the Indian villages. Massachusetts made state efforts in 1646, but they were surpassed by the individual enterprise of John Eliot of Roxbury, who had laboriously learnt the Indian tongue to accomplish this great work. Excellent as the work was, it compares but feebly with the self-denial of the Jesuits in Canada, whose missionary labours far surpassed in deeds of heroism and suffering anything that was ever undertaken by the English settlers. A progressive move was made in 1649, when Parliament incorporated the Society for the Propagation of the Gospel in New England. The work then spread more rapidly, so that in two years a convert settlement of four hundred "praying Indians" was established at Natich. The Society for the Propagation of the Gospel was encouraged to still further action when in 1662 it was granted a Royal Charter. For this reason it may be said that the Restoration stimulated missionary effort, the partial success of which is to be found in the issue of an Indian Bible and the creation of converted Indian villages in Massachusetts, New Plymouth, Martha's Vineyard, and Nantucket.

In New England the church and township were inseparable, their members being for the most part Congregationalists. In the early days a body of believers simply entered into a Church covenant and that was all. The methods of worship were somewhat peculiar, and it is asserted that for sixty years these Puritans had no marriage or funeral ceremonies.

Throughout all the colonies there was the principle that the members of the church must support their minister, and in 1637 Massachusetts issued an order to that effect. In 1650 Connecticut and in 1657 Plymouth did the same. The Churches were separate in their governance, and the synods of United Churches held at Boston in 1646, 1657, and 1662 were not viewed with entire favour by all the congregations. At first, as has already been shown, the Puritans were the most intolerant of people, and tried to enforce the law that a freeman must be a member of the Church. Gradually, however, this fanatic flame burnt itself out, and by the end of the seventeenth century the intensity of feeling on matters of Church and toleration began to relax. Fifty years later there were men in Massachusetts and elsewhere who blushed for shame at the harsh bigotry of their grandparents, and one writer is able to say "at present the Congregationalists of New England may be esteemed among the most moderate and charitable of Christian professions" [221]. Nevertheless even in that eighteenth century there was no lack of factions and parties, and this was intensified by the preaching of George Whitefield in 1739. He certainly created a religious revival amongst the dissenters, but at the same time his words drove many of the Independents into the arms of the Church of England, which, though by no means welcomed in Massachusetts, had long been tolerated in Connecticut. Even after this event, however, the Established Church never really succeeded in the colonies, for there was no colonial episcopate, and it was regarded as doing little or nothing for spiritual life. In 1758, Archbishop Thomas Seeker urged manfully "the establishment of Bishops of our Church in America," [222] but it was too late, and the fear of such an establishment was a main cause of uneasiness in New England at the outbreak of the War of Independence.

The lack of unanimity in the religious question does not seem to have existed with regard to education. Unlike the southern and middle colonies, the Puritans from the outset encouraged the education of the young with praiseworthy enthusiasm. This owed its origin to several circumstances, not the least being the fact that so many men from the two ancient Universities emigrated during the period 1630 to 1640. The foundation of Harvard, as already mentioned, [223] did something to encourage teaching.

In 1640, Rhode Island, with extraordinary promptitude, established public education, but without any definite system. Seven years later, Massachusetts went further still by creating elementary schools in small villages of fifty householders, and grammar schools in the larger and more populous towns. The same was done in Connecticut; but curiously enough New Plymouth seems to have done nothing for education until the end of the seventeenth century. Providence had its own school three years after the Restoration; and by 1693 Hartford, Newhaven, New London, and Fairfield were all in possession of state-supported schools. Connecticut's energy did not stop here; for Yale College was founded, and in 1717 was permanently established at Newhaven, where a house had been built "for the entertainment of the scholars belonging to the Collegiate School" [224]. Thus the clergy of Connecticut were freed from their dependence upon Harvard. For nothing does New England deserve more unstinted praise than for these early efforts in the cause of education, the results of which have proved so eminently satisfactory.

Whether University education had much effect upon the literature of New England it would perhaps be a little difficult to say. Connecticut, for example, even with Yale College as a starting- point, produced no great literary achievements. Nevertheless throughout the first century of New England's story there was a well-defined and living school of literature. The school naturally divided into two parts: that of theology, which to the ordinary modern critic is somewhat meaningless; and that of history. The historical section was composed for the most part of chronicles, glowing with patriotism, alive with the picture of the daily life, and filled with "a dignity of diction belonging to those who have assimilated the English Bible till their speech instinctively adopts its form" [225]. There was the work of Winthrop; the impulsive, triumphal hymn of Edward Johnson; "The Simple Cobbler of Agawam" of Nathaniel Ward, and the writings of many others. But this period of history and theology died away as the century neared its close. At the beginning of the eighteenth century Cotton Mather may be regarded as one of the best known of Boston authors. But the curious thing about the New England literature is the total absence of anything that might be called secular. The colonies, however, were not without their poets, for they had Anne Bradstreet and Michael Gigglesworth, the works of both of whom were recognised in the seventeenth century as being of real poetical merit.

This outburst of literature could never have been accomplished had it not been for the introduction of the printing-press. As early as 1638 a press was brought by Day to Boston and set up at Cambridge. A second press was introduced in 1655 by the Society for the Propagation of the Gospel. Rhode Island had its press in 1708; while Short of Boston established printing in New London, Connecticut, in 1709. By the end of the seventeenth century newspapers began to be printed, such as The Public Occurance both Foreign and Domestic at Boston in 1690, to be followed fourteen years later by John Campbell's Boston Letter.

The increase of newspapers was the natural outcome of better means of travel and circulation of news. At first the different townships had been divided by vast forests; gradually, however, roads were built and communication between the different settlements was established. As early as 1638, three bridges were ordered to be built in Plymouth, and in 1652 we read of bridges that were strong enough for horsemen. Travelling, however, was generally on foot, for coaches were very rare and were only possessed by the more wealthy citizens of Boston. A postal service was established in the reign of Charles II. between Boston and New York; but it was not until 1710 that a General Post Office, with several sub-offices, was erected by Act of Parliament. The inns were not of any particular comfort, though they were fairly numerous. The Puritan was not hospitable like his southern brother, so that throughout New England taverns were insisted upon by law.

This was probably an excellent enactment and far better than many of the extraordinary laws that stained the pages of the New England records. Numerous sumptuary laws were passed against the wearing of gold or silver girdles, ruffs, or slashed sleeves. Drunkards had to proclaim their fault by wearing a red D; while Hawthorne's Scarlet Letter has familiarised all with the cruel punishment meted out to the fallen woman. In 1658, lying, drinking, and swearing could be punished by flogging; dancing and kissing also fell under severe penalties, though Cotton does say he only condemns "lascivious dancing to wanton ditties and in amorous gestures and wanton dalliances, especially after great feasts" [226]. The attempt to prevent immorality was carried to the most absurd lengths, and even in the eighteenth century stage plays and rope dancing were forbidden as "likely to promote idleness and a great mispence of time" [227].

The laws may have been foolish, but it is perhaps uncharitable to judge them too sternly at this period. The men who passed them were undoubtedly conscientious; harsh they may have been, cruel in their punishments, but their hearts were in what they conceived to be the work of the Lord. They were bold men in a "howling wilderness"; they were the pioneers of a great nation. The American spirit to-day is compounded of much that once animated these first Americans on the eastern sea-coast. Their industry, their untiring energy, their honesty, their masculine character have been handed down through many generations to descendants not unworthy of such an ancestry as that of the Pilgrim Fathers.

Chapter 9

THE SOCIAL AND ECONOMIC HISTORY OF THE SOUTHERN AND MIDDLE COLONIES

The southern colonies in their geographical formation, their soil and climate, were of a uniform character; nor were there any decidedly marked religious differences. In the middle colonies this was by no means the case, but even here the style of life in such states as Pennsylvania, Delaware, and New Jersey had many points of resemblance. In all the colonies except Maryland and Virginia there was a heterogeneous population of English, Irish, Scots, Dutch, Huguenots, and Germans, but in New York State mixed nationalities were most apparent.

The distinction between the grades of society was well-marked in both the southern and middle colonies. In South Carolina in early times there was practically no middle class, but at the end of the seventeenth century a few Ulster Protestants settled in the colony as small farmers and remained in spite of economic conditions. In Maryland there were yeomen farmers and tradesmen, who were for the most part rude and uneducated. A professional middle class was unknown until the eighteenth century; doctors, for example, were not licensed in New York till 1760. In New Jersey there was a tendency to insist on democratic principles, though there is every reason to think that the gentleman farmer was treated with the same respect accorded to the Quaker squire of Pennsylvania, or the Dutch patroon of New York. In the South the upper classes resembled their contemporaries in England. Some were indolent, haughty, and vain, showing the greatest contempt for honest toil; many were confirmed gamblers and horse-racers. The bottle and the dice were the household deities of not a few; but they were nevertheless bountiful, generous, and patriotic, and proved themselves good specimens of England's manhood in time of peril.

Below these classes were the indentured servants and negro slaves. The former were composed of paupers and criminals sent out from England, the earliest instance being in 1618, when Ambrose Smythe, a felon, was transported to America, as a servant bound for a limited period. The life in Virginia on the tobacco plantations must have been of the hardest, but it was evidently preferable to that in the West Indian islands, as Penruddock, the conspirator against Cromwell, petitioned in 1656 to be sent to Virginia rather than to the Barbadoes. The evil of the system of indentured servants lay for the most part in the ease with which inconvenient people were got rid of, and in the kidnapping of harmless children. Fugitives from justice, guilty husbands or wives, the felon and the innocent were all to be found on those ships that sailed from Bristol. The scandal increased from year to year, so that in 1661 the new Colonial Board was obliged to make an effort to regulate indentured servants, while three years later a commission under the Duke of York was appointed to look into the whole matter. The outcome of this was a most salutary enactment by which kidnapping was made a capital offence. The inquisitorial system necessary for the proper enforcement of this Act soon came to be burdensome, as proved by a complaint of the merchants in 1682, concerning vexatious prosecutions; but that it was absolutely essential is shown by a fresh Order in Council, four years later, against kidnappers. The one great advantage possessed by the indentured servant over the negro slave was that no hereditary disqualification attached to the children of such servants, whereas in the case of the blacks the stigma of slavery passed from the parents to their offspring.

The system of binding servants for so many years tended to check the growth of slavery; but there is little doubt that during the first hundred years of American colonisation the influx of negro slaves reached alarming proportions. In 1620 a Dutch ship landed twenty negroes from the Guinea coast at the recently established Jamestown. From this small beginning the cursed traffic grew, and so rapidly that in 1637, and on many later occasions, enactments were passed to check all intercourse between whites and blacks. Within twenty years of the introduction of slavery there were in Virginia about three hundred blacks, while twelve years later the number had reached one thousand. It is not to be wondered at that the growth was so rapid, for the trade was a lucrative one, [228] and it was difficult to check when the first in the land participated in its spoils. Thus in 1662 the Royal African Company was founded with James, Duke of York, at its head, and with his brother Charles II. as a large shareholder. The negroes were in theory regarded as mere chattels, and to check risings such as those of 1678, 1712, and 1741, barbarous laws were passed against them. On the other hand, as individuals they were as a general rule comfortably clothed, fed, and housed; they had many amusements, and their work was not as arduous as has so often been described. At one time it was an understood thing in the colonies that the lord had the jus vitae necisque over his slaves, but at the beginning of the eighteenth century the Crown made the murder of a negro a capital offence, a decision vigorously upheld by Governor Spotswood. The number of slaves on each plantation varied very much; the average may, perhaps, be placed at thirty. But the largest owner in Virginia possessed 900; while in Maryland this was easily beaten by an owner with 1300. In the eighteenth century the negroes far outnumbered the whites in South Carolina; but in New York they only formed about one-sixth the total population. In Maryland and Virginia they were as one to three, while in the middle colonies it is calculated that a ratio of one to seven would give a rough estimate of their numbers.

Figures and statistics with regard to the white population can only be surmised. In 1650, Virginia, as the oldest of the colonies, may possibly have had 15,000 inhabitants. Stuyvesant's calculation for New York fourteen years later was probably exaggerated when he placed that cosmopolitan people at 10,000. At the time of the Revolution the total population of Maryland, Virginia, and the Carolinas was about 90,000; but the two first colonies had by far the largest proportion, for although Shaftesbury and Locke had worked so hard, the Carolinas had only 4000 settlers all told. The population of East Jersey at the beginning of the eighteenth century was, according to Governor Lewis Morris, "about eight thousand souls"; [229] while that of Pennsylvania and Delaware may have been 20,000, at least one-half of whom were English Quakers. Later in the century more exact figures are ascertainable. Virginia in 1724 was still the largest with 65,000; Maryland ran it close with 53,000. Pennsylvania and Delaware had steadily increased owing to immigration to 32,000; and New York, which in 1705 had had 25,000 people, had by 1724 increased to 30,000. New Jersey came next with 26,000, while North and South Carolina lagged behind with 14,000 and 9000 respectively.

With so large a population it is only natural that there were various kinds of trade. Tobacco was the staple of Virginia and of Maryland; but by 1701 Virginia tobacco was acknowledged as far superior to that from the Baltimore plantations. South Carolina for the first ninety years of its history relied mainly upon rice, the export of which was encouraged by Sir Robert Walpole in 1730. The colony was now allowed to export rice to any port in Europe, south of Finisterre, provided it was sent in British ships, manned by British seamen. "The result was that the rice of the American plantations beat the rice of Egypt and Northern Italy out of the markets of Europe" [230]. After 1741 or 1742, indigo planting became an important industry in the colony, for the seed which was then introduced was found to flourish in the swamps of the South. Iron was worked in Virginia to a small extent. Its value was pointed out by the Company in defence of their charter in 1623: "during these 4 last years that hath been expended in setting up of iron works (the oar whereof is there in great plenty and excellent) above five thousand pounds, which work being brought in a manner to perfection was greatly interrupted by the late massacre" [231]. The industry continued throughout the century, but never on a large scale. In Philadelphia a more profitable iron industry existed, while in Maryland in 1749 seventeen iron furnaces were regularly employed. New Jersey made some slight profit from working her minerals, such as iron and copper, but her chief exports were cattle and tanned hides. The exports of

Pennsylvania were even more varied, consisting of horses, pipe staves, salted pork and beef, bread-flour, peas, beans, tobacco, potashes and wax; while from Germantown in particular there was paper, glass, and coarse cloth.

New York carried on a small linen and woollen manufacture, but the chief industry, until checked by the policy of Andros, was tanning. After the revolution New York was famous for its fur trade, particularly that in beaver. Busy as most of the settlers were, yet almost every necessary of life was brought from England, including such common articles as wooden bowls. In a list of the imports of Pennsylvania at the end of the seventeenth century we find rum, sugar, molasses, silver, salt, wine, linen, household goods, and negroes. In 1733, to the annoyance of the colonists, a heavy duty was imposed on all molasses imported from foreign countries. Tobacco, at the same time, was not allowed to be exported to any European ports, save those of Great Britain. This, however, was easily evaded, for the numerous rivers and private landing-stages in the southern colonies made effective supervision impossible.

As in the case of the New England colonies, the main check to commerce lay in the serious want of money. The steady influx of coin was prevented by the lack of retail trade, and also by the fact that the planter was nearly always in debt to the merchant. In Virginia and Maryland the scarcity of specie was overcome by the use of tobacco, which, "as the staple product of the country, established itself as the accepted medium of exchange" [232]. But even in these colonies a desire for good money was shown on various occasions. The Virginia Assembly, in 1645, tried to fix the legal value of the Spanish coins which were in common use, and also proposed a copper coinage of their own. Cecil Calvert, as a careful proprietor, attempted to assist his Maryland settlers by establishing a coinage, but nothing came of it. In the eighteenth century, therefore, most of the southern and middle colonies fell under the fascinating influence of paper money; New York and Virginia being the only two to escape this economic evil.

Brief reference has been made to the educational indifference of the southern settlers. As has already been shown, Governor Berkeley thanked

God that there were no schools in Virginia [233]. To the rich planter this was not so disastrous, as his sons were either provided with a tutor or sent to England. But this absence of schools for the small freeholders presented a great difficulty. Certainly in the Carolinas the lack of education was not so marked, for there, as society was more urban, the opportunities of a school training were more numerous. "Their cohabiting in a town has drawn to them ingenious people of most sciences, whereby they have tutors amongst them that educate their youth à la mode" [234]. South Carolina was particularly famous for its educational advantages, and in one year there were no fewer than four hundred educational advertisements in the South Carolina Gazette. Although William and Mary College in Virginia was founded by Blair at the end of the seventeenth century, it remained for many years nothing more than a rather superior boarding school. In Philadelphia there was some attempt to instruct the young, not only in several German and Moravian seminaries, but also, after 1698, in the Penn Charter School. New York had its first Church of England School in 1704, but it was not until fifty years later that King's College, afterwards Columbia College, was established. A college was founded in New Jersey in 1746, but two years later Governor Belcher complained that "they are a very rustical people and deficient in learning" [235]. Owing to the energies of the indefatigable Benjamin Franklin an academy was built in Philadelphia in 1750 in which the Quaker youth of the colony had the greater part of their training.

There can be no doubt that the lack of education in the southern and middle colonies was reflected in the absence of any vigorous literary development. Virginia is easily first in its possession of three writers of repute: Robert Beverley, who wrote the history of his own colony; or the Rev. William Stith, whose work though fragmentary is never dull, and "might have been produced by a learned, leisurely, and somewhat pompous English clergyman"; [236] or finally, Colonel William Byrd, a man of education and wealth, who has left on record a witty and interesting account of his travels. New York was not without two famous names, those of William Smith, author of The History of New York, and Cadwallader Colden, who has left to posterity a chronicle of the Five Nations, filled with picturesque descriptions. Pennsylvania, unlike the other colonies, has to revere the name, not of an historian, but a poet and tragedian, in Thomas Godfrey, whose short life lasted only from 1736 to 1763.

The religion of the southern and middle colonies was not of the harsh character of the northerners. The Church of England had more power than in the Puritan settlements, though its position was a peculiar one. In New York and New Jersey up to 1693 it was supported owing to orders from the Crown. From that date its preponderance over other sects was due to the habit of the governors to appoint Church of England clergymen. In Maryland and Virginia the Church was established by acts of the colonial legislature; while in the Carolinas it owed its position to the Proprietary Charter. In the southern colonies the clergy for the most part shared the vices of the planters, and "drunkenness is the common vice" [237] is not an unusual complaint. In North Carolina the people seem to have been at first utterly indifferent; they were a lawless population and cared for none of these things. In 1703 there was no episcopalian minister, nor was there a church until 1705. Six years later Governor Spotswood reported that there was only one clergyman in the whole colony. Nor did South Carolina evince a more ardent religious spirit, for at the beginning of the eighteenth century there were only two Episcopalian churches, the one at Charlestown, the other at Goose Creek. Virginia and Maryland seem to have been better than this, for from quite early times the clergy were readily supported and paid in so many pounds of tobacco. In Virginia George Whitefield's preaching had some little effect, but on the whole he failed to arouse any great religious enthusiasm in the other southern colonies. Maryland and Pennsylvania were the most tolerant of all the colonies. In the first Roman Catholics and Protestants had lived together, though not always peaceably, since its foundation; while in the latter colony there were Quakers, Lutherans, and Presbyterians tolerating each other. After the capture of New York by Nicolls, everyone was supposed to conform to the Church of England; each township was commanded to maintain its own church and minister. At first the New York authorities were strongly against Jesuits and Popish priests, but as the eighteenth century grew in years, there is every reason to believe that within this state there were Episcopalians, Roman Catholics, Presbyterians, and Lutherans living happy lives and seeing much that was good in their religious antagonists.

Church life was in no way connected with town life as in New England, for the simple reason that towns were very uncommon, having "no place in the social and industrial economy of the south" [238]. They consisted for the most part of scattered houses, an inn, a gaol, and a court-house. They were visited by the planters nominally for business, but mostly for pleasure, and the tavern, which was in some cases enforced by law, became the meeting-place for gossip. Jamestown and Williamsburg in Virginia, St Mary's and Annapolis in Maryland, are not worth considering as busy centres of trade. They were rather the meeting-places of pleasure parties who came for balls and horse races, and when these gaieties were over they slumbered until again roused for the next joyous gathering. Charlestown in South Carolina had always been somewhat different; from its foundation it had taken upon itself the position of the most important town in the south, and it proved that it was ready to progress with the times by being the first town to possess a theatre, which was built in 1735. In the middle colonies the towns played a very considerable part in the social and economic life of the settlers, and in this way resembled the northern corporate communities. New York and Philadelphia were both good towns with wide streets lined with trees; along the edge were the orchards and gardens surrounding stone or brick houses with overhanging gables. The two other towns of importance were Germantown which was very busy, and Newport which is described as ill-built.

Such in brief were the towns, industries, and style of living of the southern and middle colonists. The English-born planter depended upon slave labour or indentured servants; he lived upon a large estate in a magnificent and often too lavish manner. But they were men of as much grit as the New Englanders; certainly they were descended from a different stock, and they looked upon the present life and the future with very different eyes, but that was all. The settlers of the middle colonies plunged with readiness into the intricacies of trade, and the merchant and tradesman were far more conspicuous figures in daily life than in either Virginia or

Maryland. The colonists were, too, far more cosmopolitan than in the north. In the Carolinas there were a few Huguenots, Swiss, and German Palatines, but in Virginia and Maryland there was little trace of any foreign element. But in the middle colonies there were regular waves of aliens from Germany and Switzerland intermixed with the earlier Dutch and English settlers. They all helped to play their little parts in the world's history, and they all came to look upon England as the home country. Then by the middle of the eighteenth century they were called upon to resist the aggressions of France; and during those years of struggle they partly learnt their power. United at last, English settler and foreigner, Northern Puritan and Southern planter, they made the one supreme effort, throwing off the yoke of England, and became no longer colonists, but Americans.

Chapter 10

THE FRENCH COLONIES IN NORTH AMERICA

"The French empire in the New World has vanished, leaving behind it ineffaceable monuments of the grand political conception of which it formed part" [239]. Frenchmen were amongst the earliest to be roused by the discoveries of Columbus, Cabot, and Vasco da Gama; but it was not until the sixth year of the sixteenth century that any real attempt at discovery was made. In that year, 1506, Denys of Harfleur sailed across the Atlantic, hoping to reach the East, but finding instead the great Gulf of St Lawrence. He was not the only adventurer, for Aubert of Dieppe followed two years later and astonished his countrymen by bringing to France some natives of North America. Baron de Léry was the first to see the advantages of colonisation, and long before Sir Walter Raleigh was born the quick-witted Frenchman had planned within his fertile brain a new France beyond the sea. He attempted to carry out his purpose in 1518, but it was bound to fail, for the time was not yet ripe for a French colony, since France itself was still unsettled and imperfectly concentrated. Francis I., realising the advantages gained by his rival Charles V. from the rich mines of Peru, employed Verrazano, a Venetian, to "discover new lands by the ocean." He sailed in January 1524, and first reached that part of America now known as the Carolinas, and then coasted as far north as

Newfoundland. "Sayling northeast for the space of 150 leagues," Verrazano writes, "we approached to the land that in times past was discovered by the Britons, which is in fiftie degrees. Having now spent all our provision and victuals, and having discovered about 700 leagues and more of new countries, and being furnished with water and wood, we concluded to return into France" [240].

Quebec from Point Levy in 1761. From an engraving by R. Short.

The year 1534 is the most memorable of all concerning those early French voyages; it is a year of the very greatest importance in the history of both France and North America; from this time may be dated the beginning of New France, for now Jacques Cartier made his first voyage to the St Lawrence. He found that the people had "great store of Mushemilions, Pompions, Gourds, Cucumbers, Peasen and Beanes of every colour.... There groweth also a certaine kind of herbe, whereof in Sommer they make great provision for all the yeere, ... and onely men use it, and first they cause it to be dried in the sunne, then weare it about their neckes wrapped in a little beast's skinne made like a little bagge, with a hollow peece of stone or wood like a pipe: then when they please they make pouder of it, and then put it in one of the ends of the said Cornet or pipe, and laying a cole of fire upon it, at the other ende sucke so long, that they fill their bodies full of Smoke, till that it commeth out of their mouth and nostrils, even as out of the Tonnell of a chimney.... We our selves have tryed the same smoke and having put it in our mouthes, it seemed almost as hot as Pepper" [241]. On his return to St Malo, Cartier brought with him some Indian children as a proof of the success of his enterprise. He was not content with this voyage, and in the following year sailed again to this land of promise. On this occasion he penetrated still further up the St Lawrence, bringing his ship to anchor beneath the cliffs where now stands the city of Quebec. "It is called," he writes, "Stadacona, ... & beyond, is as faire and plaine as ever was seen" [242]. This second voyage was marked by the naming of his discoveries, and it is recorded that the new found lands were by him called New France. Six years later Cartier sailed again to the West, associated with a royal officer of the name of De Roberval. Cartier started first and was met by his superior when returning in disgust. De Roberval, with the title of Lord of Norumbega, proceeded as he was bound to establish a colony, but by 1542 he proved unsuccessful owing to the insufficiency of supplies and his own brutal despotism. There can be little doubt that all concerned in De Roberval's venture were deeply disappointed with its disastrous failure; its chief interest lies in the fact that it marks the end of the prologue of this drama of discovery, and the curtain was rung down not to rise again for half a century.

In the year celebrated for the Edict of Nantes, the Treaty of Vervins and the death of Philip II., the French once again started their attempts to colonise Canada. In that year, 1598, the Marquis de la Roche established a small settlement of convicts on Sable Island, which lies off the coast of Nova Scotia. The settlers, however, were incapable, the callous nobleman sailed away to sunny France, and the unhappy survivors were left to quarrel among themselves, till eleven only of the original forty remained alive to be rescued after five long years of misery and starvation. The spirit of adventure was not crushed, and in 1599 Chauvin, a sea captain, and Pontgravé, a St Malo merchant, obtained a patent to colonise Canada, and so established a settlement at Tadoussac. Their object was to monopolise the lucrative fur trade, rather than to establish any permanent colony. Four years later De Chastes, a grey-haired veteran of the civil wars, associated himself with Pontgravé, and they were fortunate in obtaining the services of Samuel Champlain, whose name is the greatest in the history of French colonisation. Almost immediately the small association of Chastes was amalgamated with another under De Monts, a Huguenot nobleman of the King's household, and together in 1604 they entered the Bay of Fundy. In the next year Port Royal was established in Nova Scotia on Annapolis Basin, and the fur traders passed the winter there under the leadership of Champlain. Supplies were brought out in 1606 by an expedition, which was accompanied by Lescarbot the historian, but, as De Monts' patent was cancelled in 1607, Port Royal was abandoned.

The French colonies differed in many respects from the British, but in one particular most essentially. The story of the British settlements which has already been told is the story of the progress of communities; in the case of the French colonies the history is really composed of a long series of entrancing biographies. The record of Canada from 1608 to 1635 is in fact the biography of Samuel Champlain. His first exploit was the erection of a habitation at Quebec in 1608, his two main objects being to support exploration and encourage missionary work. He thus established the French nation in Canada less than twelve months after the settlement of the British in Virginia; the two rival nations, therefore, started their great work of colonisation at practically the same moment. The progress and results of their settlements resembled each other in no single item. Not content with founding Quebec, the adventurous Frenchmen left Pontgravé to encourage commerce and pushed up the St Lawrence. In 1609 he discovered the Lake that still bears his name; and for the first time came into direct hostile contact with the warriors of the Five Nations, whom he defeated at Ticonderoga. In the same year he returned to France, but re-sailed to Canada in 1610, leaving a few months afterwards for his native country. On landing in France he was dismayed to find that his patron, Henry of Navarre, had been assassinated by the fanatic Ravaillac in the streets of Paris. The year 1611 found the intrepid voyager once again in Canada preparing the way for a French settlement at Montreal.

The great change in France, and indeed throughout Europe, caused by Henry IV.'s untimely end, was felt with almost equal intensity in the far-distant region of Canada. A new system was immediately inaugurated, and that most unsatisfactory Regent, Marie de Medici, appointed the Count de Soissons as supreme Governor of New France. Before the Count could take over his unaccustomed duties, he died, and the Prince de Condé was nominated in his place. Champlain was at once created his deputy, with the main work of regulating the fur-trade and keeping some semblance of order amongst the turbulent French backwoodsmen. Champlain's objects, however, were neither commercial nor pecuniary. His ambition soared above the merely lucrative, and he looked to the increase of French possessions, and if possible by means of the great waterways to the discovery of a short route to China and the East. It was for this latter reason that he was persuaded by Nicholas Vignau, one of his companions who had passed the previous winter among the northern Indians, to explore toilfully the waters of the upper Ottawa in 1613; Vignau having concocted a story about an outlet to the east, a fabrication which, when discovered after many hardships, nearly cost him his life.

It is an interesting fact that behind all these adventurous expeditions undertaken by either the English or the French, there was always something of the missionary spirit. The first French attempt to convert the Indians was in 1615, when the Recollet branch of the Franciscan Order sent out a few brethren to undertake the hazardous task of instructing the savages in the doctrines of the Christian faith. The chief of this worthy band was Le Caron, who, taking his life in his hands, penetrated far into the dangerous Huron country. Ten years had still to elapse before the Jesuits embarked on a duty which, though in many ways erroneously carried out, has rightly received the admiration of the world. It so happened, in 1625, that the Viceroy of Canada, the Duc de Ventadour, was closely connected with the Jesuit order; and he celebrated the beginning of his term of office by introducing Jesuit priests and supporting them from his private purse. The difference between the newcomers and the Franciscans, who had already bought their experience, was very marked. The Franciscans, although devoted missionaries, were not bigots, and they claimed no religious monopoly; the Jesuits, on the contrary, imported religious despotism. The coming of the Jesuit fathers had two effects which may perhaps seem contradictory. They stimulated in many ways the progress of Canada and did much for her advance; but equally they retarded the true evolution of the young nation. They were brave men who were ready to sacrifice themselves for the cause; no body of men have ever shown to the savages such tactfulness and diplomacy as these members of the Society of Jesus. As map-makers and discoverers they were pre-eminent. On the other hand they were the upholders of exclusiveness and the bitterest enemies of freedom; they formulated a rigid system which was necessarily inimical to the expansion of a youthful community. Above all, deeming the Huguenots to be heretics, they excluded from Canada the very people who might have made the French in Canada a great nation. In supporting the Jesuits in this action the French Government did itself a double injury, for by debarring the best artizans of France from French colonies, it turned them in after years to the British settlements, and they thus helped to advance those very colonies which were the inveterate foes of their native land.

Between the years 1620 and 1627 the government of Canada passed through numerous hands, including those of the Duc de Montmorenci and the already mentioned Duc de Ventadour; but had it not been for the striking qualities of Champlain, all must have failed. These years were troubled by continuous squabbles, and it was only Champlain's steadfastness that saved the colony. At last in 1627 affairs began to improve. Richelieu had now become a power in France, and for the better regulation of Canada he formed the "Company of the One Hundred Associates." Even now the difficulties of Champlain appeared overwhelming, not the least being the war between England and France. Richelieu had successfully defeated the Huguenots and their English allies, and the "weathercock fancy" of Buckingham had been incapable of devising any further scheme for the protection of La Rochelle. The war, however, lingered on, and although it was extremely languid in Europe, it was waged with more smartness in the New World. David Kirke, nominally a captain in the British service, but really little more than a pirate, with his three sons entered the St Lawrence in July 1628; they attacked the French trading station of Tadoussac, and in the following year starved Champlain into surrender at Quebec. The victory proved a barren one, for before it had actually been accomplished, Richelieu had brought about a treaty with Charles I. at St Germain- en-Laye, by which the newly conquered Canada was restored to the French in 1632.

Champlain returned to his adopted country in May 1633, and for the next two years he controlled the affairs of the French Company until his death on Christmas Day, 1635. New France then lost the man to whom she owed her all, and the French nation was deprived of one who has been fitly called "the Father of French Colonisation." From thirty-six years of age to the time of his death, Champlain had given up the whole of his energies to increase the power of his native country and to encourage the welfare and prosperity of New France. He was a hardy explorer, an excellent administrator, and one of the most trustworthy writers of his time. His ambitions were lofty, his foresight keen and intelligent, while the whole of his life was pure and resolute. His biography is one of the most interesting among the many entrancing stories of colonial founders, and his memory receives the lasting respect and honour which his great works naturally demand, not only from the Frenchman or French Canadian, but from posterity throughout the civilised world. Champlain was succeeded by Monsieur de Montmagny, who arrived at Quebec in 1636. Six years later the first permanent settlement was established at Montreal, which was at first entirely of a religious character; this was soon to be followed by another at Fort Richelieu at the point where the Richelieu River joins the St Lawrence. These new settlements may be taken as an indication of the progress and general advance of the French Empire in the West. But as a matter of fact up to the year 1663 the government of Canada was far from being satisfactory, for the "Company of One Hundred Associates" had been continually checked by Indian wars, and was by no means capable of creating a great nation. Colbert, the successor of Mazarin, and chief minister of Louis XIV., realised the incapacity of the Company, and in 1663 deprived it of all rights. It is not surprising that the minister should take this action if a colony's prosperity is to be judged by its population. It has already been shown how remarkably the English settlements increased in number; but the French colony starting at practically the same time had in 1663 a meagre population of 2500. Father Christian le Clercq, writing at that time, says, "The colony far from increasing began to diminish. Some returned to France, others were taken and killed by the Indians. Many died of misery; the clearing and cultivation of lands advanced but little, and they were obliged to expect all from France" [243]. The Jesuits were to a certain extent to be blamed for this lack of population; they had for some years been expending their energies upon the spiritual needs of Canada, but what Canada wanted, as a new colony, was what the English settlements had got, married men and women who willingly found new homes, whose children grew up around them, and whose aims were to create no temporary but permanent abiding- places. The Jesuits supplied rather both by teaching and example martyrs and virgins, whose history is filled with heroic records, but whose actual value to a new colony was extremely slight. The mission of Le Moyne to the Iroquois in 1653 and the establishment of those from St Sulpice under Maisonneuve at Montreal, are both fine examples of reckless devotion and self-sacrifice, but the outlook on life of these religious enthusiasts was an erroneous one.

The clear-sighted judgment and the financial genius of Colbert was needed to remedy the mistakes in the work which had been started so rashly by Richelieu. As Le Clercq recorded, the progress of New France required "a more powerful arm than that of the gentlemen of the Company" [244]. Colbert, in 1663, supplied the "more powerful arm" by making Canada a royal province, and in the following year creating the "Company of the West." The members of the Company claimed to be the Seigniors of New France, with the right of nominating the Council for the government of Canada. The Crown, however, insisted on retaining the privileges of appointing the Governor and the Intendant. As soon as Canada became a Crown Colony with such a splendid guide as Colbert the progress and prosperity of the settlers were assured.

The government of Canada was purely despotic under the all-powerful Governor, Intendant, and Supreme Council, and the settlers were never allowed the political freedom exercised by the English colonists in New

England or the Southern States. The law was the customary law of Paris, added to which were certain ordinances and, on occasions, royal edicts which received the ratification of the Council. This body had both legislative and judicial functions, and for the better maintenance of peace and order minor law-courts were established at Quebec, Three Rivers, and Montreal. In addition to these courts the seigniors had in some cases the right to try crimes that were committed on their estates, and nominally to pass the extreme penalty of death upon their vassals. The Governor controlled the armed forces, and was in continual conflict with the Intendant, for each was jealous of the other. The latter was the King's steward, a civilian, and usually a member of the legal profession; he was President of the Council, and by controlling the sinews of war was often more powerful than the Governor. The Bishop sat in Council with these two, and was spiritually supreme in name and fact. The great defects of Canada's political system were over-centralisation and lack of popular representation. The feudal system had been transferred to Canadian territory, and by its means the seigniors attempted to tie the peasant to the soil. The whole scheme was that of a benevolent despot exercising power over a closely restricted people; and yet the system itself, which was purely artificial, proved the skill of its originators, for under it the peasants of Canada lived happy and contented lives for almost a hundred years after they had passed under British rule.

This scheme of government as devised by Colbert and Louis XIV. was put into execution by the Marquis de Tracy, who arrived at Quebec in 1665 as Lieutenant-General of all the French forces in America. His coadjutors were Courcelles, the Governor, and Talon, the Intendant. These men made numerous expeditions against the Indians, and in particular against the Iroquois; but their work was completely overshadowed by that of the next Governor. The name of Count Frontenac has been ever dear to the French Canadian from the moment that he came to administer New France in 1672. He is one of those great figures in history who are perhaps particularly human; he was not a cold image, but composed of warm flesh and blood; he was neither a villain nor a saint. His great merits are to a certain extent balanced by his great defects; his temper was most violent, his manner haughty, pretentious, and arrogant. It is said with some truth that he was not altogether clean-handed in the methods he employed in repairing his fortunes; but grave as his faults were, they were weighed down on the other side not so much by his kindness, his firm alliance with those he regarded as his friends, but because his heart warmed to the land and the people of the land to whom he had been sent as a guide and governor. Frontenac's memory remains a happy one, because, like Champlain, he believed in the great future of the Daughter of the Snows. Canada was unknown to him when he was fifty years of age; when he was appointed Governor for the second time he was twenty years older; but this long roll of years did not prevent him from adapting himself to his surroundings, and with such excellent effect that at the time of his death in 1698 he left Canada on the highroad to prosperity and greatness. In particular he must be praised for ridding Canada of murdering savages, as a means towards which he established, in 1673, an outpost at Fort Frontenac [245]. His return to France, however, emboldened the Seneca Indians, the most numerous of the Five Nations, to make frequent raids until his restoration to office in 1689. Five years later Frontenac began his great work of suppression, which was marked by an act of ferocious brutality in 1695, which has deeply stained the old man's reputation. In the same year he retook Fort Frontenac, which had been lost, and twelve months later was so successful against the Iroquois that he not only humbled their pride but actually won their respect. Ruthless he may have been; brutal in a time when brutality was common; but whatever his faults, he came to Canada when Canada cried aloud for such a man, and had the future governors been of the character and possessed the daring spirit of Frontenac, the Great Dominion might still have been the New France in the West.

Meantime, brave, devoted adventurers and Jesuits had been endeavouring to extend the French dominions west and south-west. It has already been mentioned that Champlain, in 1613, had been tempted to make an arduous journey to discover by means of the numerous waterways some route to China. The Great Lakes were first explored; but it was found that none of these vast sheets of water contained the tantalising secret that was interesting and engaging the attention of so many European seamen. From Lake Michigan, then called the Lake of Illinois, the discoverers moved to the narrows of Lake Huron and onward to the Fox River, following the course of which they came to Lake Winnebago. Moving still farther south, they found that a narrow strip of land divided them from another waterway, the Wisconsin, and that in turn they were destined to discover was a tributary of the mighty Mississippi. But some adventurers were more daring than their brethren, and instead of clinging to their canoes and following the course of streams, boldly skirted the territory of the dreaded Five Nations and found the "Beautiful" River, or Ohio.

As early as 1635 Jean Nicollet had reached Lake Michigan, and so successful was he in his explorations of the rivers and lakes that it has been supposed that he was the original white discoverer of the Mississippi. Plausible as this would seem, historians have conclusively disproved his claims; and that honour must be divided between the two famous explorers Joliet and Marquette [246]. Louis Joliet was a layman, though connected by early training with the Jesuits; he was a Canadian born, and had been employed by the Intendant Talon to discover copper in the neighbourhood of Lake Superior. His companion, Jacques Marquette, was a Jesuit in priest's orders; he was a man of pure and saintly life, and within his delicate body there burnt a fiery spirit of endeavour to convert, a spirit which consumed him, as it were, so that his life was but a brief one in labouring for his faith. He landed in Canada in 1666; two years later he was sent forward into the almost unknown wilds and established himself on Lake Superior, teaching both the Hurons and the Illinois. It was indeed from the latter that he first heard of the Mississippi. Being forced by the savages to retire from this outpost, he and his little following took refuge in 1670 at the mission station of St Ignace, now known as Mackinaw. It was here that Marquette determined to make an expedition for the discovery of the great river of which he had heard. He has left an account of his journeyings written from memory, as unfortunately he lost his papers on his return. "I embarked with M. Joliet, who had been chosen to conduct this enterprise, on the 13th May 1673, with five other Frenchmen, in two bark canoes. We laid in some Indian corn and smoked beef for our voyage.

We first took care, however, to draw from the Indians all the information we could concerning the countries through which we had designed to travel, and drew up a map, on which we marked down the rivers, nations, and points of the compass to guide us in our journey" [247]. The discoverers followed the route laid down by others as far as Lake Winnebago, but no white man had up to that time crossed over to the river Wisconsin. Canoeing down that stream, hardly realising where fortune was leading them, the plucky Jesuit and his companions were carried out on the face of the broad waters of the Mississippi on 17th June 1673. "We met from time to time monstrous fish, which struck so violently against our canoes that at first we took them to be large trees, which threatened to upset us. We saw also a hideous monster; his head was like that of a tiger, his nose was sharp and somewhat resembled a wild cat; his beard was long; his ears stood upright; the colour of his head was grey, and his neck black" [248]. But even this terrible apparition did not discourage them, and they still pushed on, hoping at first that the great river would bear them into the Gulf of California. They passed the mouths of the Illinois, the Missouri, and the Ohio, and came to the Arkansas; here they learnt their mistake. "We judged by the compass that the Mississippi discharged itself into the Gulf of Mexico. It would, however, have been more agreeable if it had discharged into the South Sea or Gulf of California" [249]. They turned back, therefore, having found out what they wanted to know, and "we considered that the advantage of our travels would be altogether lost to our nation if we fell into the hands of the Spaniards, from whom we could expect no other treatment than death or slavery" [250]. Neither Marquette nor Joliet reaped any great advantage during their lifetime for their plucky endeavour, but they have had and will have the respect of those who come after them. Marquette made one more voyage on the stream that was his own. His burning zeal for the faith made him set out in the winter of 1674-5 to carry the Christian religion to the Indians of the Illinois River. He returned to Lake Michigan in the May of 1675, but he was a dying man. Death came suddenly, and his companions rapidly interred him far away from his friends; but so great was the love inspired by this faithful priest amongst the savages that they fetched his bones and laid them, with every sign of affection, respect, and grief, in the little mission-chapel where he had laboured for the faith. Marquette was followed by a man whose name is even better known, but who was cast in a different mould. Réné Robert Cavelier, Sieur de La Salle, was born at Rouen and had landed in Canada in the same year as Marquette. His object was to discover a route to the East, and the name that he gave to his seignory, La Chine, testifies to this desire. He began his work of discovery in 1669, and in the next two years he passed from Lakes Ontario and Erie right through the Illinois country, finally discovering the Ohio. In 1675 he took up his seignory on the Cataraqui River at Fort Frontenac. He was only thirty-two years of age, but he had already made himself famous. He was a man of strong character, and as such had many enemies amongst his fellow French Canadians; his want of sympathy turned men against him, and his want of tact wounded their feelings. To the Jesuits he was most unwelcome, for they recognised in him a rival discoverer; with the merchants and traders he was no less unpopular, a fact which was possibly intensified by his seignory being one of the best positions in New France for pecuniary gain. He was in every way an austere man, solitary and self-communing; and as his mind was filled with ambitions and even statesmanlike conceptions for New France, it is not surprising that the trading element and even his own followers failed to understand him. From 1675 to 1677 this man of extraordinary energy employed himself in commerce with the Indians by means of vessels of his own construction on Lake Ontario; but such work was too petty for La Salle. He therefore, in 1678, obtained from Louis XIV. permission "to labour at the discovery of the Western parts of New France through which to all appearance a way may be found to Mexico," [251] in addition to which La Salle was strengthened in his possession of Fort Frontenac and was granted the privilege of constructing forts if necessary on his expeditions. On his enterprises he was accompanied by Henri de Tonty, an Italian officer and ever faithful to La Salle, and by Father Hennepin, a brave Flemish friar, whose overwhelming vanity tempted him in later years to try to rob his leader of the honour of first reaching the sea by the Mississippi River.

The early efforts of La Salle were unsatisfactory. He built a fort at Niagara and constructed a vessel called the Griffin, which foundered on Lake Michigan and left him in a hostile country swarming with savages, without supplies, and with mutinous followers. Nevertheless he kept on and descended the Illinois River, determined to reach the Gulf of Mexico. In 1680 his men began to desert, but Tonty and a faithful few assisted him to construct Fort Crèvecœur on the Illinois. Here the discoverer left his lieutenant for a time while he returned to Canada for supplies. The men mutinied, abandoned the fort, and followed La Salle with the intention of murdering him. Meantime he had sent out an expedition under Father Hennepin which had been captured by the Sioux Indians on the Upper Mississippi in what is now Minnesota. The Flemish friar and his followers were rescued by a Canadian backwoodsman, Du Luth, and Hennepin returned to France to write his account of the Mississippi.

Father Membré has left a record of La Salle's great expedition. "M. La Salle having arrived safely at Miamies on the 3rd of November 1681, began with his ordinary activity and vast mind to make all preparations for his departure.... The whole party consisted of about fifty-four persons, including the Sieur de Tonty and the Sieur Dautray, the son of the late Sieur Bourdon" [252]. The expedition safely passed the mouths of the Missouri and Ohio; after building a fort, the adventurers reached the Arkansas, where they were welcomed by the Indians, who knew nothing of white men. "The Sieur de la Salle took possession of this country with great ceremony. He planted a cross and set up the king's arms, at which the Indians showed a great joy.... On our return from the sea we found that they had surrounded the cross with a palisade" [253]. Passing still farther south, "we arrived on the 6th of April at a point where the river divides into three channels. The Sieur de la Salle divided his party the next day into three bands, to go and explore them. He took the western, the Sieur Dautray the southern, the Sieur Tonty ... the middle one" [254]. On the 9th of April the three parties met on the shores of the Gulf of Mexico. This success was marked by the ceremony of planting the cross and raising the arms of France. La Salle took possession of the river and all the country round in the name of the king, and amidst a volley of muskets a leaden plate inscribed with the action and the names of the discoverers was deposited in the ground. Such was the foundation of the French in Louisiana. La Salle and his party returned to the North, but he was not the man to rest upon his laurels, for in the autumn of 1682 and the spring of 1683 he is to be found busily establishing a French colony on the Illinois. Fort Louis was built on a rocky summit and promised to be a most important station in the future, always on the one condition that the connection with Canada was in no way broken, or even threatened.

Perpetual envy and jealousy tended to keep Canada weak and the French in the West powerless. When La Salle returned he found himself surrounded by enemies, and without his friend and supporter, Count Frontenac, who had retired to France. Seeing no chance of accomplishing anything in Canada, La Salle sailed to Europe to put his version of the story before King Louis. He reached Versailles at exactly the right moment for his fortunes. France and Spain in 1683 were again on the verge of war; and even before La Salle's arrival, Seignelay, the son of the late grim Colbert, had proposed to Louis a scheme for the seizure of some port on the Gulf of Mexico so as to discomfit Spain. La Salle was heard with respect and attention, and was, in fact, welcomed as the very man required to carry out the prearranged plans of the king and his minister. All La Salle's possessions in Canada were restored, and he was commissioned to conduct a party for the purpose of colonising some strip of territory upon the Mexican Gulf. The scheme was from the outset hopeless. La Salle may have seen that it was the last toss of the dice, fortune or ruin. He may have been blinded by his successful discovery; but it is impossible to imagine that a man who had always kept his ends clearly in view, and who had accurately measured the means to attain them, should now have embarked blindly upon so hazardous a task. Whatever his private opinions were, he readily undertook the leadership in conjunction with Admiral Beaujeu. The party embarked in four vessels, and sailed from La Rochelle on July 24, 1684. At the very outset their troubles began. One of the most important of the vessels carrying their supplies was captured by a Spanish buccaneer. The other three ships managed to reach San Domingo, where the little band of soldiers, artizans, and women were kept in idleness for two months owing to their leaders being stricken with fever. At last on January 1, 1685, La Salle brought the expedition to the shores of Texas, where the colony was settled within a palisade at a point called Fort St Louis. The distress of the settlement was terrible, and still further intensified by the realisation of their distance from Canada. In October, La Salle, driven to despair, set out to discover a way to the outposts of the northern colony. In March 1686 he was back again, but unsuccessful. Having rested for a month, he once more started for Canada, but after wandering until October he returned to the settlement utterly baffled. What was worse still was that he found a heavy mortality amongst the colonists; out of one hundred and eighty who had originally started he now had but forty-five followers, and very few of these he could really trust. All his ships were lost, escape to France was impossible, starvation stared them in the face. The only thing to do was to try to cut a way through to Canada. On January 7, 1687, La Salle, his brother, two of his nephews, and half his party set out; mutiny was evident from the beginning, and on March 19th, ambushed by his own men, the daring explorer was murdered. His brother, one of his nephews, and Jontel, who told the tale, escaped, and succeeded after terrible suffering in reaching Canada.

Louis XIV. and his ministers were far too busy at home to care about the death of one who had dared so much for France. The insane idea of Louis' European policy blinded him to the prospects of an empire in the West, which La Salle might, had he been properly supported, have made so great. The people in authority in Canada were equally oblivious to the loss of one of Canada's greatest sons. They were too envious of this remarkable man who had done so much. One man, however, remembered his old master. Henri de Tonty, the faithful friend, had set out in 1686 to find this man whom he regarded with such affection. When he discovered that La Salle had been murdered, he did what he knew his great leader would have done and turned his attention to the rescue of the remnant at Fort St Louis. His efforts were unavailing, for the Spaniards had learnt, and from them Tonty heard, that the few who had remained on the shores of Texas had been annihilated by the Indians. Thus the grandiose schemes of La Salle appeared to end in failure, mystery, and death; but like his forerunner

Marquette, his name still lives in Canada, where the names of his detractors have long since been forgotten. La Salle will be remembered as one of the boldest explorers, as a man who, even above any Englishman of his day, really grasped the imperial idea of a New France beyond the sea. He was the first to realise the great conception of uniting the French settlement from the snow-clad plains of Canada to the sunny shores of Mexico; and he it was who saw that should this dream be turned to reality, the Anglo-Saxon people would be confined to the narrow strip along the coast, and the illimitable expanses of the North American continent, with the enormous wealth of the West, would be the inheritance of the Gallic race.

There were, however, a few Frenchmen who had glimmerings of the dream of La Salle. As early as 1686 a party under Du Luth established a French outpost between Lakes Huron and Erie. Eight years later La Mothe Cadillac urged upon the French government the importance of holding this post, which in fact controlled the outlet of the two lakes. The consent of those in authority having been obtained, the French began in 1701 the erection of the city of Detroit. The Iroquois at last realised what was happening; they saw that, just as Fort Frontenac some years before had very seriously curtailed their rights of hunting and had indeed endangered their power, so now that they might again be trapped. To prevent this, on July 19, 1701, they ceded their hunting grounds to the King of England, retaining the right of free hunting. They were not versed in European politics; nor did they know that the magnificent Louis was gradually being ruined by William III. and Marlborough. The war of the Spanish Succession, fought for the most part in the Netherlands and Spain, had a vital effect upon those Iroquois nations of the Western prairies. The victories of Marlborough brought to England many possessions, and amongst them those lands which had been so trustingly conceded in 1701.

The Treaty of Utrecht, although it brought peace after a long and expensive war, may be said to mark a new epoch in the stories of both British and French colonial expansion. This epoch is not one of peace in the true sense; the actual fighting, when it occurred, was not always sanctioned by the home government; but the period was one of aggression on the part of the French in Canada and resistance on the part of the British colonists along the Eastern seaboard.

Chapter 11

FRENCH AGGRESSION

In a previous chapter reference has already been made to the fatality of having no form of union among the Thirteen Colonies. Every chance of concentration existed towards the end of the seventeenth century, for the colonies were contiguous, they lay in compact and continuous territory along the eastern seaboard, backed by the boundary of the Alleghanies. They were too, for the most part, inhabited by Englishmen, who may originally have been driven to emigrate for very different reasons, but who were in reality of the same stock and blood. But though everything pointed to union, the necessary concomitants were comparative only, and union was impossible. The colonies were squabbling, jarring communities, without any constitutional links; they were surrounded and separated by vast tracts of impenetrable forest; their traditions, religions, and beliefs were entirely opposed; and each colony was as much divided in thought and feeling from its neighbours as from the home country. This lack of concentration was one of the main differences between the English on the American coast and the French in Canada. This want of union was unknown in New France, where centralisation, perhaps over-centralisation, was the predominating feature. One governor at the head of all, a semi-feudal system, and an absolute reliance upon each other and upon support from home made the numerically inferior Canada in some respects superior to the Thirteen Colonies. At the end of the seventeenth and the beginning of the eighteenth centuries, therefore, the French possessed great advantages over their southern rivals; and the English, disunited and internally jealous, were likely to prove impotent against the Government of Quebec.

From the very first the relations between the colonies and Canada had been unfriendly, but the feelings of antagonism increased as the seventeenth century grew in years; and by the time that Frontenac ruled Canada and Thomas Dongan was English Governor at New York, this feeling had reached a climax. So pressing had the question become that the colonies, in 1684, held a general conference at Albany, the outcome of which, to the alarm of the French, was a firm alliance with the Five Nations or Iroquois. No greater struggle, however, resulted than an acrimonious literary warfare between the energetic Dongan and the capable Denonville concerning numerous attacks upon English and Dutch traders.

The English Revolution, the recall of Dongan, and the reappointment of Count Frontenac as governor of Canada were contemporaneous and were sufficient reasons for more trouble. The acceptance of William and Mary in England meant war in Europe; and Frontenac, seeing his opportunity, began what was called by the English settlers King William's war. The French governor made elaborate plans to attack New York, but having failed, found on his return that the Iroquois had disastrously raided Canada and massacred the people of Lachine. A fresh expedition was planned at a most unfortunate moment for the English colonists, who were suffering from the effects of the Revolution; and New York, in particular, was in the throes of the already mentioned Leisler rising. For Frontenac it was the ideal chance; now if ever he felt that he was bound to succeed against the English. His plans were well laid: his force was divided into three parties, which were to strike their blows at the same time and paralyse the settlers with terror. The first party with a band of Indians, under the famous rangers the brothers D'Iberville, started along the familiar waterway of the Richelieu River, Lake Champlain, and the Hudson, to attack Albany. By mischance they turned to the west and fell upon the little Dutch settlement of Schenectady, which was unguarded except for a few militiamen from Connecticut. The scene can only be described as one of helpless and hideous massacre; all who resisted were butchered and the place was deliberately and ruthlessly burnt. The second expedition was no less successful in carrying out their horrible task. It was mere murder. For three months they worked their way down to the settlement of Salmon Falls on the borders of New Hampshire and Maine. Here the settlers, little expecting such a terrible visit, were murdered while sleeping. Elated with these horrors, the French and Indians moved on to join their other comrades, and together, between four and five hundred strong, attacked Fort Loyal in the settlement of Falmouth, where now stands the town of Portland. Sylvanus Davies, the commander of the fort, surrendered on the promise of quarter and freedom; the promise was so much waste paper, and some of the English suffered the fate of the inhabitants of Schenectady, while others were led captive to Quebec.

The lesson learnt by the English colonists was a salutary one, and the immediate result of Frontenac's three successes was a tendency on the part of the settlers to unite. At a solemn conference held in 1690 at Albany, the colonies came to the conclusion that a combined naval and military force must attack the French at once. The authorities in Massachusetts took the lead; the "Bostonnais," as the French called them, were seamen to the backbone. They had come, as has been shown, of a sturdy Puritan stock, and as dwellers by the sea and traders on its waters, they possessed those very characteristics which the Canadians so sadly lacked. It was therefore the people of Boston who did all they could to further the attack by sea, by which the main effort was to be made; the land forces were not supported with the same enthusiasm and were thereby insufficient for the work in hand, as events afterwards proved, and instead of a magnificent military exhibition against Canada, the soldiers did little more than raid a French settlement at La Prairie. The memory of David Kirke's attack upon Quebec was still green, although sixty years had passed since that event. The aforetime ship's carpenter and sea-rover, Sir William Phipps, governor of Massachusetts, was now burning to renew the old glories of the colonial navy at the expense of France. He had already, at the time of the French attack upon Falmouth, taken possession of their one stronghold in Acadia,

Port Royal, and returned with much booty, some prisoners, and an increased reputation as a brave, patriotic man. In August 1690, with 34 ships and 2200 men, Phipps sailed from Nantucket to attack Quebec, the headquarters of the French Government. The inhabitants had been lulled by continuous peace into a sense of security, which was neither justified by past experience not by daily occurring events. The expedition, however, landed too late in the year. What happened to it was what Wolfe dreaded nearly seventy years later. It was late in October before the men had disembarked and the wet and cold season had already set in. The food supplies ran short; sickness broke out and the little party was easily outnumbered. Phipps bombarded the lower town to his heart's content, but he made the fatal mistake of trying to attack from Beauport, instead of by means of the path, which was afterwards discovered by Wolfe, and which had already been shown to the "Bostonnais" general. The failure of the gallant band from Massachusetts was complete; but there was something truly magnificent about the whole affair. The man who had once tended sheep, who had been a common seaman, and worked his way up the rungs of the ladder of fame and prosperity, now pitted himself against the Count de Frontenac, noble of France; the humble citizens of Boston, who, up to that moment, had shown more interest in religious intolerance and the rejection of any unnecessary pressure from England, had dared to attack the ancient fortress of New France, garrisoned by trained forces and skilled backwoodsmen warriors; practically one humble Puritanic colony strove against the pomp and might of his Catholic Majesty, Louis Quatorze.

The New England colonies, headed by Massachusetts, were bound to struggle against the French with more determination than any of their colonial brethren. New York did occasionally suffer severe attacks such as that which had been intended for Albany; but the French realised very clearly that their raids in this direction were always liable to be repulsed, not by the settlers themselves, but by the warlike Iroquois, who were in every way bound to the English and antagonistic to France. The Puritan colonies, on the other hand, were threatened by Indian foes just as friendly to the Canadians as the Iroquois were towards the New Yorkers. The Abenaki Indians were an ever constant danger along the New England borders, and their hostile attitude was intensified by the Jesuits, who had acquired over them an influence even greater than that which they had gained over other tribes. It was, in fact, the priests' main task, particularly during the latter years of the seventeenth century, to incite the Indians in their attacks upon the English. Wild, looting, scalping, murdering bands poured in upon the unhappy settlers who dwelt along the borders of New Hampshire and Maine. The French feared, and with reason, that unless they kept this blood-lust at fever heat, the Abenaki like the Iroquois would be won over by the English owing to the fascination of a lucrative commerce.

The onslaughts that had to be resisted were not only from the Indians. The success of Phipps at Port Royal, and his daring attack upon Quebec, forced the Canadians to cry aloud for some form of retaliation, which swiftly came. No sooner had Villebon recaptured Port Royal in Acadia, than, in 1692, a definite series of massacres were organised along the colonial sea-coast, and for years the English frontiers were swept with desolating raids. York in Maine was the first to suffer the horrors of this combined Indian and French warfare. Wells, further north, was more successful in its resistance; for here Convers and thirty militiamen drove back a party of Indians and French who had hoped to perpetrate the usual butchery. The terror began again in 1694, and the settlers at Oyster River were either immediately killed or carried into captivity. That such things were tolerated by the New Englanders, and especially by the people of Massachusetts, who had been so energetic in their naval expeditions, is extremely surprising; there can be little doubt that the settlers in the larger towns exhibited extraordinary indifference to these raids upon their more isolated brethren. Massachusetts, with a population of 50,000, was quite capable of building a strong line of forts and organising a well-equipped border police. A few forts they certainly had, but these were ill-protected and worse cared for. The only one of any importance was that of Pemaquid, which lay as a rampart in the path of any Abenaki attack on New England; but so dilatory was the conduct of the settlers that, at the very moment when they might have expected serious trouble with the French, they withdrew most of their troops and in 1689 allowed the fort to be taken by the Indians. The energetic Phipps had done his best, and in 1692 Pemaquid was rebuilt and regarrisoned. The later story of this fort is one that causes Englishmen to blush for the scandalous and dastardly action of one of their countrymen. In 1696, acting under the orders of Stoughton, lieutenant-governor of Massachusetts, Chubb tempted a party of Abenaki to come to the fort, and there killed some and kidnapped others. The French immediately seized the opportunity to revenge this cowardly treatment of the savages, and on August 14, Iberville, after making a triumphal progress from Quebec, capturing English vessels as he sailed along the coast, appeared before Fort Pemaquid. Chubb scornfully refused to surrender, and supported his vainglorious words by capitulating the very next day.

So delighted were the French by their success that in the following year they determined to capture Boston. The Marquis de Nesmond was to command the fleet, while Frontenac was to lead the land forces. Delay for one reason or another, contrary winds and stormy weather, kept the expedition back until the summer was passed, when it was found to be too late in the season to proceed. By the time that any fresh expedition could be undertaken King William's War was over, and the Treaty of Ryswick had been signed and was proclaimed in America in 1698. The importance of the treaty with regard to the American colonies is to be found only in the fact that it gave breathing-space to the combatants. Both parties regarded it as a truce more than a treaty, and both looked forward to a not far distant date when their differences might once again be decided by the arbitrament of war.

The long-looked-for day came in 1701 when James II. died, and Louis XIV., with that spirit, half- bravado half-chivalrous, declared the Old Pretender James III. of England. The real fighting that now ensued took place not in the forests of North America but in the lowlands of Europe. The Netherlands, the cockpit of Europe, were once again to be drenched with blood. The battles of Blenheim, Ramillies, Oudenarde, and Malplaquet played an important part in the history of North American colonies. Fighting, however, was not unknown in the West, and on May 4, 1702, war was openly declared. The old raiding expeditions began again, and the French led the way by an attack on Wells, situated on Casco Bay. The little town was terribly beset by the marauding Abenaki Indians, and was almost at its last gasp when succoured by an armed force by sea from Massachusetts. Then followed the historic attack upon Deerfield in 1704. It was a small town of 300 inhabitants on the north-west border of Massachusetts. The French and their Indian allies burst upon it in February. Fifty of the people were butchered and one hundred were carried into a captivity made famous by John Williams, one of the prisoners, in The Redeemed Captive returning to Sion. "The direct and simple narrative of Williams is plainly the work of an honest and courageous man" [255]. He tells of his own and his fellow-captives' sufferings; and, in particular, of how the Jesuits promised him untold wealth if he would be converted, to which he replied, "the offer of the whole world would tempt him no more than a blackberry" [256]. As years went by the captives were either exchanged or, having been converted, married Canadians and settled at Quebec or Montreal.

The disgrace of these murdering expeditions falls upon the French Government, for they were planned by French officials and were carried out for the most part by savage Indians. It must be allowed, however, that the havoc on the border settlements of Canada had been caused by the Five Nations, the friends of the English. Thus retaliation was the feeling that grew up on both sides. The Canadians cared nothing for the horrors that they perpetrated in the New England colonies; while the English settlers naturally vented their wrath upon the nearest object of attack, Acadia, for their indignation had been fanned to white heat by the unspeakable horrors of Indian war. In revenge for the massacre at Deerfield, Major Benjamin Church with a force from New England appeared before Port Royal in 1704, and burnt the French settlement at Grand Pré. Three years later Colonel John March, supported by a company of volunteers from Massachusetts, made an attack upon Acadia, which proved abortive. This expedition, together with a French raid upon Haverfield on the Merrimac, had the effect of stirring Massachusetts to more grandiose schemes, and in 1708 Samuel Vetch was sent to England to ask for the assistance of regular troops.

The emissary selected by the "Bostonnais" had been well-chosen, for in the colonies he was one of the most notable men of his day. He had lived in the tropical heats of Darien; he had sojourned amongst the French Canadians; and he had mixed with the cosmopolitan population of New York. His adventurous life had given him an intimate knowledge of the affairs and methods of the English and French colonial systems. He was a shrewd, self-made man; very impetuous and sanguine, but at the same time astute and wary. Above all he was filled with determination and ambition, and if he had his own advance at heart, it was only in conjunction with the true welfare of his country and her colonies. His great ambition was, that "Her Majesty shall be sole empress of the vast North American Continent." Vetch had the common sense to see that this glorious object could only be accomplished by a united and aggressive action against France. The firsthand knowledge that Vetch possessed seems to have had considerable influence at the English Court; and as Marlborough's victories had been so decisive in Europe, it was thought that something might be done in America. In fact, the agent was granted all that he had asked, and he returned to Massachusetts with a promise of a fleet and five regiments, amounting in all to about 3000 men. The prospect of conquering Canada now appeared less visionary than ever before; the settlers ought to have felt that they were entering on the last great struggle, had it not been for the fact that, as always, colony was divided against colony. Pennsylvania, the home of the Quaker, disapproved of war on principle; it was a safe theory for the Pennsylvanians, for they were out of reach of French attack, and they knew that they were well protected by those colonies which lay in the zone of danger. Then, too, instead of acting like true men, the people of New Jersey refused any actual help in the way of a force, though they were not so mean as the Pennsylvanians, for they did send a contribution of money. The New Yorkers exhibited a more magnanimous spirit; they threw in their lot with the people of New England and roused the Five Nations against the French. The chief expedition by land was under the command of Colonel Francis Nicholson, who wrote to Lord Sunderland in July, and said that if "I had not accepted the command, there would have been insuperable difficulties" [257]. This sentence tells its own story, for the writer knew that any other commander would have been without support owing to the shameful provincial jealousies which were the everlasting reproach and curse of the American states. Nicholson was a man of robust strength, a clear, practical brain, though ambitious, vehement, and bold. He had already proved himself a fairly capable colonial governor in Virginia, New York, Maryland, and Carolina, where, though his private life may not have been a pattern of strict morality, his conduct in official affairs was unimpeachable. With 1500 men he entrenched himself at Wood Creek, near Lake Champlain, where he was besieged by Ramesay, governor of Montreal. The settlers were able to drive back the French, but were forced to wait anxiously for news of the grand naval expedition that was to do so much; they waited in vain, day by day being struck down by disease and pestilence; and Nicholson was finally compelled to retreat, leaving behind him innumerable graves as proofs of the patience and courage of his little force.

The British squadron with the promised regiments was long overdue. The forces of Massachusetts, New Hampshire, and Rhode Island were encamped at Boston ready, on the appearance of the fleet, to sail to Quebec. From May to July they were diligently drilled, and Vetch wrote in August, "The bodies of men are in general better than in Europe and I hope their courage will prove so too; so that nothing in human probability can prevent the success of this glorious enterprise but the too late arrival of the fleet." [258] If it should not come, "it would be the last disappointment to her Majesty's colonies, who have so heartily complied with her royal order, and would render them much more miserable than if such a thing had never been undertaken" [259]. The fleet never came! To the grief and despair of the colonies, it had been sent to Portugal to meet the exigencies of the European war. Although the hearts of the English settlers had been made sick by hope deferred, yet a tenacious energy had always been one of their strongest characteristics; and the representatives of Massachusetts still urged the home Government to make a supreme effort against New France. They asked Nicholson, who sailed for Europe, to point out how much assistance was needed, how advantageous the undertaking would be to the Crown, and how impoverished and enfeebled the colony was by the long and expensive war. The last plea was true enough, for Massachusetts, New Hampshire, and Rhode Island had spent on the disastrous military schemes of 1709 no less than £46,000. Like Massachusetts, the colony of New York was equally anxious to impress the English Crown with the importance of the question at stake, and in 1710 sent five Mohawk chiefs under the guidance of Peter Schuyler to interest the English in colonial affairs, and at the same time to so impress the chiefs with England's power as to dispose them to hold fast to their alliance.

The resolution and tenacity shown by the colonies had some effect in the home country. An English force of over three thousand men was at last dispatched to Boston; and though timed to arrive in March, it did not reach that port until July. Meantime the people of Massachusetts had once again stirred themselves; raised their own militia; tempted the soldiers of 1709 to rejoin by a promise of the Queen's musket; and actually quartered troops on private houses, "any law or usage to the contrary notwithstanding" [260]. This fresh outburst of energy culminated in Nicholson again taking command and sailing for Port Royal. On September 24, 1710, he reached his object of attack; and on October 1 the French, finding themselves outnumbered, readily surrendered; the town became Annapolis, and Acadia or Nova Scotia passed permanently into the possession of Great Britain, owing to the bravery of her American colonists.

The capture of Acadia was to Nicholson merely a stepping-stone towards the greater defeat of the French and the final subjugation of New France. He returned to England to further his schemes and was there ably supported by Jeremiah Dummer, who was at that time in the service of Henry St John, Viscount Bolingbroke. The Sacheverell trial of 1710 had, amongst other things, caused the fall of the Whigs and concluded Marlborough's warlike schemes. The Tories, champions of peace, were left in power with St John and Harley as their leaders; but so ably did the two colonials plead the cause of their brethren, that in April 1711 fifteen men-of-war and forty-six transports, containing five thousand regular troops, sailed for America. To their intense surprise the officers of this great armament found on their arrival that they were regarded by the colonists with the strongest suspicion. The ships had only been provisioned to reach

America; definite orders as to their further destination had not been issued; and the French had attempted to poison the minds of the Bostonians by the idea that the British forces were to subvert colonial liberties and reduce Massachusetts, Rhode Island, and New Hampshire to the position of Crown colonies. One Frenchman wrote, "There is an antipathy between the English of Europe and those of America, who will not endure troops from England even to guard their forts" [261]. Another, Costobelle, had said as early as December 1709, "I do not think that they are so blind as not to see that they will insensibly be brought under the yoke of the Parliament of Old England; but by the cruelties that the Canadians and Indians exercise in continual incursions upon their lands, I judge that they would rather be delivered from the inhumanity of such neighbours than preserve all the former powers of their little republic" [262]. For the reasons stated in this report the New England colonists were on the horns of a dilemma; they feared the British troops, but they were equally afraid of their French neighbours.

There were, however, other difficulties. The presence of the British regulars acted as an incentive to ill-feeling, which showed itself in the deliberate lack of provisions and pilots, and in the willing shelter offered to deserters from the army. The English officers, too, failed entirely to understand now, as again in later years, the character of the colonists; they were often arrogant or at least patronising; and to the republican New Englander they appeared bumptious aristocrats. The colonist was a brave and experienced man, and it was irksome to him to find himself in an inferior position to men who really knew less than he did about Indian warfare and forest fighting. On the other hand, the English troops felt quite as bitterly as the colonists, and Colonel King wrote to St John in July 1711, "You'll find in my Journal what Difficultyes we mett with through the Misfortune that the Coloneys were not inform'd of our Coming two Months sooner, and through the Interestedness, ill Nature, and Sowerness of these People, whose Government, Doctrine and Manners, whose Hypocracy and canting, are insupportable; and no man living but one of Gen'l Hill's good sense and good nature could have managed them. But if such a Man mett with nothing he could depend on, altho' vested with the

Queen's Royal Power and Authority, and Supported by a Number of Troops sufficient to reduce by force all the Coloneys, 'tis easy to determine the Respect and Obedience Her Majesty may reasonably expect from them ... they will grow more stiff and disobedient every day unless they are brought under our government and deprived of their charters" [263].

The inhabitants of Boston may have shown many signs of coolness, but the authorities of Massachusetts loyally supported the expedition which was supposed to be about to accomplish so much. On the 30th July the fleet sailed from Boston to the St Lawrence under the command of Sir Hovenden Walker, of whom little is known, and who in no way added lustre to his name. The colonial contingent that went by sea consisted of about fifteen hundred men, led by the experienced and buoyant Samuel Vetch. Another colonial force was commanded by Francis Nicholson, whose object was to move north by way of Lake Champlain and attack the Canadian strongholds. At the head of all was General Hill, or Jack Hill, the man about town, who was no soldier, and owed his position to his sister Abigail Hill, the famous supplanter of the Duchess of Marlborough. General Hill made no attempt to gain laurels for himself or his country, and his troops struggled back to Boston disgraced, not by their own actions, but by the want of action on the part of their leader.

Walker's fleet entered the St Lawrence on the 22nd of August. The Admiral, totally ignorant of the navigation of the gulf, steered his vessels in misty weather straight for the northern shore. His own ship was saved just in time, but not so those which followed, and eight of the transports were dashed to pieces on the rocks, with a loss of almost a thousand lives. Walker, as proved by his own writings, never possessed any true ability; and he was only too ready, like Jack Hill, to look for some pretext for retreat. This horrible disaster was sufficient for the Admiral's purpose, and three days later the mighty armament turned away from Quebec, and New France was for the time saved. Walker looked upon the wreck as providential, and that the army had been saved from worse disasters. It was indeed a strange action for a British sailor to pen words of sincere gratitude for the loss of half his fleet. "Had we arrived safe at Quebec," he writes, "our provisions would have been reduced to a very small proportion, not exceeding eight or nine weeks at short allowance, so that between ten and twelve thousand men must have been left to perish with the extremity of cold and hunger. I must confess the melancholy contemplation of this (had it happened) strikes me with horror; for how dismal must it have been to have beheld the seas and earth locked up by adamantine frosts, and swoln with high mountains of snow in a barren and uncultivated region" [264]. Walker sailed back to Boston and then with his fleet returned to England, where as a final completion to the horrible fiasco, the Admiral's ship was blown up. Swift records this event as taking place in the Thames, but it more probably occurred at Spithead, owing "to an accident and carelessness of some rogue, who was going as they think to steal some gunpowder: five hundred men are lost" [265].

Every disgraceful plot deserved to come to a bad end. The ignominious conclusion of the Walker and Hill expedition was only to be expected, since its true object had been to eclipse the victories of Marlborough and bring about his entire downfall. St John and Harley had not been animated by patriotic or imperial sentiments when Mrs Masham had agreed to assist them in the backstairs attack upon the Churchill family. The price of her assistance was a high military command for her incapable brother Jack Hill. The two Tory ministers cared nothing for the success or failure of the colonies; all they required at the time was the fall of the Whigs with Marlborough at their head. The blame therefore must to a certain extent rest upon the English Crown ministers; but the incompetence of the two commanders, though not unparalleled in English history, was worse than most instances, because it bordered very closely upon cowardice. Muddle-headed as some British generals have proved themselves, it is almost impossible to find another case where the more serious charge can be brought or sustained. Marlborough had certainly fallen; but his unpatriotic enemies had not succeeded in effacing the glories of the four battles which still stand out as the chief features of the War of the Spanish Succession. Although St John's plot was disgraceful and deserved the failure that it earned, yet the disaster fell very hardly upon New England. It has been hinted that the colonials were themselves to blame, and that they were so afraid of the presence of an English force that they preferred failure to success. They feared, according to Colonel King's Journal, that "the conquest of Canada will naturally lead the Queen into changing their present disorderly government" [266]. The New Englanders could not, however, be so indifferent as is supposed, for the people of Massachusetts at any rate did their utmost to make the attack a success; and it was afterwards found that one in five of her male population was on active service in 1711; while many years had to elapse before the colony recovered from the effects of her financial exhaustion [267].

The War of the Spanish Succession in Europe had for all practical purposes ceased, and the echo of it in America was dying away. The belligerents were weary; the English began to feel the burden of their National Debt; while the French were utterly exhausted, for in 1709 even nature had turned against the omnipotent Louis, and the country was impoverished by a winter which killed the fruits and vines. In 1713 terms were at last agreed to; and the Treaty of Utrecht, the first really great colonial treaty, was the result. It is idle to speculate on what enormous gains might have fallen to the English if party spirit and spite had not cut short the remarkable career of England's great captain. Had Marlborough been allowed to continue his unbroken series of triumphant victories, and had he been permitted to select a commander-in-chief in the West, it is most probable that the Treaty of Utrecht would have contained those clauses which made the Treaty of Paris so famous half a century later. As it was, the gains to England in the colonial world were not to be despised. Acadia was surrendered to Great Britain, with Hudson Bay and Newfoundland; on the other hand, Cape Breton Island was restored to France. The great faults of the treaty, as far as it concerned the Western Hemisphere, lay first in allowing the French certain fishing rights off the shores of Newfoundland, which remained until recently "a dangerous cause of quarrel between two great nations, a perpetual irritating sore, a bar to the progress and prosperity of the Colony;" [268] and, secondly, it was unwise to restore Cape Breton to the French, as it was the key to the St Lawrence. A Frenchman pointed this out in 1745, when he said that "it was necessary that we should retain a position that would make us at all times masters of the entrance to the river which leads to New France;" [269] and even in 1713 the French Government realised something of the island's importance, and reared upon its desolate, fog-bound shore the mighty fortress of Louisburg, a stronghold that came to be regarded as impregnable, and second only in importance to that of Quebec.

"An avalanche of defeat and disaster had fallen upon the old age of Louis XIV.," [270] and he was forced into a treaty which contained many humiliations. He must, however, have realised that England had once more lost her opportunity, and that it was still possible for France to assert her supremacy in the West. Canada, the goal of the New Englander, was still New France, and for the next thirty years chronic warfare, sometimes only flickering, but never extinct, smouldered along the frontier line of the English and French settlers. The Canadians had the distinct advantage of knowing what their great object was. It was far more magnificent than that which filled the minds of the English; it was perhaps too widely extended, but it was undoubtedly grand—North America for the Gaul. To the governors of Massachusetts and New York the dream of the total defeat of the French and their banishment from Canada may have occasionally appeared; but their general outlook upon the question was as circumscribed as that of the French was diffuse; and to them the safety of their colonies, the friendship of the Five Nations, and sound, steady trade were sufficiently difficult problems for solution.

From the moment of the Treaty of Utrecht Acadia was the source of quarrels and intrigues which were entirely due to the interference of French Canadian priests. With these difficulties, however, the Thirteen Colonies had little or nothing to do, but found ample scope for their energies in resisting priestly plots elsewhere. The Canadian Government, owing to the preaching of the Jesuit priest Sebastian Rasle, succeeded in renewing their alliance with the Abenaki Indians on the New England frontier, although the chiefs of that tribe had made terms with the people of Massachusetts in 1717. Rasle was a man of zeal, of sturdy independent spirit, and fired with intense hatred of the English. The Massachusetts Government realised the danger of allowing this man, from his mission-station on the Kennebec River, to urge the Indians to acts of violence and cruelty. Letters are still preserved which prove that he was the agent of the Canadian Government, and exciting the Indians for French purposes. It seems a somewhat cowardly action, but it is evident that New France, concealing itself beneath the banner of ostensible peace, was fighting the New Englanders by means of savage allies. To crush this underhand scheme, in August 1724 a body of men under Captains Harmon, Moulton, and Brown, rowed up the Kennebec, took the Indian village, killed the Jesuit Rasle, and burnt the Indian wigwams. This blow, which was both daring and statesmanlike, had an excellent effect, and was hailed with joy by the border settlers, who saw in it the end of their troubles; and after a similar raid by Captain Heath on the tribes of the Penobscot in 1726, the Indians readily made terms of peace which lasted for many years.

The main object of the French in the West, during the first half of the eighteenth century, was to shut the English settlers in behind the Alleghanies by means of a series of forts. In spite of the strong opposition of the Five Nations, [271] the French erected one of the earliest of these permanent blockhouses at the mouth of the Niagara River in 1720. The English Colonists saw the danger, but the Legislature of New York was so mean in matters of finance that it refused any pecuniary assistance in creating a similar erection at Oswego in 1727. Governor William Burnet had therefore to find the requisite funds out of his own pocket; and although the fort proved of vital importance to New York, he was never fully repaid. In May 1727, Burnet wrote to the Board of Trade and Plantations, "I have this spring sent up workmen to build a stone house of strength at a place called Oswego, at the mouth of the Onondaga River, where our principal trade with the far Nations is carried on. I have obtained the consent of the Six Nations to build it" [272]. The establishment of this fort was a great blow to the French, who encouraged the Indians to drive out the English, but only received the reply, "Chassez-les toi-même" [273]. As a counterpoise they built Fort Rouillé at Toronto, but Oswego remained as a bastion against French aggression and as a lucrative trading station with the Indians until captured by Montcalm [274].

French Aggression

The Marquis De Montcalm. From a painting by J. B. Massé.

Even earlier than the foundation of Oswego the French had tried to establish themselves, in 1726, opposite Crown Point, where Lake Champlain contracts to the width of a river; but for the moment they were deterred by the strong opposition of Massachusetts. New Hampshire also claimed this territory, and while, with their usual jealousy, the two colonies "were quarrelling for the bone, the French ran away with it" [275]. French aggression continued, and in 1731 they seized Crown Point itself, at the instigation of the celebrated Chevalier Saint Luc de la Corne, and named it Fort St Frederic. The point was claimed by the colony of New York, but here again the settlers were too much engrossed in their chronic dispute with New Jersey to take any effective measures to prevent the loss. It was utterly futile for the New Yorkers and New Englanders to protest that the fort was a menace to British territory, for they had neither the will nor the common-sense to place petty domestic jealousies on one side and unite in driving back the French. The English found, by the year 1750, that owing to their supineness, France had succeeded in building forts at Niagara, Detroit, Michillimackinac, La Baye, Maumee, on the Wabash, St Joseph and Fort Chartres. These may have been loose and uncertain links, but they had great possibilities, and they at least connected Canada and Louisiana, and gave some appearance of the possibility of a French North America.

It seems strange that the aggressive conduct of one of the newest kingdoms in Europe should have a dire effect upon the New World; but so it was. The determination of Frederic of Prussia to aggrandise himself at the expense of Austria, caused, in 1744, the torch to be rekindled in North America, and packs of howling savages carried rapine and murder along the borderland of New France and New England. The war actually began in America in May 1744 when Duquesnel, the Governor of Louisburg, overpowered the small outpost of Canso in Acadia. The people of Massachusetts realised that to them the transference of Acadia to the French would mean a serious loss, and so planned "an enterprise second to none in colonial history" [276].

Louisburg was a menace to all the northern British colonies, and the New Englanders had been both exasperated and alarmed by the action of its governor. The fortification itself was built upon the famous system of

Vauban; it had cost 30,000,000 livres, and had taken twenty-five years to complete. Strong as this fortification was from without, owing to mutinous spirits it contained all the elements of weakness within. The honour of proposing an attack upon this scourge and curse of New England probably rests on William Vaughan, who at that period was interested in the fishing industry and dwelt at Damariscotta, Maine. Governor Shirley lent a willing ear to the daring proposal. He had, as a young barrister, come to Massachusetts in 1731, and within ten years had by his tact and cleverness been appointed chief magistrate of his colony. He laboured under the delusion that he was a military genius, and thought to prove his powers by engaging in this scheme. The Massachusetts Assembly, however, composed for the most part of grave merchants and stolid rustics, refused to undertake anything so risky and expensive. Boston and other coast towns, knowing well what a harbour of refuge Louisburg had proved to all hunters on the ocean, petitioned ardently that Vaughan's plan should be executed; and at length, after many difficulties, it was agreed that the settlers should make this one supreme effort. History immediately repeated itself, and the colonies showed their habitual want of union; and although Shirley appealed to them as far south as Pennsylvania, all with one accord made excuse, except Connecticut, New Hampshire, and Rhode Island. Once again, therefore, the burden of defeating France fell upon the New England settlements. William Pepperell, a merchant of Maine, was placed in command of the colonial land force. He came of Devonshire stock, was a colonel of militia, and fortunately possessed of good sound common-sense, for he had practically no military experience. The naval commander was Admiral Warren, who was well disposed to the American colonists, as he had married an American lady and owned property on both Manhattan Island and the banks of the Mohawk River. He was a good sailor, and in later years won for himself some renown in an engagement against the French in European waters.

Colonel Pepperell was willingly followed by colonists of sturdy character, still replete with Puritan ideas, and still further encouraged by the motto given to them by the Evangelical preacher, George Whitefield, "Nil desperandum, Christo duce" [277]. On April 30, 1745, the New

England force arrived within striking distance of Louisburg. The town itself was oblong in shape, built upon a tongue of land upon which the fortifications were erected with a due east aspect. The troops of France were composed for the most part of brave men, but they were in a state of disaffection, and their new commander, Duchambon, was pusillanimous in his decisions. The whole garrison, consisting of regulars and militia, was well under two thousand men; while the colonial army comprised four thousand in all. This superiority of force was immediately discounted by the privations undergone by the besiegers; and it has been computed that only half the army was really fit for action. The mutinous state of the French was but a poor match for the peculiar mixture of youthful impetuosity and religious fervour which stirred the colonials. A force under Vaughan occupied the Grand Battery, and still further encouragement was given by Admiral Warren's capture, on May 18, of the Vigilant, a French man-of-war of 64 guns, bringing supplies. One who took part in the siege writes, "Providence has signally smiled, and I doubt not the campaign will be crowned with success. I am willing to undergo anything for the good of our cause" [278]. The chief danger which threatened the settlers was relief from New France, but this came too late to be of any service to the garrison.

After an unsuccessful attempt against the battery on the little island at the mouth of the harbour, both Pepperell and Warren agreed that their best move would be a final assault upon the fortification. The French dreaded the effects of such an action; they were already worn out by fatigue and anxiety; the town was shattered in every direction by shot and shell. "Never," Pepperell wrote to Shirley, "was a place more mal'd with cannon and shell" [279]. Rather than sustain the horrors of a wild attack which might lead to ruthless massacre, Duchambon thought it better to accept the generous terms offered, and, on June 17th, capitulated. The town was taken over by Warren and Pepperell, and all praise must be given to the latter for the splendid way in which he preserved discipline amongst his colonials, who were forbidden to reward themselves, for their weary weeks of hardship, by loot and plunder. The capture of Louisburg was one of the greatest events of the War of the Austrian Succession; and historians are agreed that the success of the enterprise was almost entirely due to the courage and perseverance of the New Englanders, though they are ready to give all praise to Warren and his seamen. It was a remarkable feat, and it must ever be regarded as one of the most illustrious actions in American history. The Bostonians welcomed the news with joy; their brethren, they believed, had gone forth against the enemies of the Lord, and, like the Israelites of old, returned victorious. The grim Puritan had shown that though a man of peace, he was still able, when called upon, to smite the idolaters hip and thigh. Governor Shirley's schemes did not stop short at the capture of the key of the St Lawrence. After Louisburg had been garrisoned by regular troops, he intended to attack Canada. This plan failed, and he therefore turned his attention to the more feasible scheme of capturing Crown Point; but this also proved abortive. In the meantime the French made a counter-expedition from La Rochelle under the Duc d'Auville. From the outset the scheme was doomed: D'Auville died; his second in command, D'Estournel, committed suicide; while his successor, the Marquis de la Jonquière, was thoroughly defeated by Admirals Anson and Warren off Cape Finisterre.

The struggle in which the colonists had shown such gallantry slowly dragged to a close. Neither to Great Britain, nor to France had there been much gain in those six years of warfare: the glory belonged to the men of New England, who, in particular, realised the danger of the French Empire in the West. They had learnt by experience the peril that menaced them, and Shirley and Pepperell had done their best to remove that danger by direct attack. In England the enormous value of Cape Breton Island and Louisburg was not fully understood. George II. is traditionally reported to have said that Cape Breton was not his to return to France for it belonged to the people of Boston. This in a sense was true; it had been won by the men of New England and it would appear on the surface that it was for them to keep or restore that frowning outpost in the Atlantic. Peace, however, was most necessary at the moment, though it was only a breathing space in the colossal struggle of the eighteenth century; and it was realised that this peace could only be obtained by the cession of this fortification in exchange for our East Indian territory at Madras. The possibility of the growth of an Indian Empire never dawned upon the settlers in the West. They felt that this small speck in an Eastern land was nothing in comparison with the Dunkirk of North America. The New England colonies had done their best; they had given their men and their money to accomplish a great task. Their lack of unity had often stood in their way, but on the occasion of the capture of Louisburg the Puritan brotherhood had succeeded without the help of either Quaker or southern confederates; they had earned for themselves the respect of their contemporaries and the admiration of their descendants. Unfortunately, however, the abandonment of Louisburg "under the pressure of diplomatic necessity was in the eyes of the colonists an unscrupulous betrayal, and a manifest proof of total indifference to colonial interests. It gave a sting to the words of colonial demagogues and cut the sinews of colonial loyalty" [280].

Chapter 12

THE CLIMAX: THE STRUGGLE BETWEEN ENGLISH AND FRENCH COLONISTS

"If we can remove the turbulent Gallics the seat of Empire might be transferred to America" [281]. Such were the characteristically pompous words of John Adams, which nevertheless contained something of the spirit that animated a few of the thinking colonists in their final struggle with the power of France. The Conquest of Canada liberated the settlers of the Thirteen Colonies from a state of continuous and watchful alarm; but it also increased their attitude of resistance to interference on the part of England, and was an undoubted cause of the American War of Independence. The actual conquest was, however, due to British commanders, and more than half the troops employed consisted of British regulars. It is not intended to belittle the work of the colonials, for without them many of the stirring scenes which took place between 1750 and 1763 could never have been enacted; but without the discipline and experience of English leaders the great task could never have been accomplished, because of the hopeless internal jealousies of these quarrelsome communities. In the last chapter it has been shown that the burden of the war with the French fell upon the New England group, and in the period now under discussion the men of Massachusetts also played an active part; but, whereas the rapine and murder had been confined to the northern border, the stress of warfare now fell upon the western frontiers of the more southern States, and New York, Pennsylvania, Maryland, and Virginia were called upon to take a serious share in the great struggle. It had long been seen that these provinces as they grew in size must necessarily extend their borders, and the men from Pennsylvania and Virginia must come into hostile contact with the Canadian backwoodsmen who had pushed into the valley of the Ohio.

It is during this period that the want of unity between the Thirteen Colonies is more clearly evidenced than even in previous years. New York was torn by internal factions, and the history of that colony would have been infinitely more sad had it not been that its fighting contingent was led by the redoubtable William Johnson. The state of Pennsylvania was actually worse than that of New York; it was "a sanctuary for sloth, cowardice, and sordid self-interest. The humanity of Penn, the peace principles of the early Quakers, were a cloak behind which the factious and indolent citizen with no sense of public responsibility could always screen himself" [282]. The Pennsylvanians were as callous, during this colossal epoch, as if the war had been on the plains of Germany, and were not only inert themselves but endeavoured to neutralise the action of the other Colonies, so that they have earned the reputation of selfishness and disloyalty. Maryland was not like Pennsylvania in its open refusal to help; its attitude was one of indifference, which was partly due to niggardliness, and partly to the fact that it was safely screened by the colonies of Pennsylvania and Virginia. The latter colony has been severely blamed for the ineffective assistance rendered during the war. It is urged with truth that the inhabitants consisted of the very men who should have composed a fine fighting force, but that the Virginian youth exhibited an astounding supineness in following the gallant Washington. There are, however, two reasons that may be found as partial excuses for the unpatriotic attitude of the Virginian settlers. The first was an ever-present dread of a slave insurrection if the militia left the colony; while the second is to be found in the irascible temper of the governor, Robert Dinwiddie.

The year after the Treaty of Aix-la-Chapelle, the French governor of Canada, La Galissonière, had sent Celeron de Bienville to register the claims of France to the Ohio valley, and thus carry on the great scheme of shutting in the English settlers behind the Alleghany Mountains. The demonstration was purely peaceful, and for the next three years nothing serious came of it. Galissonière resigned his government to De la Jonquière, who, in turn, was succeeded by the Marquis Duquesne. In the meantime, in 1750, the Virginian traders, for the most part, had formed the Ohio Company for the exploiting of that rich valley. The work of this corporation was not of a successful character, owing to the jealousies between Virginia and Pennsylvania, both colonies trying to shift the burden of fort building on to the shoulders of the other. The French, seeing their opportunity, began to teach these bickering colonials those bitter lessons which were at last to be an indirect cause of their union. In June of 1752, the Miami Indians, a confederacy friendly towards the English, were attacked; their town was burnt, and their chief killed. This was not a mere raid upon an insignificant group of Redskins' wigwams, but was the outward and visible sign of the aggressive policy of Duquesne towards the advanced English traders in the Ohio valley. In the spring of the next year, a veteran French officer, Marin, established, by means of two forts, communication between the Great Lakes and the sources of the Ohio. This, indeed, was a direct act of trespass upon that debatable land lying on the borders of Virginia, Pennsylvania, and Maryland, and was a heavy blow at the Ohio Company and their trading station at Fort Cumberland. The French intrusion aroused the wrath of William Shirley of Massachusetts, and also of the cross-grained Governor Dinwiddie, of Virginia. Ill-tempered though the latter was, he possessed clear judgment and tenacity of purpose, and from this moment worked strenuously for the welfare of the colonies against the French.

In November 1753, George Washington, then a young land-surveyor, but already fairly prominent among the Virginians, was despatched to warn off the French trespassers. He found that what had formerly been an English trading station at Venango had been converted into a French Canadian outpost. Resistance was obviously necessary; and Dinwiddie embarked upon a zealous military policy, calling upon the Governors of Massachusetts, New York, New Jersey, Pennsylvania, Maryland, and the

Carolinas to assist in preventing the Governor of Canada becoming the master of the valley of the Ohio. Virginia responded cheerfully to the Governor's appeal, and subscribed £10,000; North Carolina gave a small sum and sent a few soldiers; South Carolina and New York also sent a contingent of militiamen; but Pennsylvania refused both men and money. Dinwiddie did what he could by despatching, in February 1754, a small force to build a blockhouse at the junction of the Monongahela and the Alleghany Rivers. The settlers were overpowered by the Canadians in April, and the fort which was erected was the work of French hands, and was called after the Canadian Governor, Fort Duquesne. With a party of Virginians, Washington was ordered to take this fresh example of Canadian insolence, then under the command of Contrecœur. His lieutenant, Jumonville, was killed in a sortie or scouting expedition, but even with this advantage Washington's little army was outnumbered. He was forced to retreat, first to Fort Necessity, and after a nine hours' fight, across the Alleghany Mountains.

The campaign of 1754 had been utterly disastrous for the English settlers, but it only encouraged the indefatigable Robert Dinwiddie to further efforts. He saw that "if the misfortune attending our forces has aroused the spirit of our neighbouring colonies, it has done more than probably a victory could have effected" [283]. He now did his best to still further arouse the united enthusiasm of the Middle and Southern colonies, and so stirred the Assembly of Virginia that it voted £20,000. The defeat of Washington also gave a stimulus to a movement towards unity that had already been made in the autumn of 1753. The delegates of the seven colonies of Massachusetts, New Hampshire, Rhode Island, New Jersey, New York, Pennsylvania, and Maryland, had met in friendly conference at Albany, and had listened to Benjamin Franklin's great scheme of union, under which a colonial Council of forty-eight members was to be formed, each colony supplying members according to its population. This Council was to have very important powers and privileges, including those of declaring peace or war. Had Franklin's statesmanlike proposals met with the general acceptance of the colonies, North America would have become one great self- governing community, having more independent powers

The Climax: The Struggle Between English and French Colonists 193

than any of the present-day colonies of Great Britain. The time, however, was not yet ripe; the colonies were still too jealous of their own petty rights and privileges; and those who were acting for the welfare of the English in America did not at the moment wish to rush into some great revolutionary change in the constitution, but desired rather a firm attitude of resistance to the French aggressions in the Ohio valley. Dinwiddie found the task difficult enough. He wrote to the Governor of Pennsylvania that the colonies "seemed satisfied to leave the French at full liberty to perpetrate their utmost designs to their ruin" [284]. But he did not despair, and asked help from New York, Pennsylvania, Maryland, and the Carolinas, and received encouraging replies from all the governors, except Glen of South Carolina. In his excellent work he was ably supported by William Shirley of Massachusetts, who, at this time, was working strenuously to stir the home government to realise the danger that threatened the Thirteen Colonies.

The combined efforts of these two men were not in vain; and although there was peace in Europe, two regiments were sent out under Major-General Braddock in January 1755. Edward Braddock has been the subject of much controversy; his character has been torn to pieces by different historians, and certainly the records point to a man of a curious combination of magnanimity and brutality. When in command at Gibraltar, he was adored by his men; whereas in America, Horace Walpole speaks of him as "a very Iroquois" [285]. William Shirley, son of the Governor of Massachusetts, said "We have a general most judiciously chosen for being disqualified for the service he is employed in, in almost every respect" [286]. This view is upheld by Burke, who wrote of him as "abounding too much in his own sense for the degree of military knowledge he possessed" [287]. It is, however, extremely doubtful if the terrible disaster associated with his name can be entirely attributed to the general's own personal character, and recent writers have shown that the charge of utter incompetence cannot be satisfactorily sustained [288].

Braddock's forces landed at Hampton, Virginia, in February 1755; and a colonial conference was at once held at Alexandria. This important meeting was attended by six of the colonial governors, including the most patriotic and energetic, Dinwiddie, Shirley, and Sharpe. They concluded that four practically simultaneous expeditions should be made against the French. The English general was to march against Fort Duquesne; two forces were to converge on Crown Point from a base of operations at Albany; while the fourth effort, under Shirley, was to be made against the French conspirators in Acadia.

The English regiments, the 44th and 48th, were reinforced by two hundred and fifty Virginian rangers, and by small detachments from New York, Maryland, and the Carolinas. The force supplied by the wealthy colony of Virginia was utterly inadequate; while Pennsylvania, as usual, sent no aid in the way of troops, and only voted a sum of money to be collected with such difficulty that it was practically valueless. George Washington, at that time recovering from a severe illness, was requested by Braddock to accompany him as one of his aide-de-camps. After a series of delays, on July 3rd Braddock unexpectedly fell in with a French force under Beaujeu on the right bank of the river Monongahela, about eight miles from Fort Duquesne. The majority of the enemy were Indians trained to forest fighting, while the English, accustomed to European methods, fought in a solid mass, their red coats affording an excellent target for their invisible foes. Braddock fought with heroic perseverance; four horses were shot under him, and it was only when he saw the approaching failure of the ammunition, and that his men were exhibiting distinct signs of panic, that he gave the order to retreat. At that moment he was mortally wounded. "I cannot describe the horror of that scene," wrote Lieutenant Leslie of the 44th, three weeks after the battle: "no pen could do it. The yell of the Indians is fresh on my ear, and the terrific sound will haunt me to the hour of my dissolution" [289]. The disaster was immediately attributed to the incompetence of Braddock. The colonials naturally praised the conduct of the Virginian detachment, the members of which had had the common-sense to conceal themselves behind trees, and fought the Indians after their own methods. Thus Washington wrote: "The Virginia companies behaved like men and died like soldiers;" [290] but there can be no doubt that Washington and other settlers were prejudiced against the English general and were filled with contempt for his scheme of fighting. They never took into consideration that Braddock's failure was partly due to the delay caused by the quarrels between Pennsylvania and Virginia, and partly owing to the utterly worthless horses supplied to him by the colonial authorities for his transports. Where Braddock's great mistake lay was in the belief that "it was better to be defeated in conformity with orthodox methods than to win by conduct which seemed lacking in courage, and by imitating the hitherto unknown tactics of colonials and barbarians" [291].

Dinwiddie, with that same wonderful energy which he had displayed during the whole of this anxious epoch, did his best to mitigate the harm done by the terrible disaster. He realised clearly what Washington pointed out to him, "the consequences that this defeat may have upon our back settlers" [292]. He again sent frantic appeals to the Governors of Massachusetts, New Jersey, New York, Pennsylvania, Maryland, and North Carolina. The apathy, at this time, of the Middle and Southern colonies was extraordinary; and "while sleek Quakers and garrulous Assembly men prated of peace and local liberties, the outlying settlements were given over to fire and sword" [293]. The New England States were, however, more energetic; and on the northern frontier an attempt was being made by Shirley and William Johnson to put into execution the other schemes arranged by the colonial conference. William Johnson was a man who had lived a semi-savage life and who had gained remarkable influence over the Iroquois, particularly the Mohawks. Governor Shirley had recognised this man's gifts, and had appointed him commander of the Massachusetts, New England, and New York levies, consisting of about 6000 men. In the early summer of 1755 Johnson rapidly constructed Fort Lyman, and in August moved slowly forward to the southern extremity of Lake George, with the intention of taking Crown Point. The French, hearing of these warlike preparations, despatched Baron Dieskau to Ticonderoga; he marched still farther south and cut off Johnson's communications with his recently constructed fort. At first the French cleverly ambuscaded a party of the English, but in an assault upon Johnson's camp they were defeated, Dieskau being wounded and taken prisoner. The results of the fight were of some slight importance, as the capture of the leader and the repulse of his men were regarded in England

and the colonies as some compensation for the disaster of General Braddock. Johnson was rewarded with a baronetcy and £5000; the little camp was converted into Fort William Henry; and the lake, hitherto known as the Lac du Sacrament, was rechristened, in honour of the King, Lake George. On the other hand, the object of the expedition, Crown Point, remained in the hands of the French, and their possibilities of aggrandisement in the West were still as illimitable as they ever had been.

The two other campaigns of 1755 were under the superintendence of Governor Shirley. In June he sent two thousand men of Massachusetts to Acadia. Their commander was the much- respected John Winslow; and by his assistance the English at last defeated the machinations of the French under De Loutre. Governor Laurence, however, was forced to take strong measures to preserve peace, and deported the intriguing and disloyal Acadians to Massachusetts, Virginia, South Carolina, and elsewhere. His action has been severely criticised and the story has been depicted in words of horror by the poet Longfellow. The expulsion of these "men whose lives glided on like rivers" was, as a matter of fact, absolutely essential for the welfare of the English nation in Nova Scotia. Winslow, who assisted in the work of deportation, recognised the necessity although he disliked the action; but he carried out his orders with the greatest humanity that could be shown under exceptionally difficult circumstances. Meantime, Shirley's second expedition, though commanded by himself, was not so successful. His troops were composed for the most part of colonials paid by the British Government. His object of attack was Fort Niagara, a place of considerable danger to the trading station at Oswego, and one of the main connecting links between Canada and the south-west. The season grew late; the troops were delayed by unexpected obstructions; and towards the end of October, having reinforced Oswego, Shirley found it better to retire.

The campaigns of 1755 had proved most unsatisfactory for the colonists. The southern confines of Virginia continued to be harried, although Washington and his little band, for the most part composed of Ulster Protestants, did what they could to preserve peace along the border-line. In much the same way the frontiers of New England were open to attack, and French animosity was by no means decreased by the skilled scouting expeditions of Robert Rogers and his bold New England rangers. The only great achievement was in Acadia, a province of more value to Great Britain than to the settlers of any particular colony. The French had not only succeeded in remaining in the coveted valley of the Ohio, but had also repulsed with enormous loss a general of some repute, which brought with it the much-desired Indian alliance. Along the shores of the Great Lakes no practical advantages had been gained; and Johnson's victory at Lake George brought rewards to the individual rather than to the New Englanders as a community. The Puritan colonists, however, came out of these campaigns with an enhanced reputation; they were distinguished from their southern brethren by a readiness to sacrifice both men and money in a great imperial cause.

In the early spring of 1756, war in Europe had not yet been declared, but border skirmishes still continued unabated in the distant West. The main effect on the colonies of the declaration of the Seven Years' War, on May 11th, was an increase in the number of regular troops sent to America. These were largely supplemented by the colonial militia and by colonial royal regiments in the pay of the Crown. Before the arrival of the regulars, the French again began their raids, and, under De Lery, captured Fort Bull, thus threatening the more important neighbouring station of Oswego. Shirley at once despatched Colonel Brodstreet with supplies and reinforcements to the traders at that fort, and for the moment baulked the Canadians. But by this time, a greater than De Lery had been sent to America, in the person of the Marquis de Montcalm, who immediately undertook the capture of Oswego. For this purpose, in July, he started from Ticonderoga, and by August 10th was in close proximity to the doomed blockhouse. The powerful artillery of the French, together with the cunning tactics of their native allies, forced Oswego to surrender after its commander, Colonel Mercer, had been killed. This success was invaluable to the French, for as Braddock's defeat had given to New France the Ohio valley, so now Montcalm's victory made her undisputed mistress of the Great Lakes.

The man who had done this great work may be regarded as the French hero of the Seven Years' War. The Marquis de Montcalm was by this time forty-four years of age, and had gained his military experience on many European battlefields. He owed his command to his own intrinsic merits and not, like so many French generals, to the influences of Court mistresses. He was a gentleman of France; a man of impetuous spirit, but possessed of many lovable characteristics; he was kind, tolerant, and gentle, and yet one of the sternest of soldiers. Owing to his ability and energy, his chivalrous courage and kindliness of manner, he was a leader who not only had his men under perfect discipline, but was also endeared to them by those very sterling qualities which they fully recognised. He hated corruption, cheating, and lying; he detested the brutality of many of his companions; and although Wolfe said that "Montcalm has changed the very nature of war, and has forced us ... to a deterring and dreadful vengeance," [294] yet in reality he did his best to lift the war from mere butchery and murder on to the higher plane of civilised methods. Montcalm, Marquis of the Château de Candiac, gave his life to an ungrateful country, which repaid him for his sacrifice by cruel and unjust charges.

To oppose so good an officer the English Government selected the unsatisfactory leaders, Colonel Daniel Webb, dilatory in taking action, General Abercromby, in Wolfe's opinion "a heavy man," and the Earl of Loudoun, who lacked tact in his treatment of the settlers, and quickness in his command of troops. To add to the English errors, the home authorities recalled Shirley, who had given up the best of his life to sturdily resisting French aggrandisement. Fortunately the colonial forces were not without their own leaders, in many instances men of merit, such as William Johnson, friend of the Mohawks, John Winslow, famous for his Acadian experiences, Colonel Brodstreet, a good and dashing soldier, and, above all, that daring and clearheaded Prince of Rangers, Robert Rogers of New Hampshire.

The individual settlers were brave and true, but the year 1757 opened with the same petty and local quarrels in the colonial Assemblies, chiefly in Pennsylvania and New York, in the former concerning the everlasting squabble about taxing the proprietors' land, in the latter on the question of billeting. The Earl of Loudoun, though his position had given him some weight and authority in the factious Assembly of New York, failed to win the respect or goodwill of the colonial forces. They doubted his capacity, and blamed him in particular for his mismanagement of what ought to have been the crisis of the war. Ever since the restoration of Louisburg by the Treaty of Aix-la-Chapelle, the settlers had been anxious to again seize that key of the St Lawrence. Loudoun recognised the importance of such an action, and, in conjunction with Admiral Holborne, in August and September endeavoured either to take the fortification, or at least to tempt the French fleet into a pitched battle. That Loudoun was unsuccessful in both schemes was partly due to those delays that have left deep stains upon colonial history, and partly because the elements warred against the British, and Admiral Holborne's fleet being shattered by storms, the expedition had necessarily to be abandoned.

Meantime Montcalm had again displayed his activity; and while Loudoun was engaged in his abortive attempts on Louisburg, the colonies received a severe blow by the loss of Fort William Henry. Towards the end of 1756, the French had made an attack upon this fort, but had been repulsed. Throughout the following July, Montcalm massed his troops at Ticonderoga, and with Lévis, his second in command, and La Corne, a noted Canadian irregular, arrived before Fort William Henry on the 4th August. General Webb ought to have pushed forward to its relief, but he felt himself too weak to cope with Montcalm's army of regulars and Indian allies. For four days the defenders made a gallant struggle; and on August 9th only capitulated on the terms of safe-conduct to Fort Edward. The Indians refused to recognise those terms, and fell upon the English. A massacre ensued, horrible in character and of revolting details, though possibly these may have been exaggerated by lapse of years. It is thought that Montcalm and Lévis did what they could to preserve order, but were unable to prevent the many coldblooded murders because of the utter indifference of the French Canadian officers, who had been hardened in the terrible school of border and Indian warfare.

The French had now reached the high-water mark of their triumph in the West; but in Europe the dawn of better things for the English people had already come, for the king had been forced to place William Pitt in office. An end was now to be put to all the dilatory conduct either of the home authorities or of the colonial Assemblies. A man had been found to save England and the Empire. Pitt's plans were not original; they had been tried before; but they were at last to succeed because proper effort was made, and able generals instead of incompetents were sent out, and chiefly because behind all was the man who inspired with his own glorious spirit every one with whom he came in contact. On December 30, 1757, Pitt addressed a letter to the Governors of the Thirteen Colonies, who cheerfully responded by raising a substantial force.

General James Wolfe from the picture by Schaak in the National Portrait Gallery.

The first expedition—in which the colonials were not employed—was the capture of Louisburg. The possession of this fortress on Cape Breton Island by the English would ensure the starvation of the Canadians, who were at this time, practically without food. The men chosen for the work were Admiral Boscawen, a hard fighter and typical English seaman; General Jeffrey Amherst, a good but cautious soldier; and three others, Whitmore, Laurence, and General James Wolfe, of "whom the youngest was the most noteworthy," [295] and whose name is so famously connected with the story of the British in North America.

James Wolfe was born in Kent in 1727. When most modern boys are still at school, he was adjutant of his regiment, and took part in the Battle of Dettingen. He then went through the arduous campaign necessitated by the Jacobite Rising of 1745. At twenty-five years of age he found himself a full colonel. There can be little doubt that he was possessed of many ennobling qualities, but his appearance was much against him, as his face, with its pointed nose and receding forehead and chin, resembled very closely the flap of an envelope. His figure was loose and ungainly, and though over six feet in height, he lacked the smart appearance of the military man. As a soldier he showed the greatest enthusiasm in everything connected with his profession; he worked hard at mathematics, tactics, and strategy, and did his best to perfect himself in the French language. The records of this man's life go to prove that he won the affection and regard of every one, and that he was almost worshipped in the different places in which he was quartered. He never, however, lost his good sense, never became puffed up with pride, never thought himself greater than others. His gallantry in the unfortunate enterprise against Rochefort in January 1758 had come to the notice of the great Pitt, and it was for this reason that he was chosen to accompany Amherst in the attempt to capture the "Dunkirk of America."

Boscawen's fleet with the transports containing the army came in sight of Louisburg in June. Since the capture of the fort by the Massachusetts militia in 1745, something had been done to strengthen its walls, and it was now regarded in Europe as impregnable, though it was probably not so formidable as it looked, since Drucour afterwards referred to it as "crumbling down in every flank, face, and courtine, except the right flank of the king's bastion, which was remounted the first year after my arrival" [296]. A town of about four thousand inhabitants nestled in false security beneath the apparently [297] massive walls; but it was of little good for them to imagine that assistance could reach them from France, for the British navy made it impossible for her to send soldiers or supplies. The English force was at last landed, and batteries were at once erected under the distinguished guidance of Wolfe. These fortified entrenchments were moved day by day nearer the doomed stronghold. The guns never ceased to bombard the wretched town that had once considered itself so secure. Within the harbour were eleven French men-of-war, but soon four of these were deliberately sunk at the mouth of the harbour by Drucour, while the rest were driven on shore or captured by a cutting-out expedition. On the 20th of July, Wolfe had erected his last battery; an enormous shell was sent into the chapel of the town, and a fearful explosion occurred. On the 27th the French, under their Governor, Drucour, were forced to capitulate, and Amherst and Wolfe entered the fortress in triumph. Shortly afterwards the vast fortifications were razed to the ground, and to this day there remains nothing save some few ruined casements and huge, grass-grown stones, lying in dismantled heaps upon the edge of the restless Atlantic, to mark the spot where once stood one of the great triumphs of Vauban's engineering art.

 The news that Louisburg had fallen was received with every expression of joy in all the colonies, and even the Quakers, who could not fight themselves, gave way to the general outburst and showed suitable signs of rapture at the victory of British arms. The news came at a moment when such glad tidings were sadly needed, for only three weeks before the colonies had been plunged into despair by the horrors of a great tragedy. General Abercromby, with a large force of regulars and colonials, had set out from Albany in May, and after tedious delays had come on July 5th to within striking distance of Ticonderoga. In a skirmish, two days before the great fight, Lord Howe, the most beloved of the British officers, was killed. On July 7th Montcalm with Lévis hurriedly erected a palisade of pines with their branches outward about half a mile from the actual fort. The English general most foolishly did not bring up his guns, fearing lest they should impede his progress. On the morning of July 8 the assault began upon this palisade manned by the trained marksmen of Canada; regiment after regiment of the English were ordered to their annihilation. The Black Watch, for example, went into action about a thousand strong; they straggled out of that awful Gehenna with only half their numbers. At last, having thrown away the lives of two thousand men, Abercromby ordered the retreat, and left Montcalm for the third time the victor.

Amongst the men who fell in that disastrous expedition, no one was so honestly mourned as Lord Howe. Pitt spoke of him as "a complete model of military virtue in all its branches," [298] but these words in no way summed up the character of one who was not only beloved by the English Army, but also by every man in the colonial contingent. Wolfe himself wrote, "if the report of Howe's death be true, there is an end of the expedition, for he was the spirit of that army, and the very best officer in the King's service" [299]. It was in winning the goodwill, respect, and admiration of the settlers that Howe differed so remarkably from his fellow officers. Burke writes of him, "from the moment he landed in America he had wisely conformed and made his regiment conform to the kind of service which the country required" [300]. In other words, he acted in a manner which would have caused Braddock to shudder; but it was the right thing to do. The long-tailed tunic of the British regular, his wonderful pigtail, his buttons and smart points were ruthlessly cut off because they were in the way. He dressed his men as nearly as possible like the colonials, for he it was who for the first time recognised that from them the English might gain experience in this new and strange warfare. He learnt much from men like Rogers the Ranger; and he taught much.

Had Lord Howe and James Wolfe been spared to give more of their short lives to the American people, the later history of the Thirteen Colonies must have been very different.

As a set-off to the Ticonderoga disaster, two great victories marked the last six months of 1758. Colonel Bradstreet, in August, with a small portion of Abercromby's army, took Fort Frontenac, thus temporarily cutting off the communication between the French in the Ohio forts with those on the upper lakes. Besides this, Bradstreet was able to destroy the presents collected for the Western Indians and all the winter provisions for Fort Duquesne. These facts considerably assisted General Forbes, who was no less successful in his undertaking. He had to contend against the squabbles of Virginia and Pennsylvania, but he managed to get both men and money. With a force of about six thousand, for the most part settlers from the southern states, but also including a Highland regiment, he set out for Fort Duquesne. His first attack was repulsed; but in November on again advancing he found that the French commander De Ligneries had been obliged, owing to Indian desertions, to evacuate and destroy the fort. A stockade was at once erected by the English to take the place of the once formidable French fortress, and was now christened by the old general, in honour of his master, Pittsburg.

The year 1759 is called "the year of victories," and one of the chief of these was the capture of Quebec. With the actual struggle for the possession of the capital of New France, the colonials had little or nothing to do; the work was entirely that of the British sailors and soldiers. The expedition against Quebec, however, was only a part of a general plan of attack upon Canada, and in this the settlers showed some activity under the leadership of the Commander-in-Chief General Amherst. In May, acting under Amherst's orders, General Prideaux, with two regiments and a small body of colonials, joined Sir William Johnson and his Mohawks at Schenectady. The plan of campaign was that this force should move forward to Fort Niagara, then commanded by Pouchot, and if possible drive out the French. Prideaux's force was quite sufficient for this, but his lack of skill seems to have delayed the surrender of the fort. On July 20 Prideaux was killed and the command devolved upon the more fiery Johnson, who first marched out and defeated a large French reinforcement, and then returned to receive Pouchet's surrender. The capitulation of Niagara was of considerable importance, as from that moment the French were debarred from exercising any influence on the lower lakes. Burke says that it "broke off effectually that communication so much talked of and so much dreaded between Canada and Louisiana" [301]. Meanwhile Amherst advanced north with a large force composed for the most part of regulars. In July he reached the deserted fort of Ticonderoga; on August 1 he found Crown Point abandoned. From this position Amherst ought to have hurried forward to the assistance of Wolfe at Quebec, but he suddenly directed his energies into wrong channels, and instead of pushing forward, employed his army in cutting paths and roads during the whole of August and September. The exertions of Robert Rogers and his New England Rangers has alone saved the expedition from contempt. Amherst lost his opportunity, and instead of being the Conqueror of Canada, by sheer sloth and lack of energy he allowed another man to do the work and win immortal glory on the Heights of Abraham.

James Wolfe had returned to England after the capture of Louisburg, but Pitt had other work for him to do, and he was dispatched to undertake the siege of Quebec. His immediate subordinates were Townshend, Monckton, Murray, and Carleton. The men who were to oppose him in this great undertaking were Montcalm and the incapable Vaudreuil, with Bougainville, upon whom his senior maliciously placed all the blame. In June 1759, Wolfe, supported by a strong naval contingent, sailed up the St Lawrence to the attack of Quebec. The town, steep and precipitous, frowned defiance upon the English; all along the Beauport shore was one vast camp, any path being strongly guarded, and the whole ridge being one long extended earthwork. Montcalm knew his business. If he could but keep Wolfe out until the winter months had come, he felt convinced that the expedition must fail. The English general, on the other hand, longed to tempt the French regulars and Canadian militia out of their snug position and beat them in open ground. In vain Wolfe established a battery upon the Ile d'Orleans, opposite to Quebec, and shattered the lower part of the town. Night after night the countryside was lighted by the fires of farmsteads and barns which were answered back by the flashing fires of Lower Quebec in flames. Nothing would tempt Montcalm to come out. His position was enormously strong, for his flank was protected by the rushing falls of Montmorency. It was at the foot of these that Wolfe made his first serious attempt on July 31, which proved a failure, not for want of bravery, but because of the rash behaviour of the grenadiers. To the astonishment of the general and his officers, the grenadiers had no sooner landed than without orders they tried to rush the hill. They clambered over the rocks, fought their way through bushes and thickets, and were then suddenly met with a withering fire from the French above them. A rain-storm came on at the moment and the army below stood petrified. The rain ceased almost as quickly as it had begun, and the cliffside was seen to be strewn with the redcoats; and worse, the Indians had rushed out and were wreaking their vengeance by their awful custom of scalping.

This success of Montcalm did not tempt him to leave his position and make an attack upon the English. The latter were now for a short time to lose all hope, for the news passed rapidly through the army that their beloved general was at the point of death owing to an incurable complaint from which he had long suffered. His indomitable spirit, however, overcame his sufferings, and rousing himself he once more spent his time gazing carefully at the beetling cliffs. On the 2nd of September he had found what he wanted and determined to start upon what seemed to him somewhat of a forlorn hope, but which was destined to form one of the most glorious pages in British history.

A path had been discovered up the cliffside—the path disclosed seventy years before to Phipps—at the top there was a small guard and nothing more. On the night of the great venture the boats slipped quietly down the river, and as the French were expecting a convoy of provisions two sentries let them go by after a first challenge. Wolfe, sitting in the stem of one of the boats, was murmuring in a solemn whisper the beautiful lines of Grey's Elegy:—

> "The boast of heraldry, the pomp of power, and all that beauty, all that wealth e'er gave, Await alike th' inevitable hour;
> The paths of glory lead but to the grave" [302].
>
> "Gentlemen," said he, "I would sooner have written that poem than take Quebec."

The Climax: The Struggle Between English and French Colonists 207

The death of General Wolfe. After the painting by B. West.

    The landing was successfully accomplished, the guard at the top was overpowered, and before Montcalm knew that the English had left their camp, four thousand five hundred men were standing in that "thin red line" upon the Heights of Abraham. The gallant Montcalm did what he could, and with surprising energy collected his troops and led them against the English. The French fired time and again upon Wolfe's men, but they stolidly awaited their advance until they could see the whites of their eyes and then let loose upon them a withering fire. The white coats of the French regulars and the gay costumes of the French Canadian trappers were ready targets and they reeled and fell. Wolfe then ordered the assault, and with a second volley the whole army charged, Wolfe leading his grenadiers. After receiving a slight wound, a fatal bullet singled out that gallant man, and he fell, unnoticed for the moment save by four of his officers, who tenderly carried him to the rear of the advancing host. "They run! They run!" cried one of the officers. "Who run?" said Wolfe. "The French," they replied. "God be praised, I die in peace."

Montcalm was also mortally wounded, and just before the city actually capitulated he passed away, happy that he should not witness the surrender. Montcalm, like Wolfe, was a hero and a patriot, but whereas Wolfe gained the love and everlasting memory of a grateful country and Empire, Montcalm's name was dragged down by unworthy men who never understood his burning zeal, who had none of his ambition for a glorious French Empire in the West. Wolfe's "star had only just arisen. For a moment something like a cloud seemed to have obscured its very dawn; when suddenly bursting like a meteor across the whole horizon of war and politics, it vanished amid a blaze of glory as splendid in a sense and as lasting as that of Nelson himself. It seemed, in truth, as if a great leader had been found and lost in a single moon" [303].

General Murray was left in command of Quebec to pass one of the most trying winters ever undergone by a garrison which was without proper clothing or supplies. At no great distance was a very capable leader, Lévis, plotting to recover the city, which he very nearly succeeded in doing, by defeating Murray outside the walls at the battle of St Foy, on April 28, 1760. The French general, however, lost his opportunity by not striking at the city itself when the garrison was confused by the defeat. Murray was saved by the timely appearance of the British fleet on May 15, and Lévis retreated. All that was now left to be done to complete the conquest of Canada and the salvation of the Thirteen Colonies from French attack was a final advance upon Montreal. Murray was the first to make a move in July; while Haviland advanced down the Richelieu River with three thousand five hundred men, including Rogers and his New Englanders. Amherst's army had already collected at Schenectady, but its progress was retarded by the slow arrival of the colonial contingent of about five thousand men. The forces at last combined before Montreal; and on September 8, just a year after Wolfe's splendid victory, the last stronghold of New France capitulated to the combined forces of England and the Thirteen Colonies.

According to Lord Chesterfield the acquisition of Canada cost the English nation four score millions. No one at the present day can think that the possession of the great Dominion, then regarded as "a few acres of snow," was not worth twenty times the sum. By the Treaty of Paris, 1763, Louis XV. ceded "in full right Canada with all its dependencies, as well as the island of Cape Breton and all other islands and coasts in the gulf and river of St Lawrence." The French had done their best, ever since the great voyage of Jacques Cartier in 1534, to build up a new French Empire in the West. They had failed, partly because of the fallacious principles of the French colonial system, but particularly for two reasons. The first was the absolute exclusion of the Huguenots, whereby the Canadians shut out the very people who would have made the Empire rich and strong; and the second reason was because their dreams were too diffuse, too magnificent, beyond the physical capacity of so small a nation. They proposed to shut within narrow limits a nation twenty times as large in population, far more energetic and industrious, and one which would by the laws of nature overflow into those very valleys and happy hunting-grounds that they had marked out for themselves.

What, then, was the effect of the capture of Canada upon the settlers of the Thirteen Colonies? We stand at the parting of the ways. The Treaty of Paris not only marked the increase of the British dominions beyond the seas, but also carried within it the germ of the future schism within the British Empire. Several of the Thirteen Colonies had for many years been filled with "a spirit of independence, puritan in religion, and republican in politics" [304]. Ever since the seventeenth century the people of Massachusetts had kicked against the pricks of the Navigation Act. The danger from the north and the west had undoubtedly had a repressive influence upon the colonists, and had kept them subservient to the English colonial system, which they hated and which was in reality at the root of their disaffection. The Peace of Paris removed all danger from Spain in the south, while the French danger was removed by the victory of Wolfe; and the rising colonies felt themselves as a new race about to start some great venture. They were (they knew it themselves, and the French recognised it most clearly) absolutely free to choose their future. The sagacious Vergennes predicted events that actually occurred. "England," he said, "will soon repent of having removed the only check that could keep her colonies in awe. They stand no longer in need of her protection. She will call on them to contribute towards supporting the burdens they have helped to bring on her, and they will answer by striking off all dependence" [305]. The defeat of New France meant the possibilities of a new nation in the Western hemisphere; and Old France revenged herself for the loss of her would-be Empire by throwing in her lot with those aforetime jealous and jarring Thirteen States. Old France, therefore, though she knew her own Empire was gone, largely assisted to create the new nation, the new people, the United States of America. The Thirteen Colonies had scarcely been taught the lessons of unity by the horrors of Indian barbarities and the French border war; but so much as they had learnt they tried to put into practice at the first Philadelphian Congress, and at the time of the Declaration of Independence. The Treaty of Paris, one of the most important of all colonial treaties, was merely the forerunner of that other great Treaty of Versailles; the former gave to us the vast area now known as the Dominion of Canada; the latter marked the disappearance of England's Thirteen Colonies, and the creation of the United States of America. It would not have been any very great or wonderful prophecy for a statesman, after the Treaty of Paris, to have foretold the rise of that new nation which has grown with such marvellous strides; and it would not have been inappropriate for him to have used the words of the poet in which to describe this great evolution, and say, "Methinks, I see in my mind a noble and puissant nation, rousing herself as a strong man after sleep, and shaking her invincible locks. Methinks I see her like an eagle viewing her mighty youth and kindling her undazzled eyes at the full midday beam."

Chapter 13

CHRONOLOGY OF COLONIAL HISTORY

1492.   First voyage of Columbus.

1496.   Charter to John and Sebastian Cabot.

1497.   John and Sebastian Cabot discover Newfoundland.

1498.   The second voyage of the Cabots.

1500.   Gaspar Corte Real sailed to Newfoundland.

1501.   Gaspar Corte Real wrecked in Chesapeake Bay.

1502.   Miguel Corte Real sailed to search for his brother.

1506.   Denys of Harfleur reached the Gulf of St Lawrence.

1508.   Aubert of Dieppe brought American Indians to France.

1523.   Verrazano sent out by Francis I.

1524.   Verrazano sailed along the coast of North America.

1527.	John Rut and Albert de Prado sailed to Newfoundland.
1534.	Jacques Cartier of St Malo sailed to the St Lawrence.
1535.	Jacques Cartier's second voyage. He reached Stadacona.
1536.	Master Hore was wrecked on Newfoundland.
1541-42.	Cartier's third voyage, joined by De Roberval.
1553.	Voyages of Sir Hugh Willoughby and Richard Chancellor.
1562.	Jean Ribault's expedition to Florida.
1564-65.	René de Laudonniere sailed to the Carolinas.
1565.	The French settlement destroyed by the Spaniard Menendez.
1576.	Martin Frobisher's first voyage.
1577.	Martin Frobisher's second voyage, and discovery of Meta Incognita.
1577-80.	Drake's voyage round the world.
1578.	Martin Frobisher's third voyage.
	Grant of a patent for colonisation to Sir Humphrey Gilbert.
1583.	Newfoundland claimed as an English colony.
1584.	Sir Walter Raleigh sends out Captains Amidas and Barlow.

Chronology of Colonial History 213

1585.   Raleigh's first Virginian colony.

1586.   The colonists brought back by Drake.

1587.   Raleigh's second attempt.

1589.   First edition of Hakluyt's Voyages published.

1598.   Second and complete edition of Hakluyts Voyages.

           Marquis de la Roche attempts to found a convict settlement.

1599.   Chauvin and Pontgravé attempt a settlement at Tadoussac.

1602.   De Chastes obtains the services of Samuel Champlain.

           Bartholomew Gosnold makes a voyage to the West.

1603.   The voyage of the Discovery and the Speedwell to America.

           De la Roche's settlers rescued from Sable Island.

           Samuel Champlain sailed up the St Lawrence.

           De Monts otained a patent to colonise Acadia.

1604.   De Chastes joined to De Monts and established Port Royal.

1605.   Samuel Champlain remained the winter in Acadia.

1606.	Relief arrived. The expedition included Lescarbot, the historian.
	The formation of the London and Plymouth Companies.
1607.	The foundation of Jamestown, Virginia.
	Popham and Gilbert's expedition to the Kennebec.
1608.	Champlain founded Quebec.
1609.	Champlain discovered Lake Champlain.
	Claude Etienne and Charles de la Tour settled on the Penobscot.
	Sir George Somers and Sir Thomas Gates sail for Virginia.
1610.	Lord De La Warr governor of Virginia.
1611.	Sir Thomas Gates governor of Virginia.
1613.	Marriage of Pocahontas to John Rolfe.
	Champlain and de Vignau follow the course of the Ottawa.
1614.	Samuel Argall sacked Port Royal in Acadia.
	Captain John Smith made a voyage to New England.
1615.	Champlain and Le Caron came to Lake Huron.
1616.	The Recollet missionaries settled in Canada.

1619.	Sir George Yeardley governor of Virginia.
1620.	Reorganisation of the New England Company.
	The voyage of the Mayflower and establishment of New Plymouth.
1621.	Sir William Alexander obtained a patent to colonise Acadia.
1622.	Sir Robert Gordon attempted to settle Cape Breton Island.
1623.	James I. demanded the surrender of the charter of the London Company.
	A fishing station at Cape Ann, Massachusetts.
	Levitt established a settlement on Casco Bay, Maine.
1625.	Jesuit missionaries first came to Canada.
1626.	Definite settlement of the Dutch on Manhattan Island.
1627.	Death of Sir George Yeardley. Harvey governor of Virginia.
	Richelieu establishes the Company of the One Hundred Associates.
1628.	David Kirke destroyed the French fleet in the St Lawrence.
1629.	David Kirke captured Quebec.

Sir Robert Heath received a grant of land south of Virginia.

The establishment of Massachusetts.

1630. Winthrop established Boston.

La Tour made governor of Acadia.

1631. Arrival of Roger Williams in Massachusetts.

Lord Saye and Sele and Lord Brooke obtain land on the Connecticut.

Sir Ferdinando Gorges formed a company for colonising Maine.

1632. Grant of Maryland to Lord Baltimore.

Treaty of St Germain-en-Laye, by which Quebec was restored to the French.

1634. Champlain built a fort at Three Rivers.

1635. Champlain died.

Maine granted to Sir Ferdinando Gorges.

Captain John Mason established New Hampshire. Foundation of Providence by Roger Williams. Winthrop, the younger, governor of Connecticut.

Harry Vane, Mrs Anne Hutchinson, and John Wheelwright come to Massachusetts.

The Pequod War.

1636.	The foundation of Harvard College.
	De Montmagny succeeded Champlain.
1637.	The foundation of Rhode Island.
	Theophilus Eaton founded New Haven.
1638.	Minuit's Swedish settlement.
1640.	Union of Rhode Island and Providence.
1642.	Conformity Act in Virginia.
	Fort Richelieu (Sorel) founded.
1643.	The New England Confederacy.
1647.	Peter Stuyvesant made governor of the New Netherlands.
1649.	Toleration Act in Maryland.
1650.	Sir William Berkeley commissioned by Charles II.
1651.	Sir George Ayscue sent to subdue the West.
1651-58.	The towns of Maine under the jurisdiction of Massachusetts.
1652.	Richard Bennet governor of Virginia.
1653.	Le Moyne, the Jesuit, sent as an envoy to the Iroquois.

1654.	War with the Nyantic Indians.
	Stephenson took Acadia.
1655.	Peter Stuyvesant captured the Swedish settlements
	Edward Digges, Governor of Virginia
	Victory of the Protestants at Providence, Maryland.
1657.	Lord Baltimore restored in Maryland.
1659.	Josias Fendall, Governor of Maryland.
1661.	Royal Commissioners sent to the colonies.
1662.	Charles Calvert made Governor of Maryland.
	Charter granted to Connecticut.
1663.	Charter granted to the Lords Proprietors of the Carolinas.
	Canada became a Royal Province.
1664.	Colbert created the Company of the West.
	Richard Nicolls captured New Amsterdam.
1665.	Attempt of De Ruyter to retake New Amsterdam
	Marquis de Tracy made Lieutenant-General of Canada.
1666.	Courcelles attacked the Iroquois.

           The Treaty of Breda.

           La Salle arrived in Canada.

1667.   Locke's Fundamental Constitutions for the Carolinas.

           Terrific gale in Maryland and Virginia.

1668.   Francis Lovelace made Governor of New York.

           Jacques Marquette, a missioner on Lake Superior.

1669.   La Salle supposed to have discovered the Ohio.

1670.   Incorporation of the Hudson Bay Company.

           William Sayle came from the Barbadoes to South Carolina.

1671.   Sir John Yeamans, Governor of South Carolina.

1672.   Count Frontenac made Governor of Canada.

           Grants in Virginia to Lords Arlington and Culpeper.

1673.   Cornelius Eversen retook New York.

           The establishment of Fort Frontenac.

           Joliet and Marquette reach the Mississippi.

1674.   Death of Marquette.

The Treaty of Westminster restored New York to the English.

Carteret and Berkeley given rights in New Jersey.

Joseph West made Governor of South Carolina.

1674-1676. King Philip's War.

1675. Death of Cecil, Lord Baltimore.

1677. The end of Berkeley's rule in Virginia.

Thomas Eastchurch, Governor of Carolina.

1678. Massachusetts purchased all rights over Maine.
La Salle given leave to discover the western parts of New France.

La Salle, De Tonty, and Father Hennepin allied as discoverers. Fort Niagara built.

1679. La Salle sailed up Lakes Erie and Michigan.

1680. La Salle built Fort Crèvecœur on the lower Illinois.

Father Hennpin travelled on the upper Mississippi.

Edward Byllinge and certain Quakers encouraged to colonise Delaware.

1681. William Penn founded Pennsylvania

Limitation of the franchise in Maryland.

1681-1682. La Salle descended the Mississippi to the Gulf of Mexico.

1682. End of Frontenac's first government of Canada.

Formation of the "Compagni du Nord."

1682-1683. La Salle established a French colony on the Illinois.

1682-1684. New Hampshire governed by Edward Cranfield.

1683. Seth Sothel, Governor of North Carolina.

Thomas Dongan, Governor of New York.

1684. La Vallière, Governor of Acadia, succeeded by Perrot.

Lord Howard of Effingham, Governor of Virginia.

The Five Nations allied with the English at Albany.

1684-1685. La Salle's expedition to Texas.

1684-1687. The Mississippi Scheme.

1685. The Marquis de Denonville, Governor of Canada.

The English colonies lose their charters.

Francis Nicholson, Deputy-Governor of New York.

Revocation of the Edict of Nantes.

1686. Sir Edmund Andros in Massachusetts.

1687.	Death of La Salle.
	The Marquis de Denonville defeated the Iroquois.
1688.	The Revolution in England.
	Sir Edmund Andros plundered Pentegost.
1689.	Denonville destroyed Fort Frontenac.
	Count Frontenac appointed Governor of Canada for the second time.
	Count Frontenac sent three raiding parties into New England.
	Du Luth defeated the Iroquois on the Ottawa. William Penn lost his proprietary rights. Leisler's rising in New York.
1690.	Congress of the colonies at Albany.
	Colonel Sloughter suppressed Leisler's rising.
	Port Royal taken by Sir William Phipps.
	Sir William Phipps led an expedition against Quebec.
1691.	Successful attack of the English on La Prairie New Plymouth incorporated within Massachusetts.
	Maryland placed under the direct control of the Crown.

1692.	Benjamin Fletcher, Governor of New York. Andrew Hamilton, Governor of New Jersey. Villebon re-occupied Port Royal.
	French attacks on the coast of Maine.
1693.	Canadians and Indians attacked the Mohawk towns.
	D'Iberville reconnoitred Fort Pemaquid.
	English expedition to recover the forts on James Bay.
	Establishment of William and Mary College, Virginia.
1694.	Proprietary rights restored to William Penn.
	End of the rule of Sir William Phipps in Massachusetts.
	La Mothe Cadillac sent to command Michillimackinac.
1695.	Fort Frontenac was re-occupied.
	Sir William Phipps died.
1696.	Frontenac, Callières, and Vaudreuil attacked the Iroquois.
	D'Iberville took Fort Pemaquid from Chubb.
1696-1726.	Rhode Island governed by Samuel Cranston.
1697.	Abortive French expedition under the Marquis de Nesmond against Boston.
	D'Iberville took Fort Nelson.

                The Treaty of Ryswick.

1698.   Establishment of a college in Connecticut.

                Frontenac died at Quebec.

1698-1701.   Massachusetts, New York, New Jersey, New Hampshire governed by Lord Bellomont.

1699.   First colonisation of Louisiana by Le Moyne d'Iberville.

1701.   La Mothe Cadillac founded Detroit.

                Penn left Pennsylvania.

                Execution of the pirate Captain Kidd.

                Lord Cornbury succeeded Lord Bellomont.

1702.   The Proprietors resigned their rights over New Jersey.

1702-1713.   Queen Anne's War.

1703.   Separation of Delaware from Pennsylvania.

                Colonel Moore's attack upon St Augustine.

1704.   Colonel Moore's attack upon Apalachee.

                The French attacked Deerfield.

                Major Church threatened Port Royal.

1706.   The French and Spanish attacked Charleston.

Chronology of Colonial History 225

1707. Colonel March threatened Port Royal.

1708. The French attacked Haverfield on the Merrimac.

Lord Cornbury recalled.

1709. Samuel Vetch advocated combined attack on New France.

Colonel Francis Nicholson attacked near Lake Champlain the forces of Ramesay, Governor of Montreal.

1710. Colonel Francis Nicholson took Port Royal.

1711. The Walker-Hill expedition against Canada.

North Carolina attacked by the Tuscarora Indians.

1712. Birth of Montcalm at Nîmes.

1713. The Treaty of Utrecht.

1715. Proprietary rights over Maryland restored to the fourth Lord Baltimore.

1716. North Carolina attacked by the Yamassee Indians.

1718. Death of William Penn.

Bienville, brother of D'Iberville, founded New Orleans.

1720. Settlement of German Palatines in New York.

Louisburg on Cape Breton began to be important.

> The French built a permanent fort at Niagara.

1723. The Jesuit Charlevoix recommended a mission among the Sioux.

1724. Sebastian Rasle, a Jesuit priest, killed on the Kennebec.

1726. Peace between the Indians and New Englanders.

1727. Birth of James Wolfe at Westerham, in Kent.

> The English established a trading centre at Oswego.

> Fort Beauharnois built in the Sioux country.

1729. Death of Governor Burnet.

1731-1740. De la Verendrye built forts from Rainy Lake westward.

1731. Saint Luc de la Corne built Fort St Frederic (Crown Point).

1732. General Oglethorpe established Georgia.

1734. Salzburg Germans came to Georgia.

1736. John Wesley in Georgia.

1738. George Whitefield in Georgia.

1739-1742. War in Georgia with the Spaniards.

1742. The Spaniards attacked St Simons, Carolina.

1743. General Oglethorpe left Georgia.

Chronology of Colonial History

1743-1753. George Clinton, Governor of New York.

1744. War between England and France.

Canso taken by the French.

1745. Shirley, Pepperell, and Warren take Louisburg.

1747. Warren and Anson defeated the French off Cape Finisterre.

1748. Treaty of Aix-la-Chapelle.

1749. Celeron de Bienville registered the claims of France to the Ohio valley.

Establishment of Fort Rouillé (Toronto).

Establishment of Halifax.

1750. Le Loutre burnt Beaubassin.

1752. The Marquis Duquesne became Governor of Canada.

Georgia passed into the hands of the Crown.

1753. Proposal to unite the Thirteen Colonies.

Duquesne sent Marin to build forts between the Lakes and the Ohio. Washington sent on a counter expedition.

1754. The French built Fort Duquesne.

Death of Jumonville.

Washington built Fort Necessity, but obliged to retreat.

1755. Braddock's disaster on the Monongahela.

William Johnson's expedition against Crown Point.

Shirley's advance on Lake Ontario.

Beausejour taken and renamed Fort Cumberland.

Transportation of the Acadians.

Vaudreuil appointed Governor-General of Canada.

1756. Outbreak of the Seven Years' War.

Oswego, under Bradstreet, taken by Montcalm.

Recall of William Shirley.

1757. Loudoun and Holborne made an abortive attempt on Louisburg.

Fort William Henry taken by Montcalm and Levis.

William Pitt joined Newcastle.

1758. Louisburg under Drucour taken by Boscawen, Amherst, and Wolfe.

Abercromby defeated at Ticonderoga. Death of Lord Howe.

Fort Frontenac taken by Bradstreet.

Amherst appointed Commander-in-chief in North America.

Fort Duquesne taken by Forbes and renamed Pittsburg.

1759.   Stanwix sent to Duquesne and Prideaux to Oswego.

Fort Niagara taken by Johnson.

Ticonderoga and Crown Point taken by Amherst.

The capture of Quebec. Deaths of Wolfe and Montcalm.

1760.   The Battle of St Foy. Levis forced the English into Quebec.

Relief of Quebec.

Surrender of Montreal to the forces of Amherst, Haviland, and Murray.

1763.   The Peace of Paris.

Chapter 14

BIBLIOGRAPHY

A SHORT BIBLIOGRAPHY OF THOSE WORKS WHICH CAN BE OBTAINED EASILY

Large Bibliographies

Larned, J. N. (editor). The Literature of American History, Boston, 1902.
Harrisse, H. Notes pour servir à l'histoire, à la bibliographie, et à la cartographie de la Nouvelle France, etc., Paris, 1872.
Cambridge Modern History, vol. vii., Cambridge, 1905.

General

Calendars of Colonial State Papers in the English Record Office. Bancroft, G. History of the United States, 6 vols., New York, 1883-85.
Doyle, J. A. The English in America, 3 vols., London, 1882-87; The Middle Colonies, London,
1907; The Colonies under the House of Hanover, London, 1907.
Egerton, H. L. Short History of British Colonial Policy, New York, 1898; Origin and Growth of English Colonies, Oxford, 1903.

Hart, A. B. (editor). American History told by Contemporaries, 4 vols., New York, 1897-1902. Winsor, J. (editor). The Narrative and Critical History of America, 8 vols., Boston, 1886-89.

Discoveries

Fiske, J. The Discovery of America, 2 vols., Boston, 1892.
Hakluyt, R. Principal Navigations, voiages, etc. (1598), 12 vols., Glasgow, 1904-5. Payne, L. J. Voyages of Elizabethan Seamen to America, 2 vols., London, 1893. Prowse, D. W. History of Newfoundland, London, 1895.

The Thirteen Colonies

Bradley, A. G. Captain John Smith (English Men of Action), London, 1905. Brown, J. The Pilgrim Fathers of New England, New York, 1895.
Browne, W. H. Maryland: the History of a Palatinate, Boston, 1884. Bruce, H. Life of Oglethorpe, New York, 1890.
Bruce, P. A. Economic History of Virginia in the Seventeenth Century, 2 vols., New York, 1896. Clarkson, T. Memoirs of William Penn, 2 vols., London, 1813.
Fiske, J. The Beginnings of New England, Boston, 1889; Old Virginia and her Neighbours, 2 vols., New York, 1897; Dutch and Quaker Colonies in America, 2 vols., Boston, 1899.
Johnston, A. Connecticut, Boston, 1887.
Jones, C. C. History of Georgia, 2 vols., Boston, 1883. M'Clintock, J. History of New Hampshire, Boston, 1889.
M'Crady, E. History of South Carolina, 4 vols., New York, 1897-1903. Neill, E. D. History of the Virginia Company of London, Albany, 1869. Rickman, J. Rhode Island, its Making and Meaning, 2 vols., New York, 1902. Roberts, E. H. History of New York, 2 vols., Boston, 1887.

Saunders, W. L. (editor). Colonial Records of North Carolina, 16 vols., Raleigh, 1886. Shurtlegg, N. B. Records of Massachusetts Bay, 1628-86, 5 vols., Boston, 1853-54. Weeden, W. B. Economic and Social History of New England, 2 vols., Boston, 1890. Williamson, W. D. History of Maine, 2 vols., Hallowell, 1832.

Wenson, J. Memorial History of Boston, 1630-1880, 4 vols., Boston, 1880-82. Canada.

Bourinot, Sir J. G. Historical and Descriptive Account of the Island of Cape Breton, Trans. Roy. Soc. Can., Montreal; 1892, Canada under British Rule, Camb., 1900.

Bradley, A. G. Wolfe (English Men of Action), London, 1889; The Fight with France for North America, London, 1900.

Green, W. William Pitt (Heroes of the Nation), New York, 1901. Kingsford, W. The History of Canada, London, 1888.

Lucas, C. P. Historical Geography of the British Colonies, vol. v., Oxford, 1901. Parkman, F. Collected Works, edited by W. Kingsford, London, 1900-1.

Wright, R. Life of Major-General J. Wolfe, London, 1864.

REFERENCES

[1] Hakluyt's Voyages (ed. 1904), vii. p. 154.
[2] Hakluyt's Voyages, vii. p. 143.
[3] Bacon's Works (ed. 1870), vi. 196.
[4] Hakluyt's Voyages (ed. 1904), vii. p. 153.
[5] Barrett, History and Antiquities of Bristol (1789), p. 172.
[6] Hakluyt's Voyages (ed. 1904), vii. p. 155.
[7] It is thought by some that Cabot sailed to Greenland. Cf. Biggar, Voyages of the Cabots and of the Corte Reals (Paris, 1903).
[8] Hakluyt's Voyages, vii. p. 150.
[9] Ibid., viii. p. 37.
[10] Hakluyt's Voyages, viii. p. 3.
[11] Ibid., viii. p. 5.
[12] Ibid., viii. p. 7.
[13] Hakluyt's Voyages, x. p. 2.
[14] Ibid., viii. p. 9.
[15] Ibid., viii. p. 10.
[16] Hakluyt's Voyages, vii. p. 149.
[17] Fletcher, Cornhill Magazine, Dec. 1902.
[18] Hakluyt's Voyages, ii. p. 178.
[19] Hakluyt's Voyages, vii. p. 212.
[20] Ibid., vii. p. 320.
[21] Ibid., vii. p. 321.

[22] Ibid., vii. p. 38.
[23] Hakluyt's Voyages, viii. p. 54.
[24] Hakluyt's Voyages, viii. p. 74.
[25] Ibid., x. pp. 6, 7.
[26] Egerton, Origin and Growth of the English Colonies, p. 65.
[27] Hakluyt's Voyages (ed. 1904), viii. p. 123.
[28] Hakluyt's Voyages (ed. 1904), viii. p. 141.
[29] Ibid., viii. pp. 298 and 305.
[30] Hakluyt's Voyages, xi. p. 25.
[31] Quoted by Professor Raleigh in Introduction to Hakluyt's Voyages (ed. 1904), xii. p. 24.
[32] Hakluyt's Voyages (ed. 1904), vol. vii. p. 190.
[33] Hakluyt's Voyages (ed. 1904), vol. i. p. xviii.
[34] Quoted by Doyle, The English in America, Virginia (1882), p. 145.
[35] American Historical Review, vol. iv. No. 4, pp. 678-702.
[36] Quoted by Doyle, op. cit., p. 147.
[37] Doyle says 143 colonists; neither Percy nor Newport mention the exact number; Bradley, in his life of Captain John Smith, says 105.
[38] Cf. footnote, Doyle, op. cit., p. 149.
[39] Smith's Letter to the Virginia Company.
[40] Quoted by Bradley, Captain John Smith (1905), p. 144.
[41] Force, Tracts (1836-46), vol. i.
[42] Gates, A. True Declaration of the Estate of the Colonie in Virginia (1610).
[43] Force, Tracts (1836-46), vol. iii.
[44] Sir Thomas Dale was Governor 1611 and 1614 to 1616. Sir Thomas Gates as Governor organised the colony 1611 to 1614. See Dictionary of National Biography, xxi. p. 64.
[45] Hamor, A. True Discourse of the Present Estate of Virginia (ed. 1860).
[46] Hamor, A. True Discourse of the Present Estate of Virginia (ed. 1860).
[47] The characters of the two parties is controversial owing to the scarcity of documentary evidence.

- [48] Doyle, op. cit. p. 220.
- [49] Ibid., p. 226.
- [50] There was no question of abandoning the colony itself, which was what Spain desired.
- [51] Doyle, op. cit. pp. 242, 244.
- [52] Gardiner, History of the Commonwealth, i. 317.
- [53] Neill, Virginia Carolorum (1886), p. 215.
- [54] Cromwell's Speech V., Sept. 17, 1656.
- [55] Hening, Statutes at Large (New York, 1823), ii. p. 517.
- [56] Calendar of State Papers, Colonial, 1669-1674, p. 64.
- [57] Calendar of State Papers, Colonial, 1669-1674, p. 530.
- [58] Strange News from Virginia (1677), p. 8.
- [59] Calendar of State Papers, Colonial, 1677-1680, p. 64.
- [60] Ibid., p. 67.
- [61] Ibid., p. iv.
- [62] Fortescue, Introduction to Calendar, 1677-1680, p. v.
- [63] Calendar of State Papers, Colonial, 1677-1680, p. 589.
- [64] See p. 93.
- [65] Calendar of State Papers, Colonial, 1697, p. 642.
- [66] Itinerant Observations, p. 62.
- [67] Hammond, Leah and Rachel (London, 1656), p. 20.
- [68] White, A Relation of the Colony of the Lord Baron Baltimore in Maryland (ed. 1847).
- [69] Ibid.
- [70] Hammond, ut supra.
- [71] Bozman, History of Maryland, 1633-60 (1837), vol. ii. p. 661.
- [72] Hammond, ut supra.
- [73] Calendar of State Papers, Colonial, 1661-1668, p. 119.
- [74] Calendar of State Papers, Colonial, 1697-1698, p. 246.
- [75] Letters, vol. i. p. 135.
- [76] Hakluyt's voyages (edit. 1904), vol. ix. p. 17.
- [77] Saunders, editor of Colonial Records of North Carolina, p. 99.
- [78] Ibid., p. 100.
- [79] Calendar of State Papers, Colonial, 1669-1674, p. 186.

[80] Calendar of State Papers, Colonial, 1669-1674, p. 187.
[81] Ibid., p. 297.
[82] Doyle, Cambridge Modern History (1905), vol. vii. p. 35.
[83] Fortescue, Calendar of State Papers, Colonial, 1677-1680, p. ix.
[84] Ibid., p. ix.
[85] Calendar of State Papers, Colonial, 1669-1674, p. 620.
[86] Ibid., p. 130.
[87] Calendar of State Papers, Colonial, 1669-1674, p. 137.
[88] Ibid., p. 187.
[89] Ibid., p. 169.
[90] Ibid., p. 70.
[91] Ibid., p. 86.
[92] Calendar of State Papers, Colonial, 1677-1680, p. 455.
[93] Ibid., p. xi.
[94] Historical Collections of South Carolina (New York, 1836).
[95] See p. 24.
[96] Smith, A. Description of New England (1616), p. 1.
[97] Macaulay, Essays (ed. 1891), p. 23.
[98] Calendar of Domestic State Papers, 1591-1594, p. 400.
[99] Bradford, History of the Plimoth Plantation, p. 15.
[100] Bradford, History of the Plimoth Plantation, p. 16.
[101] Ibid., p. 17.
[102] Ibid.
[103] Quoted by J. R. Green, Short History of the English People (1893), iii. p. 1051.
[104] Smith, A Description of New England (1616), p. 27.
[105] Quoted by J. R. Green, op. cit., p. 1049.
[106] Bradford, op. cit., May 12.
[107] Bradford, op. cit.
[108] Young, Chronicles of the Pilgrim Fathers (ed. 1841).
[109] Thwaites, The Colonies, 1492-1750 (1891), p. 123.
[110] Calendar of State Papers, Colonial, 1661-1668, p. 36.
[111] Ibid., p. 344.
[112] Macaulay, Essays (ed. 1891), p. 23.

References

239

[113] American Historical Review, vol. iv. No. 4, p. 689.
[114] Ibid., p. 702.
[115] Doyle, The English in America (1887), vol. i. p. 119.
[116] A History of New England (1654), p. 38.
[117] Winthrop, The History of New England from 1630 to 1649. [1633, Feb. 17.]
[118] Doyle, Cambridge Modern History (1905), vol. vii. p. 17.
[119] Simplicities Defence against Seven-Headed Policy (1646), p. 2.
[120] Massachusetts Historical Society, Collections, i.
[121] Winthrop, The History of New England from 1630 to 1649 (1853), vol. i. p. 170.
[122] Ibid., vol. i. p. 213.
[123] New England's First Fruits (1643), p. 12.
[124] Ibid.
[125] Journal of a Voyage to New York in 1679-80.
[126] Calendar of State Papers, Colonial, 1661-1668, p. 344.
[127] Ibid., p. 9.
[128] Calendar of State Papers, Colonial, 1661-1668, p. 32.
[129] Burrough, A Declaration of the Sad and Great Persecution and Martyrdom of the ... Quakers, etc. (1660).
[130] Burrough, A Declaration of the Sad and Great Persecution, and Martyrdom of the ... Quakers, etc. (1660).
[131] Hutchinson, A Collection of Original Papers, etc. (1769).
[132] The Warr in New-England Visibly Ended (1677).
[133] Fortescue, Introd. Calendar of State Papers, Colonial, 1677-1680, p. xiv.
[134] Calendar of State Papers, Colonial, 1677-1680, p. xviii.
[135] Ibid., p. 545.
[136] Fortescue, Calendar of State Papers, Colonial, 1677-1680, p. xxi.
[137] Hutchinson, A Collection of Original Papers relative to the History of the Colony of Massachusetts Bay (1769).
[138] Egerton, A Short History of British Colonial Policy, p. 62.
[139] 139] Mather, Magnalia Christi Americana, II. (1702).

[140] O'Callaghan, editor, Documents relative to the Colonial History of the State of New York (1854).
[141] Bryce, American Commonwealth.
[142] Underhill, Newes from America (1638).
[143] Ibid.
[144] Calendar of State Papers, Colonial, 1661-1668, p. 88.
[145] Calendar of State Papers, Colonial, 1677-1680, p. 577.
[146] Ibid.
[147] Calendar of State Papers, Colonial, 1685-1688, p. 472.
[148] Calendar of State Papers, Colonial, 1677-1680, p. 398.
[149] Quoted by Doyle, Puritan Colonies (1887), vol. i. p. 249.
[150] Calendar of State Papers, Colonial, 1661-1668, p. 343.
[151] Arnold, History of the State of Rhode Island and Providence Plantations (1859).
[152] Ibid.
[153] Winthrop, History of New England (1853), vol. i. p. 226.
[154] Johnson, A History of New England, etc. (1654).
[155] Ibid.
[156] Mass. Hist. Col., Series iii., vol. viii. p. 171.
[157] American Historical Review, vol. iv, No. 4, p. 683.
[158] Josselyn, An Account of Two Voyages to New England (1675).
[159] Ibid.
[160] Calendar of State Papers, Colonial, 1661-1668, p. 315.
[161] Calendar of State Papers, Colonial, 1661-1668, p. 348.
[162] Ibid., 1669-1674, p. 579.
[163] Josselyn, ut supra.
[164] Calendar of State Papers, 1677-1680, p. 211.
[165] Calendar of State Papers, 1677-1680, p. 488.
[166] Seeley, Growth of British Policy (1897), vol. ii. p. 25.
[167] Seeley, Growth of British Policy (1897), vol. ii. p. 25.
[168] Quoted by Fitchett, Fights for the Flag (1900), p. 3.
[169] Description and First Settlement of New Netherland (1888).
[170] The Representation of New Netherland (ed. 1849).

References

[171] Documents relative to the Colonial History of the State of New York (1877).
[172] Calendar of State Papers, Colonial, 1661-1668, p. 227.
[173] Documents relative to the Colonial History of the State of New York (1858).
[174] Doyle, Cambridge Modern History (1905), vii. p. 41.
[175] Calendar of State Papers, Colonial, 1661-1668, p. 337.
[176] Ibid., p. 606.
[177] Calendar of State Papers, Colonial, 1669-1674, p. 111.
[178] Calendar of State Papers, Colonial, 1669-1674, p. 525.
[179] Hazard, Historical Collections (1792).
[180] Calendar of State Papers, Colonial, 1689-1692, p. 209.
[181] A Letter from a Gentleman of the City of New York (1698).
[182] Calendar of State Papers, Colonial, 1696-1697, p. 5.
[183] He was also governor of Massachusetts, and died in 1729.
[184] A Brief Narrative of the Case and Tryal of John Peter Zengler, etc. (1738).
[185] Document relative to the Colonial History of the State of New York (1855).
[186] Documents relative to the Colonial History of the State of New York (1855).
[187] Calendar of State Papers, Colonial, 1677-1680, p. 587.
[188] Compare the N.J. Archives, ii., p. 420.
[189] Quoted in the Enc. Britannica.
[190] Janney, Life of William Penn (1852).
[191] Pastorius, Geographical Description of Pennsylvania (1850).
[192] New Jersey Historical Society, Proceedings (1849-1850).
[193] The Voyages and Adventures of Captain Robert Boyle, etc. (1726).
[194] Force, Tracts (1836).
[195] Ibid.
[196] Force, Tracts (1836).
[197] Massachusetts Historical Society, Collections (1814).
[198] Wesley, Journal, June 22, 1736.
[199] Wesley, Journal, December 2, 1737.

[200] Force, Tracts (1836).
[201] Ibid.
[202] Doyle, Cambridge Modern History (1905), vol. vii. p. 63.
[203] An Account of the European Settlements in America (1760).
[204] Words of Stoughton, Lieutenant-Governor of Massachusetts.
[205] Calendar of State Papers, Colonial, 1677-1680, p. 529.
[206] New England Historical and Genealogical Register (1870), xxiv. p. 62.
[207] Adam Smith, Wealth of Nations (ed. 1845), p. 254.
[208] Ibid., p. 240.
[209] Calendar of State Papers, Colonial, 1661-1668, No. 50.
[210] Calendar of State Papers, Colonial, 1677-1680, p. 529.
[211] History of New England, II. (1720) ch. xiv.
[212] New Hampshire Historical Society, Collections, i. p. 228.
[213] Morley, J., Walpole, Twelve English Statesmen (1896), p. 168.
[214] Green, W., William Pitt, Heroes of the Nations (1901), p. 258.
[215] Smith, A., Wealth of Nations (ed. 1845), pp. 245 and 249.
[216] O'Callaghan, Documents relative to Colonial History of State of New York (1855), v. p. 738.
[217] Winthrop, History of New England (ed. 1853), i., Nov. 1633.
[218] Doyle, The English in America, vol. ii. p. 64.
[219] Ibid., p. 506.
[220] Knight, Journal (1825), p. 40.
[221] Quoted by Thwaites, The Colonies, 1492-1750 (1891), p. 189.
[222] O'Callaghan, ut supra, vii. 348.
[223] See p. 93.
[224] Clap, The Annals or History of Yale College (1766), p. 22.
[225] Doyle, Cambridge Modern History (1905), vol. vii. p. 60.
[226] Mass. Hist. Coll., Series II. vol. x. p. 183.
[227] Quoted by Doyle, Colonies under the House of Hanover (1907), p. 13.
[228] So lucrative did the slave trade become that, even after the Abolition Act of 1807, slave dealers realised an enormous profit if one ship out of three with its living cargo reached an American port.

[229] New Jersey Historical Society, Proceedings (1850), iv. p. 118.
[230] Morley, Walpole, Twelve English Statesmen (1896), p. 168.
[231] A Declaration of the Present State of Virginia, etc.
[232] Doyle, The English in America, Virginia, etc. (1882), p. 525.
[233] See p. 46.
[234] Lawson, p. 3.
[235] Quoted by Thwaites, op. cit., p. 221.
[236] Doyle, Colonies under the House of Hanover (1907), p. 289.
[237] Meade, Old Churches of Virginia (1861), i. p. 385.
[238] Doyle, The Colonies under the House of Hanover (1907), pp. 42-43.
[239] Bateson, Cambridge Modern History (1905), vol. vii. p. 70.
[240] Hakluyt's Voyages (1904), viii. 438.
[241] Hakluyt's Voyages (1904), viii. p. 242.
[242] Ibid., p. 244.
[243] Le Clercq, First Establishment of the Faith in New France (1881), p. 52.
[244] Le Clercq, First Establishment of the Faith in New France (1881), p. 52.
[245] The modern Kingston.
[246] These men were the first to explore the river, but it was undoubtedly reached in 1659 by two fur traders, Radisson and Des Grosseilliers.
[247] French, Historical Collections of Louisiana (1850), Part II.
[248] Ibid.
[249] Ibid.
[250] Ibid.
[251] Parkman, La Salle (edition eleven), p. 112.
[252] French, Historical Collections of Louisiana (1850), Part IV.
[253] Ibid.
[254] French, Historical Collections of Louisiana (1850), Part IV.
[255] Parkman, Half a Century of Conflict, vol. i. p. 79.
[256] Ibid.
[257] Parkman, Half a Century of Conflict, i. p. 139.
[258] Parkman, Half a Century of Conflict, i. p. 144.
[259] Ibid.

[260] Parkman, Half a Century of Conflict, i. p. 144.
[261] Parkman, Half a Century of Conflict, vol. i. p. 161.
[262] Ibid., p. 157.
[263] Parkman, Half a Century of Conflict, vol. i. pp. 166, 167.
[264] Walker, Journal, Introduction.
[265] Swift, Journal to Stella, October 16, 1711.
[266] Parkman, Half a Century of Conflict, vol. i. p. 169.
[267] Ibid., p. 182.
[268] Prowse, History of Newfoundland (1896), p. 258.
[269] Wrong, translator and editor of Lettre d'un habitant de Louisburg, p. 26.
[270] Parkman, Half a Century of Conflict, vol. i. p. 183.
[271] The Five Nations were sometimes called the Six Nations after being joined by the Tuscaroras.
[272] O'Callaghan, Doc. Hist. of New York, vol. i. p. 447.
[273] Parkman, Half a Century of Conflict, vol. ii. p. 54.
[274] See p. 266.
[275] Mitchell, Contest in America, p. 22.
[276] Lucas, Hist. Geo. of Brit. Colonies, Canada, part i. p. 198.
[277] Belknap, vol. ii. p. 160.
[278] Samuel Curwen, Journal and Letters, p. 13.
[279] Doyle, The Colonies under the House of Hanover (1907), p. 532.
[280] Doyle, The Colonies under the House of Hanover (1907), ch. 534.
[281] Adams's Works (ed. 1856), vol. i. p. 23.
[282] Doyle, The Colonies under the House of Hanover (1907), pp. 544, 545.
[283] Dinwiddie Papers, vol. i. p. 258.
[284] Dinwiddie Papers, vol. i. p. 306.
[285] Letters of Horace Walpole (Ed. 1861), vol. ii. p. 459.
[286] Parkman, Wolfe and Montcalm (1901), vol. i. p. 188.
[287] Annual Register, 1758, p. 4.
[288] Bradley, The Fight with France for North America (1905), pp. 81-99.
[289] Quoted by J. A. Harrison, Washington (1906), p. 95.
[290] Letter of Washington to Dinwiddie, July 18, 1755.

[291] Doyle, The Colonies under the House of Hanover (1907), p. 575.
[292] Letter of Washington to Dinwiddie, July 18, 1755.
[293] Lucas, Hist. Geo. of British Colonies, Canada, part i. (1901), p. 240.
[294] Wright, Life of Wolfe (1864), pp. 440, 441.
[295] Parkman, Wolfe and Montcalm, vol. ii. p. 48.
[296] Drucour's letter, Annual Register, 1758, pp. 179-81.
[297] Bradley, The Fight with France for North America (1905), p. 217, says a million sterling had been spent on the fortifications since 1745.
[298] Grenville Correspondence, vol. i. 262.
[299] Quoted by Bradley, ut supra, p. 245.
[300] Annual Register, 1758, pp. 72, 73.
[301] Burke, Annual Register, 1759, p. 34.
[302] Major W. Wood, in The Siege of Quebec (1904), doubts the truth of this picturesque story.
[303] Bradley, Life of Wolfe (1895), p. 208.
[304] Hunt, Political History of England, 1760-1801 (1905), p. 141.
[305] Bancroft, History of the United States (1891), i. p. 525.

INDEX

A

Abenaki Indians, 170, 173, 181
Abercromby, General, 198, 202, 203, 228
Abraham, Heights of, 205, 207
Acadia, 27, 169, 171, 173, 176, 180, 181, 184, 194, 196, 197, 213, 214, 215, 216, 218, 221
Adams, John, 189
Africa, 5, 97
Agriculture, 22
Aix-la-Chapelle, Treaty of, 190, 227
Alatamaha River, 118
Albany, 38, 99, 101, 103, 104, 168, 169, 170, 192, 194, 202, 221, 222, 232
Albemarle, Duke of, 48
Alcazar, Battle of, 7
Alexander VI., rule of, 5
Alexandria (America), 193
Alleghany Mountains, 191, 192
Alleghany River, 192
Allen, Nathaniel, 113
Allen, Samuel, 92
Alva, Duke of, 2
Amelia Island, 120
Amherst, Jeffrey, 201
Amidas, Captain, 13, 16, 18, 47, 212

Amsterdam, 59, 98, 99
Andros, Sir Edmund, 74, 75, 83, 102, 103, 110, 221, 222
Annapolis, 146, 152, 176
Anson, Admiral, 187, 227
Apalachee, 54, 224
Aquedneck, 84, 130
Archangel, 7, 13
Archdale, Joseph, 53
Argall, Samuel, 26, 27, 214
Arlington, Lord, 35
Arnold, History of the State of Rhode Island, etc., 240
Ashley River, 49, 51
Association for the Defence of the Protestant Religion, 45
Aubert (French voyager), 149, 211
Augusta, 118
Austrian Succession, War of, 186
Ayscue, Sir George, 217

B

Bacon, Nathaniel, 36
Bacon, Sir Francis, 24
Bahamas, the, 117
Baltic Company, 86

Baltimore, first Lord, 41
Baltimore, fourth Lord, 46, 225
Baltimore, second Lord, 42
Barbadoes, the, 48, 51, 71, 140, 219
Barbary, 7
Barlow, Captain, 13, 18, 47, 212
Barrett, History and Antiquities of Bristol, 235
Bateson, Cambridge Modern History, 243
Beaujeu, Admiral, 163, 194
Beauport, 170, 205
Belcher, Governor, 144
Belknap, 244
Bellomont, Earl of, 77, 105
Bennet, Richard, 34, 217
Berkeley, Lady, 36
Berkeley, Lord, 99, 109
Berkeley, Sir William, 32, 33, 36, 48, 217
Bermudas, 24, 26, 48
Berry, Sir John, 36
Beverley, Robert, 144
Beza, John, 113
Bienville, C. de, 190, 227
Biggar, Voyages of the Cabots, etc., 235
Bigot, 127
Black Watch, 203
Blair, Commissary, 38, 39
Blake, Joseph, 53
Blenheim, Battle of, 172
Block Island, 80
Bolingbroke, Viscount, 176
Bolzius, Martin, 118
Boscawen, Admiral, 201, 228
Boston, 66, 70, 71, 73, 75, 76, 82, 85, 87, 104, 107, 126, 127, 130, 134, 135, 136, 169, 172, 175, 176, 178, 179, 185, 187, 216, 223, 231, 232, 233
Bougainville, 205
Bozman, History of Maryland, 237
Braddock, General, 193, 196
Bradford, William, 59, 61
Bradley, Captain John Smith, 236

Bradley, Fight with France for North America, 233, 244, 245
Bradley, Life of Wolfe, 245
Bradstreet, Anne, 136
Bradstreet, Colonel, 203
Braintree (America), 127
Branford, 82
Brayne, Henry, 51
Brazil, 5, 6, 13
Breda, 33, 219
Brewton, Colonel, 54
Bristol, 3, 4, 5, 88, 91, 115, 140
British Columbia, 11
Brodhead, 100
Brooke, Lord, 79, 91, 216
Brown, Captain, 182, 232
Browne, Samuel, 67
Bryce, American Commonwealth, 240
Bulkeley, Peter, 73
Burnet, Governor, 106, 131, 226
Burrough, Edward, 71
Byllinge, Edward, 110, 220
Byrd, Colonel, 144

C

Cabot, John, 3
Cabot, Sebastian, 3, 4, 6, 211
Cadillac, La Mothe, 165, 223, 224
California, Gulf of, 160
Calvert, Cecil, 143
Calvert, George, 41
Calvert, Leonard, 42
Cambridge (America), 65, 66, 68, 136, 231
Campbell, John, 136
Canada, 59, 104, 127, 133, 151, 152, 153, 154, 155, 156, 158, 159, 162, 163, 164, 166, 167, 168, 169, 173, 174, 180, 181, 184, 187, 189, 190, 192, 196, 203, 204, 208, 209, 214, 215, 218, 219, 221, 222, 225, 227, 228, 233, 244, 245

Canary Islands, 5
Canso, 184, 227
Cape Ann, 64, 215
Cape Breton Island, 180, 187, 201, 215
Cape Cod, 60, 61
Cape Fear, 48, 50
Cape Finisterre, 187, 227
Cape Henry, 20
Carlile, Captain, 12
Carolina, North, 13, 39, 48, 52, 145, 192, 195, 225, 233, 237
Carolina, South, 39, 47, 48, 54, 55, 117, 120, 139, 141, 142, 144, 145, 146, 192, 193, 196, 219, 220, 232, 238
Carr, Sir Robert, 89, 91, 99
Carteret, Philip, 44, 99, 110
Carteret, Sir George, 99, 109, 110
Cartier, Jacques, 150, 209, 212
Cartwright, 99
Carver, William, 61
Cary, Thomas, 54
Casco Bay, 88, 173, 215
Castle Island, 66
Cataraqui River, 161
Cathay, 3, 7, 8
Cathay, Company of, 8
Cavendish, 13, 16
Cecil, Robert, 24
Champlain, Samuel, 152, 213
Chancellor, Richard, 7, 212
Charles I., 31, 41, 48, 70, 80, 88, 90, 98, 155
Charles II., 33, 34, 35, 45, 63, 69, 71, 85, 89, 96, 98, 102, 109, 130, 136, 141, 217
Charles V., 6, 149
Charlestown, 52, 54, 55, 66, 75, 145, 146
Chauvin, 151, 213
Chesapeake Bay, 20, 211
Chesterfield, Lord, 208
Chicheley, Sir Henry, 37
Chubb, 172, 223

Clap, The Annals or History of Yale College, 242
Clarke, George (Junior), 107
Clarke, George (Senior), 107
Clayborne, William, 43
Clinton, George, 107, 227
Clothmaking, 127
Coddington, William, 84
Colbert, 155, 156, 157, 163, 218
Columbus, Christopher, 2, 4
Company of the One Hundred Associates, 154, 215
Company of the West, 156, 218
Conant, Roger, 64
Condé, Prince de, 153
Connecticut, v, 69, 75, 79, 80, 82, 83, 84, 87, 93, 96, 98, 125, 127, 130, 131, 132, 134, 135, 136, 169, 185, 216, 218, 224, 232
Connecticut River, 79, 80
Contrecœur, 192
Convers, 171
Coode, John, 45
Coram, Thomas, 117
Cornbury, Lord, 106, 112, 224, 225
Cosby, William, 107
Costobelle, 177
Cotton, John, 68
Cranfield, Edward, 92, 221
Cranston, Samuel, 86, 223
Crispen, William, 113
Culpeper, Lord, 35, 37
Curwen, Samuel, 244
Cutts, John, 92
Cuyler, 104

D

Dale, Sir Thomas, 25, 27, 28, 236
Damariscotta, 185
Dare, Eleanor, 16

Darien, 174
Dautray, Sieur, 162
Davenport, John, 87
Davies, Sylvanus, 169
De Chastes, 152, 213
De Lery, 197
De Loutre, 196
De Monts, 152, 213
De Roberval, 151, 212
De Ruyter, 100, 218
Declaration of Indulgence, 75
Deerfield, 173, 224
Defoe, Daniel, 115
Delaware, 82, 97, 99, 109, 110, 112, 113, 114, 115, 139, 142, 220, 224
Delaware River, 114
Delawarr, Lord, 25, 26, 214
Denonville, 168, 221, 222
Denys, the voyager, 149, 211
Detroit, 165, 184, 224
Diaz, Bartholomew, 2
Dieskau, Baron, 195
Digges, Edward, 34, 218
Dinwiddie, Governor, 191
Dongan, Thomas, 103, 168, 221
Dorchester (America), 64, 66, 80
Doughty, Thomas, 11
Dover (America), 91
Doyle, Cambridge Modern History, 238, 239, 241, 242
Doyle, Colonies under the House of Hanover, 242, 243
Doyle, The English in America, 236, 239, 242, 243
Drake, Sir Francis, 16
Du Luth, 162, 165, 222
Duchambon, 186
Dummer, Jeremiah, 176
Duquesne, Marquis, 191, 227
Duquesnel, 184
Dutch West India Company, 96, 97, 99
Dyre, William, 89

E

East Greenwich, manor of, 82
East India Company, 13, 19, 96
Eastchurch, Thomas, 50, 220
Eaton, Theophilus, 86, 217
Edward VI., 6
Egerton, A Short History of British Colonial Policy, 239
Egerton, Origin and Growth of the English Colonies, 236
Eldorado, 2
Eliot, John, 133
Elizabeth, Queen, 8, 9, 15, 18, 34
Endecott, John, 64
Eversen, Cornelius, 102, 219
Exeter (America), 91

F

Fabian, Robert, 4
Fairfield, 135
Falmouth, 169
Fendall, Josias, 44, 45, 218
Fenwick, John, 110
Ferrars, John, 28
Fitchett, Fights for the Flag, 240
Five Nations (see also Iroquois), 103, 144, 152, 158, 159, 168, 173, 174, 181, 182, 221, 244
Fletcher, Benjamin, 77, 105, 114, 223
Fletcher, Cornhill Magazine, 235
Florida, 4, 7, 48, 53, 55, 117, 119, 120, 212
Forbes, General, 204
Fort Bull, 197
Fort Casimir, 98
Fort Chartres, 184
Fort Christina, 97
Fort Crèvecœur, 162, 220
Fort Cumberland, 191, 228
Fort Duquesne, 192, 194, 204, 227, 229

Index

Fort Edward, 199
Fort Frontenac, 158, 161, 165, 203, 219, 222, 223, 228
Fort James, 102
Fort Loyal, 169
Fort Lyman, 195
Fort Necessity, 192, 228
Fort Niagara, 196, 204, 220, 229
Fort Orange, 99
Fort Pemaquid, 172, 223
Fort Richelieu, 155, 217
Fort Rouillé, 182, 227
Fort St Frederic, 184, 226
Fort St Louis, 164
Fort William Henry, 196, 199, 228
Fortescue, Calendar of State Papers, Colonial, 238, 239
Fox River, 159
Francis I., 149, 211
Franciscans, the, 153
Franklin, Benjamin, 144, 192
Frederica, 118, 120
French, Historical Collections of Louisiana, 243
Frobisher Bay, 8
Frobisher Sir Martin, 8, 212
Frontenac, Count, 157, 163, 168, 219, 222
Fundy, Bay of, 152

G

Gainsborough, 59
Gardiner, History of the Commonwealth, 237
Gates, Sir Thomas, 19, 24, 25, 214, 236
George II., 187
George III., 74
Georgia, v, 39, 109, 116, 117, 119, 120, 121, 122, 124, 226, 227, 232
Germantown, 143, 146
Gigglesworth, Michael, 136

Gilbert, Raleigh, 58
Gilbert, Sir Humphrey, 4, 8, 9, 15, 212
Godfrey, Thomas, 145
Goelet, Captain Francis, 126
Goffe, William, 87
Gondomar, 29
Goose Creek, 145
Gorges, Ferdinando, 89, 90, 91
Gorges, Sir Ferdinando, 19, 64, 88, 90, 216
Grand Pré, 173
Granville County, 55
Green, J. R., Short History of the English People, 238
Green, W., William Pitt, 242
Greenland, 8, 235
Greenwich, 5, 82
Grenville Correspondence, 245
Grenville, Sir Richard, 16
Guildford (America), 87
Guinea, 11, 141

H

Hakluyt, Richard, 6, 12, 17, 19
Hall, John, 130
Hamilton, Andrew, 111, 223
Hammond, John, 41
Hamor, Ralph, 26
Hampton, 39, 91, 193
Hankey, Sophia, 118
Hardy, Captain, 55
Harley, 176, 179
Hartford, 80, 83, 135
Harvard, 68, 75, 134, 217
Harvard, Mr, 68
Harvey, Governor, 31, 32
Haverfield, 173, 225
Hawkins, Sir John, 11
Hayes, Edward, 9
Hazard, Historical Collection, 241
Heage, William, 113

Heath, Captain, 182
Heath, Sir Robert, 48, 216
Hening, Statutes at Large, 237
Henrico, 26
Henry of Navarre, 152
Henry VII., 2, 5, 6
Henry VIII., 6
Hiacoomes, 133
Hill, Abigail, 178
Hill, General, 178
Holborne, Admiral, 199
Holstead, Captain, 49
Hooker, Thomas, 68
Hore, Master, 5, 212
Howe, Lord, 202, 203, 228
Howe, Thos., 113
Hudson Bay, 180, 219
Hunt, Political History of England, etc., 245
Hutchinson, A Collection of Original Papers, 239
Hutchinson, Mrs Anne, 68, 84, 216
Hyde, Edward, 54

I

Iberville, 168, 172, 223, 224, 225
Iceland, 13
Illinois River, 160, 162
Indian Bible, 133
Ingle, 43
Ingoldsby, Major Ralph, 104
Ipswich (America), 75
Iron, 128, 142
Iroquois (see also Five Nations), 99, 103, 156, 157, 165, 168, 170, 193, 195, 217, 218, 222, 223

J

Jack the Feather, 29
James I., 18, 19, 29, 60, 62, 98, 215
James II., 74, 76, 83, 86, 103, 105, 112, 114, 172
James III. (the Old Pretender), 172
James River, 20, 38
Jamestown, 20, 22, 26, 34, 35, 36, 141, 146, 214
Janney, Life of William Penn, 241
Japazaus, 26
Jeffreys, Sir Herbert, 37
Jenkinson, Anthony, 7
Jesuits, the, 41, 42, 133, 145, 153, 156, 158, 159, 171, 173
Johnson, A History of New England, 240
Johnson, Edward, 135
Johnson, William, 190, 195, 198, 204, 228
Johnstone, Sir Nathaniel, 54, 55
Joliet, Louis, 159
Jonquière, Marquis de la, 187
Josselyn, An Account of Two Voyages to New England, 240
Josselyn, John, 90

K

Keith, Mr, 115
Kennebec River, 181
Kent, Isle of, 43, 44
Kidd, Captain, 77, 224
King, Colonel, 177, 180
Kirke, David, 41, 154
Knight, Mrs, 132
Knight, Sir John, 35

L

La Baye, 184
La Chine, 161
La Corne, 199
La Galissonière, 190
La Prairie, 169, 222
La Rochelle, 154, 163, 187

Index

La Salle, Sieur de, 161
Labrador, 5
Laconia Company, 90
Lake Champlain, 168, 175, 178, 184, 214, 225
Lake George, 195, 197
Lake Huron, 159, 214
Lake Michigan, 159, 162
Lake Ontario, 161, 228
Lake Superior, 159, 219
Lake Winnebago, 159, 160
Lane, Ralph, 16
Laud, Archbishop, 66
Laudonnière, 47
Laurence, Governor, 196
Laurie, Gawen, 111
Le Caron, 153, 214
Le Clercq, First Establishment of the Faith in New France, 243
Le Moyne, 156, 217, 224
Lead, 127
Leete, William, 82
Leisler, Jacob, 104
Léry, Baron de, 149
Lescarbot, 152, 214
Leslie, Lieutenant, 194
Leverett, Governor, 71
Lévis, French General, 199, 202, 208
Levitt, 88, 215
Leyden, 59, 60, 62
Literature, 231
Locke, John, 49
Logan, James, 116
Lok, Michael, 8
London Company, 19, 24, 58, 215
Long Island, 86, 96, 98, 100, 102
Loudoun, Earl of, 198
Louis XIV., 102, 103, 155, 157, 161, 164, 172, 181
Louis XV., 209
Louisburg, 181, 184, 186, 187, 199, 201, 202, 205, 225, 227, 228, 244

Louisiana, 124, 163, 184, 204, 224
Lovelace, Francis, 101, 102, 219

M

Macaulay, Lord, 64
Magellan, Straits of, 11
Maine, v, 6, 27, 58, 69, 79, 88, 89, 90, 169, 171, 185, 215, 216, 217, 220, 223, 233
Maisonneuve, 156
Malplaquet, 172
Manhattan Island, 96, 185, 215
Manning, Captain, 102
Manoa, city of, 2
March, Colonel, 225
Marie de Medici, 153
Marin, 191, 227
Marquette, Jacques, 159, 219
Martinique, 54
Maryland, v, 41, 43, 44, 45, 46, 47, 55, 79, 112, 139, 141, 142, 143, 145, 146, 147, 175, 190, 191, 192, 194, 195, 216, 217, 218, 219, 220, 222, 225, 232, 237
Masham, Mrs, 179
Mason, Captain John, 81, 90, 216
Mason, family of, 91
Massachusetts, v, 57, 64, 65, 66, 67, 68, 69, 70, 71, 73, 75, 76, 77, 79, 81, 83, 84, 85, 86, 89, 90, 92, 93, 101, 103, 106, 125, 127, 128, 130, 131, 132, 133, 134, 135, 169, 170, 171, 173, 174, 175, 176, 177, 178, 180, 181, 184, 185, 189, 191, 192, 193, 195, 196, 201, 209, 215, 216, 217, 220, 221, 222, 223, 224, 233, 239, 241, 242
Mather, Cotton, 135
Mather, Increase, 75, 76
Mathews, Samuel, 34
Mathews, Virginian settler, 31
Maumee, 184
Maverick, 101

254   Index

Mayhew, Thomas, 133
Meade, Old Churches of Virginia, 243
Membré, Father, 162
Menendez, 47, 212
Mercer, Colonel, 197
Merry Mount, 65
Meta Incognita, 8, 212
Metacam, 71
Mexico, 7, 124, 160, 162, 163, 165, 221
Mexico, Bay of, 59
Miami Indians, 191
Michillimackinac, 184, 223
Milford (America), 87
Miller, Thomas, 50
Minuit, 97, 217
Mississippi River, 161
Mitchell, Contest in America, 244
Mohawk River, 185
Mohawks, 195, 198, 204
Montcalm, Marquis de, 197
Montmagny, 155, 217
Montmorenci, Duc de, 154
Montreal, 152, 155, 157, 173, 175, 208, 225, 229, 233
Moore, Colonel, 54, 224
Moore, James, 53
Morris, Lewis, 115, 142
Morton, 65
Moryson, Colonel Francis, 36
Murray, General, 208
Muscovy Company, 7

N

Nantucket, 133, 170
Narragansett Bay, 69
Naumkeag, 64
Navigation Acts, 38, 72
Neale, Daniel, 127
New Albion, 11
New Amstel, 98

New Amsterdam, 96, 98, 218
New Brunswick, 76
New England Company, 58, 62, 64, 79, 88, 215
New England Confederacy, 69, 71, 217
New Hampshire, v, 76, 77, 79, 90, 92, 106, 128, 169, 171, 175, 177, 184, 185, 192, 198, 216, 221, 224, 232, 242
New Haven, v, 69, 79, 82, 86, 87, 96, 97, 98, 102, 217
New Inverness, 118
New Jersey, 77, 99, 102, 106, 107, 109, 111, 115, 139, 142, 144, 145, 174, 184, 191, 192, 195, 220, 223, 224, 241, 243
New London, 83, 135, 136
New Netherlands, 98, 102, 217
New Plymouth, 63, 64, 71, 79, 84, 130, 132, 133, 135, 215, 222
New Somersetshire, 88
New Sweden, 96, 97
New York, iv, 46, 55, 77, 83, 99, 100, 101, 102, 103, 105, 106, 107, 111, 114, 115, 136, 139, 141, 143, 144, 145, 146, 168, 170, 174, 176, 181, 182, 184, 190, 191, 192, 194, 195, 198, 219, 220, 221, 222, 223, 224, 225, 227, 231, 232, 233, 237, 238, 239, 240, 241, 242, 244
New York Weekly Journal, 107
Newcastle (America), 98, 115, 228
Newcastle, Duke of, 107
Newfoundland, 4, 5, 6, 7, 9, 12, 13, 41, 150, 180, 211, 212, 232
Newport (America), 21, 38, 84, 85, 86, 126, 146, 236
Newport, Christopher, 20
North-East Passage, 6
North-West Passage, 7
Nyantic Indians, 70, 218

O

Oglethorpe, James, 116, 117
Ohio Company ., 191
Oldham, John, 80
Onondaga River, 182
Opechancanough, 29, 32
Oregon, 11
Oswego, 182, 184, 196, 197, 226, 228, 229
Ottawa, 153, 214, 222
Oudenarde, Battle of, 172
Oyster Point, 52
Oyster River, 171

P

Paris, Treaty of, 180, 209
Parkhurst, Anthony, 6
Parkman, Half a Century of Conflict, 243, 244
Parkman, La Salle, 243
Parkman, Wolfe and Montcalm, 244, 245
Pastorius, Geographical Description of Pennsylvania, 241
Patagonia, 7
Pawtuxet, 85
Peckham, Sir George, 12
Penn, Thomas, 116
Penn, William, 110, 113, 115, 116, 220, 222, 223, 225, 232
Pennsylvania, 109, 111, 112, 114, 115, 116, 139, 142, 143, 145, 174, 185, 190, 191, 192, 194, 195, 198, 204, 220, 224
Penobscot, Indians of the, 182, 214
Pepperell, William, 185
Pert, Sir Thomas, 6
Peru, 7, 11, 149
Philadelphia, 109, 113, 115, 142, 144, 146
Philip II., 2, 151
Phipps, Sir William, 76, 169, 222, 223
Pilgrim Fathers, 41, 60, 61, 64, 76, 79, 137, 232
Pitt, William, 129, 199, 228, 233
Pittsburg, 204, 229
Plymouth, v, 11, 19, 57, 58, 60, 63, 64, 69, 79, 80, 125, 126, 127, 134, 136, 214
Plymouth Company, 19, 58
Pocahontas, 22, 26, 214
Pokanoket Indians, 71
Pontgravé, 151, 152, 213
Popham, George, 58
Popish Plot, the, 74
Port Royal, 27, 47, 53, 117, 152, 170, 171, 173, 176, 213, 214, 222, 223, 224, 225
Portland, 169
Portsmouth (America), 84, 85, 92
Portugal, 5, 7, 128, 175
Potomac, the, 26
Pouchot (French commander), 204
Powhattan, 21, 22, 25, 26, 29
Prado, Albert de, 5, 212
Prideaux, General, 204
Pring, Martin, 17
Providence, v, 44, 79, 84, 85, 86, 135, 186, 216, 217, 218, 240
Prowse, History of Newfoundland, 244
Puritans, the, v, 57, 58, 60, 64, 66, 68, 71, 77, 124, 133, 134

Q

Quaker settlements, 109, 114
Quakers, the, 70, 72, 83, 85, 86, 87, 105, 109, 110, 112, 115, 142, 145, 190, 195, 202, 220, 239
Quebec, 151, 152, 155, 157, 168, 169, 171, 173, 175, 178, 181, 204, 205, 206, 208, 214, 215, 216, 222, 224, 229
Quincy, Samuel, 117
Quinipiac River, 86

R

Raleigh, Professor, 236
Raleigh, Sir Walter, 12, 15, 16, 17, 18, 47, 149, 212
Ramillies, Battle of, 172
Randolph, Edward, 53, 72
Rasle, Sebastian, 181, 226
Ratcliffe, Captain John, 20
Religion, 58, 118
Rhode Island, v, 72, 76, 79, 84, 85, 86, 127, 128, 130, 131, 132, 135, 136, 175, 177, 185, 192, 217, 223, 232
Richebourg, 38
Richelieu, 154, 155, 156, 168, 208, 215
Richelieu River, 155, 168, 208
Richmond, 21
Rigby, Edward, 88
Rio de la Plata, 6
Roanoke, 13, 16
Robinson, John, 59, 61
Roche, Marquis de la, 151, 213
Rogers, Robert, 197, 198, 205
Rolfe, John, 27, 214
Rowley, 127
Roxbury, 133
Royal African Company, 141
Rut, John, 5, 212
Ryswick, Treaty of, 172, 224

S

Sable Island, 151, 213
Saco, 88
Salem, 64, 67, 110
Salmon Falls, 169
Salzburgers, 121
San Domingo, 163
Sandford, Peleg, 86
Sandys, Sir Edwin, 19, 28
Savannah River, 12, 117
Saye and Sele, Lord, 79, 91, 216
Sayle, William, 51, 219
Schenectady, 103, 168, 204, 208
Schuyler, Peter, 176
Scrooby, 59
Seeley, Growth of British Policy, 240
Seignelay, 163
Seneca Indians, 158
Shaftesbury, Earl of, 48
Shirley, Governor, 185, 187, 195, 196
Sioux Indians, 162
Slaughter, Colonel, 104
Slye, Gerald, 46
Smith, A Description of New England, 238
Smith, Adam, 126, 129, 242
Smith, Adam, Wealth of Nations, 242
Smith, Captain John, 20, 21, 30, 58, 61, 214, 232, 236
Smith, Thomas, 53
Smythe, Ambrose, 140
Society for the Propagation of the Gospel, 133, 136
Somers Islands, 26
Somers, Sir George, 19, 24, 214
Sothel, Seth, 50, 221
Southampton, Earl of, 17
Spithead, 179
Spotswood, Alexander, 39
St Augustine, 54, 119, 120, 224
St Foy, Battle of, 208, 229
St Ignace, 159
St John, 4, 176, 177, 179
St Joseph, 184
St Lawrence, Gulf of, 12, 124, 149, 150, 152, 155, 178, 180, 187, 199, 205, 209, 211, 212, 213, 215
St Sulpice, 156
Stamford (America), 87
Standish, Miles, 61
Stith, Rev. William, 144
Stone, William, 43, 44
Stoughton, William, 73

Stukeley, Thomas, 7
Stuyvesant, Peter, 97, 217, 218

T

Tadoussac, 151, 155, 213
Talon, the Intendant, 159
Tew, Captain, 105
Texas, 164, 221
Thomas, Gabriel, 114
Thompson, David, 90
Thorne, Master, 8
Three Rivers, 157, 216
Thwaites, The Colonies, 238, 242
Tison, Thomas, 11
Tobacco, 90, 129, 142, 143
Tonty, Henri de, 161, 164
Toronto, 182, 227
Townshend, Lord, 129
Trade and Plantations, Committee of, 73, 127
Tull, Jethro, 129
Tuscarora Indians, 39, 54, 225

U

Ulster Protestants, 139, 196
Underhill, Newes from America, 240
Usselinx, William, 97
Utrecht, Treaty of, 54, 165, 180, 181, 225

V

Van der Douch, 97
Van Twiller, 97
Vane, Henry, 68
Vasco de Gama, 2
Vauban, 185, 202
Vaughan, 185, 186
Venango, 191

Venice, 3
Ventadour, Duc de, 153, 154
Vergennes, 209
Verrazano, 149, 211
Vervins, Treaty of, 151
Vetch, Samuel, 173, 178, 225
Villebon, 171, 223
Virginia, v, 13, 15, 16, 17, 18, 20, 21, 24, 25, 27, 28, 30, 31, 32, 33, 34, 35, 37, 38, 41, 43, 44, 46, 47, 48, 52, 55, 57, 60, 65, 71, 79, 127, 139, 140, 141, 142, 143, 144, 145, 146, 152, 175, 190, 191, 192, 193, 194, 196, 204, 214, 215, 216, 217, 218, 219, 220, 221, 223, 232, 236, 237, 243
Virginia Company, 232, 236

W

Walker, Journal, 244
Walker, Sir H., 178
Walpole, Horace, 193, 244
Walpole, Sir Robert, 129, 142
Walsingham, Francis, 12
Ward, Nathaniel, 135
Warren, Admiral, 185, 186
Warwick, Earl of, 8
Washington, George, 191, 194
Watertown, 66, 75
Wells, 171, 173
Wentworth, Governor, 128
Wesley, John, 118, 226
Wesley, Journal, 241
West Indies, 4, 11, 92, 123, 127
Westminster, Treaty of, 102, 110, 220
Wethersfield, 80, 81
Whalley, Edward, 87
Wheelwright, John, 68, 216
White, Father, 42
White, John, 64

Whitefield, George, 46, 122, 134, 145, 185, 226
Whitmore, 201
William and Mary College, 38, 144, 223
William III., 45, 104, 165
Williams, John, 173
Williams, Roger, 67, 81, 84, 85, 216
Williamsburg, 39, 146
Williamson, Mr, 118
Williamson, Sir Joseph, 101
Willoughby, Sir Hugh, 7, 212
Windsor, 80
Wine, 117
Winslow, Edward, 61, 62
Winslow, John, 75, 196, 198
Winthrop, John, 65, 67, 80, 82
Wolfe, General James, 201
Wood Creek, 175
Wood, Siege of Quebec, 245
Woodward, Thomas, 49
Wright, Life of Wolfe, 245

Yale College, 135
Yamassee Indians, 55, 225
Yeamans, Sir John, 51, 219
Yeardley, Sir George, 28, 31, 215
York, 77, 98, 99, 100, 101, 102, 104, 105, 106, 107, 109, 110, 112, 114, 140, 141, 142, 143, 144, 145, 168, 171, 175, 182, 190, 192, 193, 195, 199, 232
Young, Chronicles of the Pilgrim Fathers, 238